Gardening Under Lights

TIME
LIFE
BOOKS
®

Other Publications:

THE ENCYCLOPEDIA OF COLLECTIBLES

WORLD WAR II

THE GREAT CITIES

HOME REPAIR AND IMPROVEMENT

THE WORLD'S WILD PLACES

THE TIME-LIFE LIBRARY OF BOATING

HUMAN BEHAVIOR

THE ART OF SEWING

THE OLD WEST

THE EMERGENCE OF MAN

THE AMERICAN WILDERNESS

LIFE LIBRARY OF PHOTOGRAPHY

THIS FABULOUS CENTURY

FOODS OF THE WORLD

TIME-LIFE LIBRARY OF AMERICA

TIME-LIFE LIBRARY OF ART

GREAT AGES OF MAN

LIFE SCIENCE LIBRARY

THE LIFE HISTORY OF THE UNITED STATES

TIME READING PROGRAM

LIFE NATURE LIBRARY

LIFE WORLD LIBRARY

FAMILY LIBRARY:
   HOW THINGS WORK IN YOUR HOME
   THE TIME-LIFE BOOK OF THE FAMILY CAR
   THE TIME-LIFE FAMILY LEGAL GUIDE
   THE TIME-LIFE BOOK OF FAMILY FINANCE

Gardening Under Lights

by
Wendy B. Murphy
and
the Editors of TIME-LIFE BOOKS

TIME-LIFE BOOKS, ALEXANDRIA, VIRGINIA

Time-Life Books Inc.
is a wholly owned subsidiary of
TIME INCORPORATED

FOUNDER: Henry R. Luce 1898-1967

Editor-in-Chief: Hedley Donovan
Chairman of the Board: Andrew Heiskell
President: James R. Shepley
Vice Chairman: Roy E. Larsen
Corporate Editors: Ralph Graves, Henry Anatole Grunwald

TIME-LIFE BOOKS INC.

MANAGING EDITOR: Jerry Korn
Executive Editor: David Maness
Assistant Managing Editors: Dale M. Brown, Martin Mann,
John Paul Porter (acting)
Art Director: Tom Suzuki
Chief of Research: David L. Harrison
Director of Photography: Robert G. Mason
Planning Director: Philip W. Payne (acting)
Senior Text Editor: Diana Hirsh
Assistant Art Director: Arnold C. Holeywell
Assistant Chief of Research: Carolyn L. Sackett

CHAIRMAN: Joan D. Manley
President: John D. McSweeney
Executive Vice Presidents: Carl G. Jaeger (U.S. and
Canada), David J. Walsh (International)
Vice President and Secretary: Paul R. Stewart
Treasurer and General Manager: John Steven Maxwell
Business Manager: Peter G. Barnes
Sales Director: John L. Canova
Public Relations Director: Nicholas Benton
Personnel Director: Beatrice T. Dobie
Production Director: Herbert Sorkin
Consumer Affairs Director: Carol Flaumenhaft

THE TIME-LIFE ENCYCLOPEDIA OF GARDENING

EDITORIAL STAFF FOR GARDENING UNDER LIGHTS:
EDITOR: Robert M. Jones
Assistant Editor: Sarah Bennett Brash
Text Editors: Bonnie Bohling Kreitler, Bob Menaker
Picture Editor: Jane Jordan
Designer: Albert Sherman
Staff Writer: Susan Feller
Researchers: Loretta Britten, Susan F. Schneider,
Judith W. Shanks
Art Assistant: Edwina C. Smith
Editorial Assistant: Kristin Baker

EDITORIAL PRODUCTION
Production Editor: Douglas B. Graham
Operations Manager: Gennaro C. Esposito
Assistant Production Editor: Feliciano Madrid
Quality Control: Robert L. Young (director),
James J. Cox (assistant), Michael G. Wight (associate)
Art Coordinator: Anne B. Landry
Copy Staff: Susan B. Galloway (chief), Kathleen Beakley,
Tonna Gibert, Elizabeth Graham, Florence Keith,
Celia Beattie
Picture Department: Dolores A. Littles, Barbara S. Simon

CORRESPONDENTS: Elisabeth Kraemer (Bonn);
Margot Hapgood, Dorothy Bacon (London); Susan Jonas,
Lucy T. Voulgaris (New York); Maria Vincenza Aloisi,
Josephine du Brusle (Paris); Ann Natanson (Rome).
Valuable assistance was also provided by
Carolyn T. Chubet, Miriam Hsia (New York). The editors
are indebted to Linda Tokarz Anzelmo,
Lea Guyer Gordon, Barbara Ann Peters, Karen Solit and
Glenn White for their help with this book.

THE AUTHOR: Wendy B. Murphy is a writer whose diverse interests range from gardening to architectural history. Formerly an editor with TIME-LIFE BOOKS, she contributed to *The Art of Sewing, The Time-Life Library of Boating* and *The Emergence of Man.* She divides her time between an island home in Maine and a 150-year-old farmhouse in Connecticut.

GENERAL CONSULTANTS: Author of 13 of the volumes in the Encyclopedia, co-author of two additional volumes, and consultant on other books in the series, James Underwood Crockett has been a lover of the earth and its good things since his boyhood on a Massachusetts fruit farm. He was graduated from the Stockbridge School of Agriculture at the University of Massachusetts and has worked ever since in horticulture. A perennial contributor to leading gardening magazines, he also writes a monthly bulletin, "Flowery Talks," that is widely distributed through retail florists. His television program, *Crockett's Victory Garden,* shown all over the United States, is constantly winning new converts to the Crockett approach to growing things. Dr. James W. Boodley is Professor of Floriculture at Cornell University, Ithaca, N.Y. George A. Elbert, past president of the Indoor Light Gardening Society of America and a member of the Illuminating Engineering Society, is author of *The Indoor Light Gardening Book* and co-author of *The Miracle House Plants.* Virginie F. Elbert, past president of the New York Metropolitan Chapter of the Indoor Light Gardening Society of America, is a former senior editor of Alfred A. Knopf, Inc., and co-author of *The Miracle House Plants.* George A. Kalmbacher was Plant Taxonomist at the Brooklyn Botanic Garden. Dr. William Louis Stern is Professor of Botany at the University of Maryland, College Park.

Watercolor illustrations for this book were provided by Adolph Brotman, Richard Crist, John Murphy, Trudy Nicholson, Eduardo Salgado, and artists of the Garden Studio, London.

THE COVER: Under softly diffused fluorescent light thrives a rainbow of flowering plants, including a Sassy Pink achimenes *(top),* salmon-suffused Rieger begonias *(center),* red-leaved firefern oxalis with yellow flowers *(foreground)* and a silver-leaved Miss Kitty begonia *(left).*

CONTENTS

The wonders of sunless gardening 1

There is in all of us a need to touch, to smell and to see living plants, and the more urbanized we become the more urgently we long to bring their color and vitality into our homes. Who would not be cheered by the sight of a bright red impatiens blossoming in December? Or a lush gloxinia in January, flourishing in a sunless corner of a house or apartment?

Until about 40 years ago, the chief obstacle to such accomplishments was the impossibility of producing the right kind of light at the right time in sufficient intensity to make tropical and semitropical plants (the vast majority of indoor ornamentals) feel at home. Successful indoor gardening was limited to areas near windows or to the few plants that require a very low level of light.

Then came the revolution in indoor gardening that ended those dark ages: the introduction of artificial light—especially fluorescent fixtures—as a supplement or substitute for sunlight. Today, hundreds of plants that once were limited to their native climes are easily cultivated under electric lamps. Plants that do particularly well under artificial light include desert-blooming succulents, most tropical foliage plants, and such tropical flowering plants as begonias, bromeliads, orchids and gesneriads.

Artificial lighting has also permitted an almost unlimited choice of locations for plants, from such an obvious spot as the living room to a seemingly impossible site like a windowless basement. Any place will do where you can install a light fixture and maintain a daytime temperature of 70 to 80° for tropical plants, 65 to 75° for those native to temperate zones.

Well-lit plants thrive in unexpected places. Scientists at a United States base 20 feet under the permafrost of Antarctica have a flourishing light garden, as does a Michigan family that uses an old bomb shelter as an underground greenhouse. A grade school teacher on the island of Savoonga, Alaska, just south of the Bering Strait,

To determine optimum growing conditions, scientists cultivated dieffenbachias and African violets (opposite) under progressively stronger light. The specimens in front got four times more light than the smallest plants.

grows flourishing crops of ivy, gesneriads, coleuses and marigolds.

Tour your own household: you should be able to find several first-rate locations. A drab, anonymous foyer, for example, could become instantly more inviting with a graceful fern as a piece of living sculpture in one illuminated corner. A wall of books and hi-fi equipment in the living room, handsome but sterile, takes on new life when a couple of shelves are filled with an assortment of top-lighted African violets and columneas. Or a discarded TV cabinet—one inventive light gardener stripped an old set of its black-and-white innards, rewired it for two 20-watt fluorescent fixtures, and turned it into a color set with flowers and foliage.

If none of these situations catches your fancy, you might want to consider portable planters, each with its own built-in light source. You can construct your own or buy them ready-made. If practicality is your prime concern, such a planter filled with dramatically lit greenery is hard to surpass as a room divider. The fluorescent tubes can be neatly concealed with baffles or valances *(opposite),* and the light from the garden will add to the illumination of the room.

FRESH HERBS FOR FLAVOR

Many gardeners have been attracted to artificial light gardening because they wanted to grow herbs in their kitchens. On a countertop no wider than a dishwasher, you can have a garden as utilitarian as it is ornamental, planted with winter and summer savory, tender basil, pineapple sage, thyme and other herbs that will be ready for plucking at the toss of a salad or the simmering of a stew. You can easily create such a kitchen herb garden by mounting a two-tube, 24-inch fluorescent fixture under a kitchen cabinet and placing potted plants underneath it on a tray of wet pebbles. The moist pebbles will increase the humidity; to keep the garden thriving, just water, fertilize and provide light for 14 to 16 hours a day.

Once your appetite for light gardening has been whetted in the kitchen, you probably will be drawn to more ambitious installations. A basement, an insulated attic or a heated garage are ideal locations to set up a couple of work tables with a number of 48-inch fluorescent fixtures suspended above them. In a pinch, even a closet—with louvered doors to provide the proper ventilation—will do. A typical setup requiring minimal wiring and carpentry is shown on page 15.

A PAYOFF IN UTILITY

Such a working indoor garden, which costs far less than comparable greenhouse space, need not look pretty in its out-of-the-way location. It can be a staging area for nursing ailing plants, for propagating new ones, for maintaining plants in a state of dormancy and for forcing others toward the edge of flowering before they are moved to a more public location for display. A utilitarian light garden can also be a valuable adjunct to an outdoor garden as a place to start seeds of flowers and vegetables weeks before it is warm enough to plant them outdoors. Many a light gardener harvests the first crop of basement-started lettuce from his outdoor garden while neighbors are still searching for the pale green shoots of their conventionally sown lettuce. Some light gardeners in northern latitudes even have success raising long-season plants by this combination of indoor starting and outdoor maturity. By adding three weeks to the front end of a melon's life span, for example, a gardener in Minnesota can raise 110-day honeydews in a 90-day growing zone, harvesting them just before the first autumn frost.

It was this spirit of experimentation that led Liberty Hyde Bailey, a pioneering American horticulturist, to try using artificial light to stimulate plant growth. In 1893, Bailey built a pair of glass-

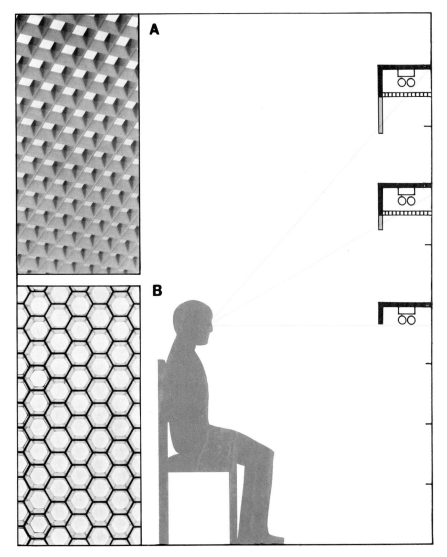

roofed "forcing houses" at Cornell University's school of agriculture and equipped one with the kind of arc light that cities were beginning to use to light their streets. He reported cautiously that "the electric light . . . can be advantageously used upon lettuce to piece out the sunlight in midwinter." A commercial grower in Boston took this advice and harvested each of three successive winter crops of lettuce a week earlier than usual. Bailey's work led many other scientists to experiment with "electro-horticulture," but few home gardeners heard of Bailey's notion of piecing out the winter sun.

THE BIRTH OF A BOOM

Interest in artificial light gardening revived in 1938 when the first fluorescent tubes were marketed. Agricultural specialists quickly recognized that the lamps had practical applications for commercial growers far beyond Bailey's wildest dreams. They found that cool-burning fluorescent bulbs could be used to produce high light intensities for long periods without drying out plants the way hot incandescent bulbs did. Fluorescents were also relatively inexpensive to operate and they spread their light evenly over large areas. The long tubular shape paired very efficiently with plants grown in rows. Further experimentation showed that a combination of those early fluorescents, which emphasized the blue end of the light spectrum, and incandescents, which were strong in red rays, worked better than either type alone.

AFRICAN VIOLETS ARRIVE

World War II brought a temporary halt to light-gardening experimentation, but when peace returned, research resumed and amateur indoor gardeners soon became as curious about the use of artificial light as the commercial growers. Henry M. Cathey, a light-gardening expert with the U.S. Department of Agriculture's Research Service, has credited amateur African violet fanciers for developing much basic data on growing house plants under artificial light. The *Saintpaulia* genus, to which these gesneriads belong, then represented the bulk of flowering tropical plants in this country. It was discovered in the moist uplands of East Africa in the 1890s, and 10 varieties were introduced in the United States in 1936. Despite the care lavished on them, African violets rarely did well except in a greenhouse. They were inhibited either by too much light or by too little; their natural habitat on the forest floor gave them tree-filtered sunlight, a difficult environment to simulate on a window sill.

Fluorescent lamps proved a lifesaver for African violets, providing a quality and quantity of light that approximated the intensity the plants preferred. Light-grown African violets became known as miracle plants. They could be kept in bloom throughout the year, and individual blossoms lasted up to 50 per cent longer than those of plants that had been grown in greenhouses.

Since those early days, thousands of amateurs have learned how to grow splendid collections of begonias, African violets and gloxinias under lighting as simple as a low-cost tabletop fluorescent lamp. The practice of gardening under lights has progressed from a hit-or-miss novelty to an everyday gardening procedure whose miracles are easily understood and mastered.

The best results require more than the flick of a switch, however. To design a light regime that suits the particular needs of particular plants, you must know how to obtain the intensity of light needed, how long to leave the light on each day and—if you want to go an extra scientific step—how to choose light bulbs or tubes that emit the best balance of colors. Moreover, since plants grow faster and more constantly under artificial lights, such cultivation techniques as watering and feeding have to be custom tailored, too.

If you ask an avid light gardener for the secret of his success, he might talk about maintaining high humidity or using a special fertilizer—like any other gardener—but he might also discuss red and far-red wavelengths, nanometers, lumens and other arcane-sounding terms having to do with light.

To appreciate the role of light in plant growth, you need to

A SCIENCE AND AN ART

LIGHTING UP A FIREPLACE

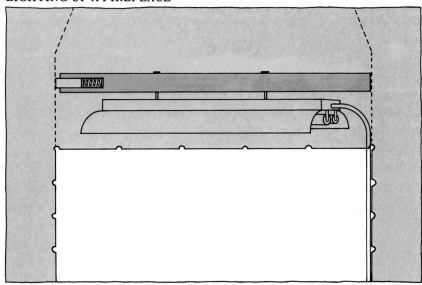

To mount a fluorescent fixture in a fireplace, cut a 2-by-2 half an inch shorter than the inside width of the fireplace. In one end, drill a ⅝-inch hole about 5 inches deep. In the hole, place a compression spring 3 inches long and ½ inch in diameter, plus a dowel pin ½ inch in diameter and long enough to compress the spring and hold the 2-by-2 in place. Attach a two-tube, 24-inch fixture equipped with a reflector to this mount and wedge it into the fireplace, spring end first, high enough to hide the fixture.

For starters, a basic tabletop assembly

A light garden that is little more than a fixture above and a tray below can satisfy the needs of many kinds of plants. The unit at right, 4 feet long, 1 foot deep and adjustable up to 18 inches between the tray and the lamps, displays 15 species, from a flavorful sweet basil to a spectacular African blood lily. Yet it was built in a few hours.

The frame, of 1- by 2-inch redwood, is fastened with wing nuts and bolts to electrical conduit tubing ¾ inch in diameter. The light is provided by a two-tube, 40-watt workshop fixture that is hung on chains with S hooks so it can be raised or lowered easily. A reflector increases the light intensity *(page 28)*. Pots are set on a plastic grid of the type used to diffuse fluorescent light. Beneath this grid is a plastic tray. When the plants are watered, the runoff drains into the tray, then raises the humidity as it evaporates.

This microcosm of a light garden accommodates a plaid cactus, perched atop an overturned pot so it gets strong light, as well as a coleus (far right), which prospers in the weaker light near the tubes' ends. The dwarf pomegranate needs regular pruning to keep it within the unit.

AGLAONEMA 'SILVER QUEEN'   ECHEVERIA SUCCULENT   BALL CACTUS

EYELASH BEGONIA   SWEET BASIL   AFRICAN VIOLET 'PIXIE BLUE

PLAID CACTUS   DWARF POMEGRANATE   AFRICAN BLOOD LILY   CRAPE MYRTLETTE   COLEUS

ANGEL WING BEGONIA 'MATHILDE'   CISSUS SUCCULENT   AICHRYSON SUCCULENT   OXALIS REGNELLII

understand the physical nature of light itself. Light is radiant energy that travels through space—be it the cosmos or a corner of your living room—as electromagnetic waves. In nature, this energy originates in the sun, where it is generated by nuclear fusion and is radiated in waves of different lengths, varying from ultra-high-frequency short waves to low-frequency long waves. The waves that influence plants occupy a narrow band near the center of this range.

Light waves are measured in nanometers (a nanometer is one billionth of a meter—about four hundred millionths of an inch), and the length of a wave determines its color. Blue is moderately short, about 450 nanometers, while red is longer, about 650 nanometers.

THE ROLE OF THE SPECTRUM When scientists first began to recognize the crucial role of sunlight in photosynthesis in 1779, they assumed that plants subsisted on the same sunlight that humans can see, no more and no less. But experiments have since revealed that plants respond to a significantly wider spectrum of light (from 280 to 800 nanometers) than do humans, whose visible light range is 380 to 760 nanometers, and that plants respond selectively to the components of that spectrum. What humans see as colors, plants respond to as specific stimulants to various growth activities: food production, flowering, dormancy, seed germination, the manufacture of chlorophyll and such other activities as branching and leaf thickening. In 1959, Department of Agriculture scientists isolated phytochrome, the plant pigment that controls many of these functions, and they found that it responds like an off-on switch to the red and far-red wavelengths of light. Today, we know that plants depend on three spectral colors for their survival: red and blue waves to energize chlorophyll, and red and far-red to stimulate phytochrome.

The gardener who confines his efforts to growing plants outdoors will find this news of little practical use. Light in nature changes constantly and plants are conditioned by natural selection to take it as it comes: so much brilliance, so much of each color component and so many hours each day, depending on weather, season and air purity. But indoor gardeners can control these factors and thus control many of a plant's growth characteristics.

LIVING FOOD FACTORIES To start, you can supply part or all of the light needed for photosynthesis, the most important chemical process on earth. Photosynthesis not only makes plants grow by transforming radiant energy into chemical energy and ultimately into food for the plant, it also forms the basis of the food chain for all other living things. The key to photosynthesis is a microscopic pale green body known as a chloroplast, containing minute concentrations of a light-sensitive pigment, chlorophyll. Up to 1,000 chloroplasts are scattered in each leaf cell where photosynthesis takes place; there they act as super-efficient food factories. Very sensitive to waves of red light, and only slightly less so to blue, the chlorophyll pigments use these segments of radiant energy as fuel. Water and carbon dioxide, the raw materials of photosynthesis, are continuously drawn into plant tissues, split into hydrogen, oxygen and carbon molecules, and re-arranged into nutritious carbohydrates. Oxygen and excess water are then released as waste products of this process, improving the air we breathe and returning water vapor to the atmosphere.

A GROWTH EXPERIMENT

For a simple demonstration of how light affects growth, buy two coleuses of equal size. Place one 6 inches below a two-tube fluorescent fixture. Place the other in the same room where it will get only incidental light. Water them equally. In two months, the artificially lighted plant will show signs of efficient photosynthesis: rich green leaves with colorful markings and compact growth. The other plant will be dull in color, leggy with smaller leaves.

Foliage plants such as philodendrons and ferns require much lower light levels than do flowering plants such as African violets and begonias. In nature, you are likely to find a foliage plant growing in the shade of other plants, while a flowering plant seeks full sunlight. In a tropical setting, different varieties of the same species some-

EASY-TO-BUILD MOUNT FOR A FLUORESCENT FIXTURE

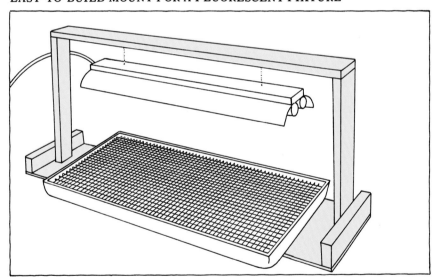

To make this mount for a fluorescent fixture 48 inches long, use 2-by-4 lumber and a base of ½-inch exterior-grade plywood, 67 inches long and as wide as necessary to hold the plant tray. The uprights are 30 inches long and the top bar 63½ inches.

Join the pieces with sixpenny nails, reinforcing the corners with right-angle braces. Suspend the fixture on chains, using S hooks so the height can be adjusted. The humidity tray is 2 inches deep; in it is a plastic grid to keep pots from standing in water.

times take root in ascending light zones, using the humus-filled crotches of tall trees to find maximum illumination.

In an artificial light garden, though, plants with differing requirements grow best in separate microclimates. Plants that prefer low light levels include the Chinese evergreen, cast-iron plant, dracaena and parlor palm. Medium-level ornamentals include the dieffenbachia, herbs, ferns and African violets. High light levels are needed by most cacti, crotons, orchids and geraniums, among others.

LONG DAYS AND SHORT

Whether you are growing ferns or figs, the length of the time a plant is exposed to light in a 24-hour span—known as the photoperiod—is as important as the intensity and color of light it receives. In nature, this photoperiod is determined by the seasonal tilt of the earth and by latitude. Areas near the equator know little change in day length from one season to the next; days and nights are roughly 12 hours each. But polar regions have 24-hour days near the summer solstice and 24-hour nights during the winter solstice.

The United States and southern Canada, which lie mostly between the 30th and 50th parallels, experience moderate changes in day length with the changing seasons. Winnipeg, Manitoba, somewhat surprisingly, gets more than 3 additional hours of natural daylight in late June than St. Petersburg, Florida. In winter, the situation is reversed.

Any gardener knows there is a relationship between the seasons and plant flowering or fruiting, though fortunately not all plants mature at the same speed. The idea that an individual response to the photoperiod was responsible for the time at which plants will flower was demonstrated more than half a century ago. In 1918, W. W. Garner and H. A. Allard, two plant physiologists at the Department of Agriculture's experiment station in Beltsville, Maryland, began working with Virginia tobacco to see if it was suited to cultivation in more northerly latitudes. The tobacco variety chosen, a mutant called Maryland Mammoth because of the size it attained in the Beltsville fields, puzzled them. Despite its apparent vitality, they could not get it to produce the flowers necessary for regeneration. But when Garner and Allard propagated the tobacco by cuttings and grew it in a greenhouse over the winter, it flowered and bore seed by the time it was only half the normal size.

That summer, following up on their experience, they built a small shed and sealed it to prevent any light from entering. They planted some tobacco in the field and some in portable trays. Each day they set the trays out in the sun for eight hours, then returned them to the shed for 16 hours of total darkness. By the end of the summer, the tobacco that had been growing under the artificially controlled short-day, long-night routine was flowering prolifically. But the plants that were grown in the field, like those the summer before, had no flowers. Similar tests with soybeans produced similar results, so the two horticulturists concluded that in many plants, the duration of light, which they called the photoperiod, was the key to producing the flowers that would enable the plants to bear seeds. Thus, plants could be made to bud and bloom out of their normal seasons if the photoperiod could be manipulated under controlled conditions. And that is exactly what is done in many light gardens.

Since the original studies, hundreds of plants have been classified according to their photoperiodic response. Garner and Allard created four general categories: short-day plants, long-day plants, daylength-intermediate plants and daylength-neutral plants. Techniques you can use to supply the day-length requirements of your plants are described in Chapter 2. Specific requirements of many popular light-garden plants are given in the encyclopedia that begins on page 79, but it is worth noting here that something as seemingly harmless as a streetlight casting a pale glow into a room full of short-day plants can upset their timing and prevent blooming.

In general, short-day plants should have 13- to 14-hour nights to form buds and subsequently to flower. House plants in this category quite logically include plants that would bloom in fall or winter in their natural habitat: for example, Rieger and eyelash begonias, the zebra plant and certain bromeliads including *Aechmea fasciata*. Long-day plants, such as late spring- and summer-blooming annuals, need six to 10 dark hours to bloom. Daylength-intermediate plants flower within a narrow range of day-night lengths, generally around 12 hours of light and 12 hours of dark. Fortunately, this cranky category is extremely small and includes no house plants. The long-day, short-day and daylength-intermediate plants all have individual cultural requirements but any one of them would be compatible with the undemanding day-neutrals. With normal care, plants in this group simply reach a certain age or size, then set buds. Many of the most popular house plants are day-neutrals, including the gesneriads, coleuses and most geraniums. Tomatoes, which grow well under artificial light, are also day-neutrals.

Meeting a plant's photoperiod requirements—whether it is a day-neutral or daylength-intermediate plant—is just one of the steps the canny light gardener takes to get the plant to grow as well as if it were in the land of its native origin, and maybe even better. He must also know how to choose the right lamps, set them at the proper distance and maintain them at top performance, the basic skills of sunless gardening described in the following chapter.

A NEED FOR DARKNESS, TOO

What makes your garden glow 2

An oil executive whose house plants thrived in a sunny contemporary house in Houston almost gave up his hobby after being transferred to New York. The building next to his high-rise apartment cut off almost all daylight from the windows that faced east. And the cold and dreary winter light that filtered in from the north seemed not the least bit conducive to plant cultivation. He was almost ready to switch to raising tropical fish when a thoughtful neighbor welcomed him to the building with a gift—a beautiful potted African violet covered with blooms. She had grown it in her apartment under artificial light, which the executive had never needed for the plants that had thrived in his Texas home.

After reading a voluminous amount of literature about light gardening, he filled his apartment with a variety of bulbs and tubes—fluorescent, incandescent, even costly mercury-vapor and sodium lamps—determined to spare his plants no amenity that science and electric-supply salesmen could offer. He tried special tubes with spectral output weighted in favor of blue, to stimulate plant growth, or red and far red, to induce flowering. He tried bulbs that produced little heat and bulbs that were designed to deliver extra wide swaths of light.

After months of experimenting, and after about as many failures as successes, he reached the conclusion held by virtually all experienced light gardeners: a combination of standard cool-white and warm-white fluorescent tubes, available at any housewares store, gives excellent results with most flowering and foliage house plants and also provides a very pleasant effect. ("Warm" and "cool" refer to the amount of red or blue light waves the tubes give off, not their heat output, but the color variations are small; the plants would thrive under either type of tube.)

Many a skilled light gardener, when asked how he tends his garden, will respond with, "by guess and by golly," or some other

Oblivious to the snow piled outside her Massachusetts farmhouse, Rita Arapoff grooms some of the 50 kinds of plants she grows under industrial-type fluorescent lights in a room next to her kitchen.

inexplicable green-thumb system. Years of trial and error have taught him the regimen that works for him. His plants let him know when he is doing things right and when he needs to change some part of his routine. Nevertheless, a working acquaintance with lumens, watts, foot-candles and spectral output will be useful and time-saving when you are shopping for a fixture or reading instructions for growing light-garden plants.

Watts are units of energy expended in operating a light or other electrical device. Your monthly electric bill is based on kilowatt (thousands of watts) hours of electricity consumption. Fluorescent light tubes and incandescent bulbs are rated in watts, but because each brand performs differently, comparing them by wattage alone can be misleading. The best way to gauge a light's efficiency is by lumens, a measure of its light output at the source. One 40-watt tube may produce 2,800 lumens, for example, while a more efficient 40-watt tube on the next shelf will produce 3,200 lumens and is a better buy—if the prices are comparable. The lumen rating is not printed on the tube but is generally available in catalogues at stores that stock fluorescent fixtures.

INCHES AND CANDLE POWER

You should also be familiar with foot-candles, a measure of the brightness of light at the point where it strikes an object such as a plant. The closer a plant is to a source of artificial light, the higher the number of foot-candles it receives. Noon sunlight falling on a plant outdoors in summer can measure 10,000 foot-candles or more. Indoors, optimum artificial lighting rarely exceeds more than 1,300 foot-candles, and a foot-candle level as low as 100 may be adequate for such low-light plants as ferns and Chinese evergreens because the light is delivered to them at a constant, dependable level for as much as 16 hours a day.

If you know the lumen rating of a 4-foot (40-watt) fluorescent tube, you can calculate the number of foot-candles two such tubes will deliver at various distances directly below them. Multiply the lumen rating by .23 at a distance of 6 inches, by .11 at 12 inches, by .068 at 18 inches. A pair of 3,200-lumen tubes, for example, can be expected to provide 736 foot-candles at 6 inches, 352 foot-candles at 12 inches, and 218 foot-candles at 18 inches.

Sometimes a combination of natural and artificial light gives better results than either does alone. One gardener who wanted her Lady Washington geraniums to be in bloom for a March flower show put them near a window in a cool room and gave them five hours of sunlight and 11 hours of artificial light each day during the months of January and February. By the time of the flower show, her geraniums were covered with blossoms, four weeks ahead of schedule.

Spectral output, another light-gardening term, describes the colors a lamp emits; a color that is used by a plant may be invisible to the human eye. Different models of fluorescent tubes emit light of various colors, depending on the phosphor compound with which the inside of the tube is coated. Growth lamps, those special fluorescent tubes designed for use in light gardens, include colors that make flowers and foliage attractive to look at, but these lamps may deliver light less efficiently than conventional tubes.

If fluorescent tubes had been invented with light gardening in mind, they could not have come much closer to filling the needs of indoor gardeners. From the time they were first marketed in 1938 they were ideal (except for an inadequate amount of red and what scientists call far-red emissions, compensated for in early light gardens by supplemental incandescent bulbs). In time the spectral-output problems were solved, and fluorescent tubes became the standard illumination in virtually all home light gardens.

One of the reasons fluorescents are popular is the low cost of keeping them turned on for long periods of time, even in the face of escalating energy costs. For example, in the late 1970s a 40-watt fluorescent lamp operated for 14 hours added less than two cents to an electric bill. It produced between 2,100 and 3,200 lumens, depending on the brand and model.

If you want to calculate the cost of operating a light garden in your home, multiply the combined wattage of the lamps needed by the number of hours you would operate them each day. Add 10 per cent for the fluorescent ballast and divide by 1,000 to get the daily electricity consumption in kilowatt-hours. Multiply that figure by your power company's residential cost of electricity per kilowatt-hour (this information is usually printed on the electric bill, expressed as KWH) to get your daily operating cost. As shown in the table on page 23, a fluorescent tube is approximately six times more efficient in light output than an incandescent bulb of the same wattage, and it should last 10 to 15 times longer (9,000 high-performance hours instead of 750) if it is turned on and off once each day, as happens in most light gardens. The chief wear and tear on a fluorescent tube comes from a slight erosion of the coating on its terminals each time it is started.

Another advantage of fluorescents is their long, tubular shape, ideal for the shelf design of most light gardens. The light is shed with relative uniformity along a wide elliptical plane, while an incandescent bulb concentrates its light in a small area.

By mounting fluorescent tubes side by side with their centers 3 to 6 inches apart above your plants, you can maintain uniformly high

LIFE UNDER CITY LIGHTS

Urban gardeners who are puzzled when a tree fails to leaf out on one side in the spring may find the cause in the powerful high-pressure sodium street lamps being installed in many cities. These lamps can turn streets into gigantic light gardens. When fall weather is mild, some trees respond to the bright light at night by growing longer than they should. The tender new growth is killed by the winter frost; damage becomes evident the following spring in the dieback of twigs on the side of the tree facing the street lamp. Trees especially sensitive include Norway maple, paper birch, catalpa, sycamore, American elm and zelkova. Less sensitive are sweet gum, willow oak and American holly.

FUNCTION FOLLOWS FORM

light levels over most of a rectangular garden. The 6 inches at each end of a fluorescent tube produce diminished light, however, so these ends are good places to locate the plants needing the least amount of light. (That is why one 48-inch tube is more efficient than two 24-inch tubes placed end to end.)

Among the many fluorescent tubes commonly available are 20-watt, which are 24 inches long; 30-watt, 36 inches long; 40-watt, 48 inches long and so on, up to a very-high-output 215-watt tube, 96 inches long, that requires special wiring in the fixture. The longest tubes are most efficient, but they are too unwieldy for most home installations. Fluorescent lights also come as circular or U-shaped tubes. Some are twisted or grooved to increase light output, some are thinner than average, and some even have built-in reflective coatings shielding half the tube. In general, these specialty fluorescents command premium prices without providing any appreciable advantage for a light garden.

It is essential, though, that tubes and fixtures match. Most tubes sold have paired prongs to fit into rapid-start fixtures, but some older fixtures with separate starters require the kind of tube that has a single prong at each end. The tube must be the proper diameter for the fixture as well. A designation such as T-12 on a tube translates into its diameter in eighths of an inch. Thus the T-12, which fits a rapid-start fixture, is 1½ inches in diameter.

"White" light is most commonly used in light gardening, but the term encompasses many variations. In addition to the original bluish-toned cool-white light, you can choose among de luxe cool-white, daylight, white, warm-white and de luxe warm-white. The names, standard in the lamp industry, do little to indicate their effects on plants and people. As a light gardener, all you really need to know is that cool-white and warm-white give a pleasing effect in combination and work well together.

KEEPING PLANTS COOL

Whatever its spectral output, a fluorescent tube produces less heat than other kinds of lamps, a major consideration when fixtures are kept on for 14 to 16 hours a day within a few inches of plants. Heat is low in a fluorescent tube because nothing burns inside it except filaments in the cathode at each end. Instead, an electric current arcs in a glass envelope from one cathode through a mixture of inert gases to the other cathode. This arcing produces ultraviolet radiation, causing a phosphor compound coating the inside of the tube to glow. The potentially harmful ultraviolet waves are held captive inside the tube.

In addition to the tube, a fluorescent light fixture consists of a housing that carries the wires; a pair of projecting tube sockets; and a ballast, a small black box within the fixture that transforms house current to the low voltage that the tube uses. These parts are factory assembled and usually can be installed without modifications. The ballast does generate some heat, however, so you may want to separate it from the holder and relocate it some distance away if, for example, the lamp is used in a setup such as a terrarium where the heat is not easily vented.

Incandescent bulbs, by their very design, are too hot for a small or confined light garden. Thomas A. Edison described one of his first incandescent bulbs as "a hot hair pin in a bottle." If you put your hand close to one, you will be reminded of just how hot it becomes as its high-resistance tungsten filament burns. Most of the electrical energy that goes into an incandescent bulb is dissipated as heat; only 5 per cent comes out the other end as visible light. That light is mostly red; it is deficient in the blue waves that are needed to stimulate the growth of plants.

Nevertheless, there are places where a fluorescent tube can not be camouflaged and only an incandescent bulb is appropriate for decorative purposes. For instance, you might want to display a large foliage plant such as a holly fern in an entrance hall or on a stairway landing, where an unobtrusive light fixture is desirable to supple-

MORE HEAT THAN LIGHT

EFFICIENCY OF INCANDESCENT AND FLUORESCENT LIGHTS	INCANDESCENT	FLUORESCENT
Consumption of electricity in watts: by light	40	40
by ballast	0	6
Output in lumens	450	3,200
Light output per watt	11	70
Visible light radiation	5%	20%
Invisible radiation	80%	32%
Energy absorbed by fixture and ballast	15%	48%
Total power consumption	100%	100%

A fluorescent tube and ballast use slightly more energy than an incandescent bulb of comparable wattage, but emit over six times more light, as shown in this chart based on a U.S. Department of Agriculture study. A tube also converts four times as much of its energy consumed into visible light radiation and lasts 10 to 15 times longer—making it a better value despite higher initial cost.

ment natural light. An incandescent spotlight recessed in the ceiling is a logical and attractive solution. Or you may have a palm, another low-light plant, growing with only moderate success in natural light from a nearby window. An incandescent spotlight fixture attached to the top of the window frame would give it supplemental light on dark days and in the evenings.

Manufacturers have developed incandescent bulbs that project the light forward while deflecting much of the heat. These devices reduce the risk of leaf shrivel caused by too much heat. But they should always be used in special fixtures that are equipped with adequate ventilation, lest you fry the fixture—and risk a fire—while trying to save the plant.

As a general rule, any incandescent bulb should be kept several feet from a plant to keep the heat within the range the plant will tolerate. This, of course, also cuts down on the foot-candles of light reaching the plant. Incandescents, therefore, are generally suited only for supplementing daylight or for maintaining a plant rather than stimulating growth.

Whenever you place incandescent spotlights or floodlights at an angle above plants for a decorative effect, remember to rotate your plants occasionally to maintain an even rate of growth on all sides. Most plants can retain a handsome aspect for several weeks under incandescent lights before you need to move them back to the light garden for a revivifying fluorescent treatment.

High-intensity lamps—mercury vapor, metal halide and sodium—are used by some commercial growers, but for most home hobbyists they are too bulky or too expensive, or the light they deliver is too harsh. One common high-intensity lamp, the sun lamp that is used for warming and tanning, has a destructive effect on plants because it produces ultraviolet radiation as well as excessively hot infrared rays.

PREFABRICATED SETUPS

You can build your own simple fluorescent stand (*page 15*). But if you are a novice you may prefer to buy a commercial unit that needs only to be plugged into an electrical outlet. Many types of prefabricated light-garden setups are on the market. Before you buy, browse through seed-company and garden-supply catalogues and gardening magazines, then survey the kinds of fixtures that are available at garden supply centers and hardware stores in your area. If you decide to buy a light fixture that is combined with a stand for holding plants, here are some things to keep in mind:

● Be sure the unit is strong enough to support the considerable weight of moist potting mix. The best stands are designed with the greater part of the weight on the bottom to prevent tipping.

● Buying a single-tube model is false economy, since one tube sheds an effective light path only 6 inches wide, too narrow to keep many plants healthy.

● Select a stand that will allow you to adjust the distance between the tube and the plants. The stand may have a stationary plant tray with telescoping supports for the light fixture, or the fixture may be hung on chains with S hooks so that you can adjust the height of the tube link by link.

● The lamp fixture should have a white-painted reflector; it will increase by one third the amount of light reaching the plants.

● Most good ready-mades come with a three-wire cord and a three-pronged plug so you can ground the electric current for safety in the event of a short circuit. If your outlets are not equipped to handle a three-pronged plug, you can buy an adapter at any hardware store, but be sure to attach the adapter's grounding clip to the screw that secures the outlet's face plate.

Tabletop setups typically come in 20-, 30- and 40-watt sizes. Straight fluorescent tubes are used in most light gardens, but stands with circular tubes, sold at 8-, 12- and 16-inch diameters, work well for single prized plants or small collections.

GROWING ON MANY LEVELS

Prefabricated light garden units on a grand scale, with several shelves, are available. These may be movable carts or they may be stationary bookcase-style units to be set against a wall or used as room dividers. Some permit you to adjust the light level by moving the shelves rather than the fixtures. Such a stand is usually large enough to accommodate two or four tubes ranged side-by-side under a single reflector umbrella. It may have a plastic honeycomb or cube-shaped louver below the light tubes to reduce glare. The main advantage of a movable cart is that you can wheel it about to give your garden sunlight if you like or to take it to the sink for watering, repotting or grooming your plants.

When you reach the level of commitment that a multilevel garden involves, you may want to build a unit suited to your decorating and gardening needs. You can find a variety of design suggestions in pamphlets that are available from the Indoor Light Gardening Society, the Department of Agriculture and your state agricultural extension service.

An old television cabinet, if it is attractively designed, can be adapted to make a good container for a light garden. A buffet or record cabinet is also suitable if you remove the back to improve ventilation. One enthusiast has a light garden in his efficiency apartment in such a discarded cabinet. When the front doors are closed, it is impossible to tell that a score of plants are thriving inside.

There are many other light garden arrangements that require more ingenuity than expertise:

● One gardener put two 40-watt tubes and a reflector on a rugged-looking sawhorse-shaped stand with a cedar-shingled awning masking the reflector. The fixture illuminates a plant tray 18 inches wide by 48 inches long. The owner has had success with begonias and gesneriads on a 13-hour-a-day light regimen.

● Another gardener installed five pairs of 40-watt fluorescent fixtures on the undersides of the five adjustable shelves in a built-in bookcase 6 feet high and 8 feet long. He painted the entire enclosure flat white to ensure the high light levels needed to raise *Paphiopedilum* and *Phalaenopsis* orchids.

● Rather than look at empty fireplaces all summer, many gardeners

A selection of light-garden plants for beginners

When you choose plants for a light garden your dilemma is like that facing a child in a candy store: there are so many choices and they all look good. Some plants, however, are more amenable than others to the trials and errors that a beginning light gardener is likely to put them through. The list at right will provide a varied, interesting and compatible selection of foliage and flowering house plants. All the plants are under 12 inches tall or can be kept less than that by pinching back. All are sold at garden centers or by mail· order. All tend to be resistant to pest attacks. The plants are also tolerant of frequent adjustments in light levels and feeding and watering schedules.

Plants should be grown under two 2-foot or two 4-foot fluorescent tubes, depending on the number of plants. One tube should be cool-white and the other warm-white, in a reflectorized fixture, with the light on for 14 to 16 hours a day. The plants marked with an asterisk need the most light and should be placed directly below the center of the tubes, propped up if needed so the top foliage is as close as possible to (but not touching) the tubes. This treatment should foster early blooming; for example, one dwarf crape myrtle, crape myrtlette, may start to bloom when it is only 3 inches tall. Plants needing less light can be placed under the ends of the tubes and toward the edges of the light swath, where the light level drops off.

Foliage plants

ALUMINUM PLANT
Pilea cadieri

BLUNT-LEAVED PEPEROMIA
Peperomia obtusifolia

BUSH BASIL
Ocimum minimum

COLEUS
Coleus blumei hybrids

FRECKLE-FACE PLANT
Hypoestes sanguinolenta

PRAYER PLANT
Maranta leuconeura

SILVER-NERVED FITTONIA
Fittonia argyroneura

SWEDISH IVY
Plectranthus australis

*ZEBRA HAWORTHIA
Haworthia fasciata

*PEARL PLANT
Haworthia margaritifera

Flowering plants

AFRICAN VIOLET
Saintpaulia hybrids

ARABIAN VIOLET
Exacum affine

*CRAPE MYRTLETTE
Lagerstroemia indica
Crape Myrtlette

*DWARF POMEGRANATE
Punica granatum nana

*FLAMINGO FLOWER
Anthurium scherzerianum

*IMPATIENS
Impatiens wallerana

OXALIS
Oxalis regnellii

WAX BEGONIA
Begonia semperflorens

suspend two-tube, 20-watt fixtures inside, just below the closed dampers *(page 11)*. One such gardener kept a half-dozen caladiums clustered below the lights on a 16-hour cycle timed to coincide with evening use of the room. The tubes selected have a purple glow, which, against a black background, creates the illusion that the foliage is floating in space.

● A gardener hung two-tube, 20-watt fixtures underneath every third step of an open staircase. Plants that need the most light are clustered below the lowest stair lamps, and taller, less demanding plants are under the higher units. An ivy hanging from the top step and under it a dieffenbachia 3 feet tall fill the nearly 6-foot rise between the top fixture and the floor. Such an arrangement makes it easy to fill each plant's light needs precisely, placing it at just the proper distance from the tubes.

The amount of light a plant needs and how far it should be from the tubes depends on the kind of plant, its age and the age of the tube, as well as on temperature, humidity and air quality. One indoor gardener reported that when he moved from Detroit to a town 50 miles away, the plants he had grown three inches from their lights in the city could now be grown a foot away in the cleaner, moister, cooler air in their new home.

But for all the variables, there are still some guidelines for positioning lights and plants, subject to how well the plants respond:

● The number of rows of tubes is determined by the depth of the shelf, table or terrarium that the garden is to occupy. Provide two tubes for approximately each foot of depth.

● The length of the tubes and their fixtures should correspond to the length of the garden. Provide a minimum of 20 watts per square foot. Not all tube lengths are readily available, however, so find out which ones are customarily stocked by your local hardware or lighting store, then plan your garden accordingly.

● The space between adjacent tubes should be 3 to 6 inches on center so the swath of high-intensity light produced by each tube intersects with that of its neighbor. If placed closer than 3 inches together, the tubes reflect each other's light as heat, reducing the number of foot-candles available to the plants and raising the temperature in the light garden.

● The vertical distance between the tubes and the plants should be determined by the plants' foot-candle needs *(Chapter 5)*.

● The first plants you choose to grow in your light garden should be compact and not more than 12 inches high, since plants of this type are the easiest to light evenly. Listed in the box on the opposite page are 18 house plants that are especially suitable for the beginning

METERING FOOT-CANDLES

Using arithmetic and a camera that is equipped with a built-in light meter, you can measure the foot-candles of light reaching a plant. Put opaque white paper on a stack of books at the same height as the top of the plant. Set the film speed at any ASA setting and aim the camera so that the paper fills the viewing frame. Adjust the lens opening (f-stop) and shutter speed until the meter shows a perfect exposure. Calculate the number of foot-candles with this formula: $10 \times f^2 \div t \times ASA$, in which f is the f-stop number, t the shutter speed in seconds, ASA the film speed. For example, with the ASA at 25 and the shutter speed at $^1/_{60}$ of a second, a lens opening of f/2 indicates illumination of approximately 100 foot-candles; and f/11, 2,800 foot-candles.

REFLECTED CANDLE POWER

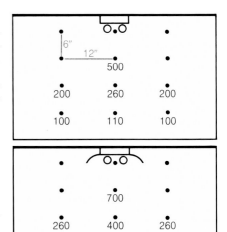

A reflector will increase light output from a fluorescent fixture without increasing your electric bill, as these efficiency measurements from a U.S. Department of Agriculture study show. A plant 6 inches directly below two 40-watt cool-white tubes without a reflector (top line, top chart) gets 500 foot-candles. With a reflector (top line, bottom chart) the plant gets 700 foot-candles. Figures on the second and third lines represent the amount of light a plant would get 12 and 18 inches below the tubes and 1 foot to either side. To take full advantage of this efficiency, keep the fixture dust-free.

light gardener. Some are flowering plants and some are foliage plants, but all are of a size that is easy to manage. Tall plants are also within the realm of light gardening, but they require supplemental lighting that is aimed at the middle and lower ranks of leaves to make the plants grow symmetrically.

PLANNING A LIGHT DIET

Many plants can be classified by their light requirements. Low-level plants need 75 to 200 foot-candles, measured at the top leaves; medium-level plants require 200 to 500 foot-candles; high-level plants need more than 500 foot-candles. Surprisingly, a large number of plants have never been categorized as to their light needs because light gardening is such a young science. Patient experimentation and close observation are likely to be your best guides in determining your plants' light needs.

For example, a foliage plant such as a kangaroo vine can be placed as far as 2 feet below a pair of fluorescent tubes and toward the darker areas at the ends, while a crossandra may need to nuzzle as close as 3 inches to the center of the tubes in order to bloom. In planning your garden, you will get best results if you group together plants that have similar light requirements, putting the most demanding ones in the center of the garden where the light is more intense. If it turns out that one plant will not thrive without a particularly large amount of light, it can be moved still closer to the tubes by setting its pot on a prop.

If you decide to grow orchids that require the extremely high light levels of 1,500 to 3,000 foot-candles in order to bloom, be prepared to make a larger investment. You may need what are known as high-output or very-high-output fluorescent tubes. Plants

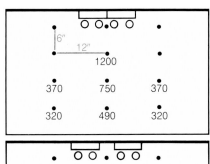

For plants like cacti that need bright light to bloom, four 40-watt fluorescent tubes efficiently positioned can deliver nearly twice the light of two. The charts at the left summarize tests conducted in a light chamber. When four tubes were mounted at 3-inch intervals in a white chamber (top left), the light intensity 6 inches below the fixture was 1,200 foot-candles, compared with 700 beneath a two-tube reflectorized fixture (opposite page). When the middle tubes were 6 inches apart (bottom left), the effective swath of light was slightly widened but the intensity directly below was sharply reduced.

placed 6 inches directly below such tubes will receive 30 to 100 per cent more foot-candles than plants under the same number of standard fluorescent tubes of the same length. But these special tubes have only three fourths to one half the life expectancy of standard tubes, and they cost about five times as much. Furthermore, they require special fixtures that are three or four times as expensive as the mass-produced workshop fixtures. Then, since these higher light levels introduce additional heat, you may need to add forced ventilation to bring the temperature of your light-garden environment under control.

THE BRIGHTEST CORNER

If space permits, you can grow plants with high light requirements under large banks of standard fluorescent tubes, alternating cool-white and warm-white tubes spaced 3 inches apart. At a distance of 6 inches from the plants, eight 4-foot tubes will deliver about 1,500 foot-candles, the equivalent of six high-output or four very-high-output tubes of the same size. The light given off by 10 standard tubes, 3,000 foot-candles, is the equivalent of eight high-output or six very-high-output tubes.

You can measure the foot-candles reaching your plants with a photographic light meter *(page 27)*. But such a reading will be approximate at best. If you need to make a more accurate measurement for a certain plant, you may want to purchase a foot-candle light meter designed especially for light gardeners. Or you can use the tables above and opposite, plus the recommendations in the individual encyclopedia entry *(Chapter 5)* to make an initial calculation, then observe the plant's condition and make more precise adjustments accordingly.

If your plants are not faring well, the fluorescent tubes may be past their prime. The lumen, or brightness, rating given fluorescent tubes represents their average performance. Fluorescents produce about 10 per cent more lumens than their average rating for the first 100 hours of operation but considerably fewer lumens after they pass 9,000 hours.

There are several ways to phase tubes in and out of action. Commercial light gardeners and scientists routinely retire tubes on a yearly basis, even though tubes are designed to last for nearly three years. They are willing to incur the extra expense in order to reduce the chances that diminishing light might spoil a critical experiment or a crop. For the home gardener, a more practical system is to mark the date of the tube's installation on the tube with a grease pencil. As the tube reaches the last stretch—say the 9,000-hour mark, which at a working time of 14 hours a day would be in the 22nd month— watch for darkening at tube ends. When darkening becomes clearly perceptible, replace the tube.

Be sure to align the guide creases on the ends of the new tube with the slit in the tube holder. If the tube is not properly seated, its life will be shortened. Since the new tube will initially deliver 110 per cent of its average rated foot-candles, you might want to raise the fixture or lower the garden shelf an inch or so for the first 100 hours (about a week on a 14-hour routine).

DUST: THIEF OF LIGHT

If you have provided all of the foot-candle and spectrum needs of your plants but they still are not doing well, the problem may simply be poor housekeeping. Dust accumulation on fluorescent tubes, reflective surfaces and the plants themselves is a persistent problem. Wipe the fixture surfaces clean once each week, and dust or rinse plants when they need it.

Your plants may not be at their peak because the reflector and the walls surrounding your light garden need a new coat of paint for optimum light reflection. Flat white paint is good and titanium pigment is desirable because it is nonyellowing.

One of the thorniest problems a light gardener must work out is timing. The amount of light or darkness some plants require to form flower buds, for example, can baffle even an expert. Fortunately, you can avoid such problems if you concentrate on the long-day and daylength-neutral plants such as those listed in the encyclopedia that begins on page 79. Gesneriads, many kinds of begonias, Natal plum and lavender will thrive and bloom almost constantly with 14- to 16-hour days, matching your own day-night regimen. Plants that would naturally bloom outdoors in summer, including annuals and vegetables, generally require 18 hours of light each day. Seedlings will tolerate a 24-hour day, but operating lights for more than 18 hours a day wastes energy.

Plant scientists have found that they have considerable leeway in giving some plants a longer time under lights rather than a higher level of light intensity. In an experiment at Ohio State University, for example, African violets in identical gardens received different amounts of light on two different schedules. Plants receiving 300 foot-candles of light for 12 hours a day were as large and had as many flowers and leaves as plants receiving 600 foot-candles for six hours a day. As it happened, the African violets fared best when they were lighted at 600 foot-candles for 18 hours a day, but the experiment was not designed to test alternate time-and-intensity schedules for this optimum regimen.

If you decide to try a short-day plant such as a strawberry geranium, which needs 12 to 14 hours of uninterrupted darkness in each 24-hour period in order to bloom, you may end up having to put it in a closet to seal out all illumination, since even a glimmer of light can throw off a plant's internal clock.

Any light schedule is easier to maintain with an inexpensive timer. If you buy one, make sure it is rated for more than the total wattage of all the fixtures you plan to attach, in order to allow a margin for the surge of current needed to start fluorescent tubes. To use a timer, set the clock dial to the on-and-off hours you desire, plug it into an electrical outlet and plug the lights into the timer. If you forget, or go away for the weekend, your artificial sun will still shine on cue. In fact, a timer can be used imaginatively in modifying the schedule of your light garden. One New York musician leaves his orchids under the care of a friend for a month every winter when the orchestra is on tour. To make the plant-sitting chores as easy as possible, the musician resets his timer to reduce the lights-on time from a normal 16 hours a day to only 10 hours. This so abbreviates the period of photosynthesis that the plants require far less water and fertilizer than they need during the longer days. The orchids seem to benefit from the rest; many of them come into bloom soon after the normal light schedule is resumed.

Most light gardeners prefer to have the periods of light coincide as much as possible with daylight hours, but if you prefer night lighting, the choice is yours. In some areas electricity is cheaper at night. Just be sure the plants get the number of dark hours they require. Though plants do not go to sleep, as humans do, they do need darkness, with cooler night temperatures. It is during these dark hours that they do most of their growing, assimilating the food they have manufactured by photosynthesis during the hours of light.

MECHANIZED TIMING

Decorating with a light touch

Many avid indoor gardeners are reluctant to undertake the installation of a light garden because in their mind's eye they visualize bulky industrial-type hanging fluorescent fixtures emitting light that turns skin tones an ugly gray or purple and distorts the natural colors of walls, furniture and other objects it falls on. As these pages demonstrate, a light garden need not be an eyesore.

The source of illumination for a light garden can be completely hidden by grids, valances or sheets of translucent material. The light itself, when produced by a combination of warm-tone and cool-tone fluorescent tubes, can be as flattering to people as it is good for plants. There are even special growth lamps that enhance the natural colors of whatever they illuminate—people, plants and any surrounding objects.

In the living room opposite the louvered shutters that ensure privacy also sharply limit natural light. Above the window, concealed fluorescent fixtures supply light for the two billowing Boston ferns suspended below as well as for the owner, who likes to read his newspaper in this comfortable spot. To sustain the room's uncluttered, contemporary look, the ceiling-mounted fixtures are framed with wood that is painted to match the adjacent walls.

With artificial light, you can enjoy the color and texture of living plants even in the darkest corner of your home. Solitary sculptural plants or banks of flowers can be placed anywhere. In a living room a mass of patterned foliage fills an unused fireplace. An awkward space under a stairway is turned into the focal point of a room. Walls of flowers line the entrance hallway of an apartment and the walls of a kitchen.

The artful light gardener can actually use his avocation to help solve decorating problems. By choosing lighting fixtures and plants as carefully as he chooses complementary furniture and carpeting, he can satisfy his esthetic tastes as completely as his botanical interests. And in so doing, he can achieve a plant-filled home where the sun forever shines.

The spare design scheme of this living room relies on a few dramatic accents, among them two huge Boston ferns brought to near perfection under lights.

Walls 12 feet high in a long, narrow kitchen invited this display of more than 50 kinds of begonias, succulents and ferns. They are sustained by three kinds of light. Those on the left are illuminated by fluorescent tubes concealed behind 4-inch-wide pine valances. Plants on the chrome-and-glass etagère on the right receive natural light from the window, supplemented by a ceiling spotlight.

An awkward corner beneath an open spiral stairway becomes an eye-catching light garden with fluorescent fixtures attached to the underside of each lower tread. In this townhouse, such plants as oxalis, false aralia, begonia and dieffenbachia thrive in pots set atop white pebbles in copper trays. The pebbles are kept moist to raise the humidity.

The problem of what to do about the gaping maw of an unused fireplace is solved here with clever camouflage. Caladiums, ferns and a poinsettia seem to float in the fireplace because their planter is painted black, as is the inside of the fireplace. A four-tube fluorescent fixture is concealed just below the damper.

An abundance of natural light streams into this greenhouse through a glass roof and end walls. The side walls, built of solid masonry in conformance with local building codes, were turned into an asset by the addition of redwood shelves, where hundreds of begonias and gesneriads grow under reflectorized fluorescent fixtures. When the plants outgrow their lighted quarters, they are moved somewhere else in the greenhouse.

Parallel light gardens create a dramatic entrance hall at the door of a city apartment. Four-tube fixtures are concealed by opaque valances made of white plastic. Backing mirrors give an illusion of depth, while end supports of clear plastic make the gardens visible from the living room beyond.

A world of endless springtime 3

It is always spring in a light garden, with unceasing budding and blooming made possible by a controlled regimen of light, temperature, moisture and humidity. But many of the plant-care techniques you use outdoors, where your plants' light source, the sun, is 93 million miles away, have to be modified when the light source is only 6 to 12 inches away and shines for as much as 18 hours a day.

You may have to water more frequently, for example, because in most of the country indoor air under lights is likely to be drier than that outdoors. The soil of your outdoor garden is too heavy for use in a light garden. Even the plants you buy for a light garden should be selected by applying different standards from those for plants you plan to grow outdoors.

When you buy a flowering plant for a light garden, for example, pick a young specimen that has yet to bloom for the first time; it will adjust more quickly to the new environment than a mature plant. If you buy a plant noted for unpredictable flowering characteristics, however, such as an African violet, it is better to choose a slightly older specimen with proven performance. Buy a plant that will not crowd the space reserved for it. By starting with small specimens, you can train the plant while you enjoy it and you will not have to perform harsh surgery to keep it from overrunning your garden.

It is desirable to isolate new plants for two weeks or so to avoid introducing pests or diseases into the light garden, but this is practical only if you are willing to maintain an extra garden unit as an isolation ward. A simpler, cheaper approach is to cover your new plant with a clear plastic bag in which you have punched two or three ¼-inch ventilation holes before placing it in your light garden. After two weeks inspect the plant with a magnifying glass; if you detect no sign of trouble, take off the plastic cover.

Your new plant probably came from the nursery potted in a mixture of leaf mold, loam, sand or perlite, and charcoal or pebbles.

A garden unit with adjustable shelves and fixtures makes it possible for a begonia fancier to fill the light needs of relatively tall species on one level and compact plants and cuttings on another.

Most light gardeners, however, prefer the so-called "soilless soils" because they weigh only a fraction as much as organic soils—an important consideration when you cluster a dozen or more pots on a narrow shelf or table.

Soilless potting mixes are largely composed of perlite, vermiculite and sphagnum peat moss, ingredients that provide a noncompacting, nonsoggy but water-retentive material in which plants will root easily and still have sufficient support. Soilless ingredients are sterile when they are purchased, so they do not harbor uninvited pests, diseases or weed seeds. And, although soilless mixes contain few nutrients, this deficiency is easily remedied by adding organic and chemical fertilizers.

TAILORING A PLANTING MIX

You can buy some soilless mixes neatly packaged and labeled for use on particular types of plants, such as those prepared for African violets or cacti. If you need a mix that is not prepackaged, however, it is easy enough to have a supply of sphagnum peat moss, vermiculite and perlite on hand so you can whip up a custom-made batch of mix whenever you need it.

Perlite is a white aggregate formed when volcanic glass or obsidian is heated rapidly to more than 1,400°. It is used in making concrete and plaster, but its gritty texture also has won it a place of honor in potting soil. Perlite performs the same service as coarse sand in aerating soil but a comparable volume weighs only one tenth as much as sand does.

Vermiculite is mica processed from ore containing silica, magnesium, aluminum oxides and other minerals. When the mica is heated, the moisture inside it changes to steam and explodes, expanding the particles. Vermiculite's structure helps the potting mix retain moisture without compacting. Both vermiculite and perlite are sold in an agricultural grade that is cleaner than the grade used by the building trade.

Sphagnum peat moss is partly decomposed plant matter that is gathered in bogs and dried to a fluffy consistency. It is popular in soil mixes because its fibers help retain water and add bulk, yet they do not soak up so much moisture that the mix becomes soggy. The chunky moss that is imported from Germany or Canada is the best kind to use in potting mixes.

There are many formulas for soilless mixes, and depending upon the general moisture, aeration and drainage needs of your plants, you can experiment with components until you strike a balance that works best for them. Here are three popular formulas recommended by the Indoor Light Gardening Society of America. (The parts indicated are by volume, not weight.)

MIX I is for tropical plants with coarse, tuberous or rhizomatous roots (that would include most bromelaids, dieffenbachias, gesneriads, hoyas and peperomias). A lean mix, it holds water for a relatively short period and will dry rapidly between waterings.

> 1 part perlite
> 1 part vermiculite
> 1 part sphagnum peat moss
> 1 teaspoon ground limestone per quart of mix

MIX II is for succulents (cactus, aloe and agave, for example). This mixture drains quickly, making it ideal for plants that require low moisture retention. It feels sandy to the touch.

> 2 parts perlite
> 2 parts vermiculite
> 1 part sphagnum peat moss
> 1 teaspoon ground limestone per quart of mix

MIX III is for plants with fine root systems (such as African violets, ferns, oxalis, most begonias, coleuses, marantas, pileas and ficuses). This is a mix that retains moisture well.

> 1 part perlite
> 1 part vermiculite
> 2 parts sphagnum peat moss
> 1 teaspoon ground limestone per quart of mix

These mixes are somewhat acid, a condition preferred by most house plants. The lime used in the three mixes reduces the acidity of the sphagnum peat moss; crushed eggshells can be used instead of lime, with one quarter of a cup of eggshells doing the job of one teaspoon of lime. Some plants, such as the gardenia, need a very acid soil; omit the lime source in their potting mixes.

If you want to check the chemical balance of your mix, buy an inexpensive soil-testing kit at any garden-supply center; it will give you a precise reading. For a less exacting check use litmus tape, sold at most aquarium shops. If the tape turns pink when inserted in wet mix, the mix is alkaline; if it turns blue, the mix is acid. More lime can be used to sweeten a mix that is too acid; various forms of sulfur are sold to reduce excessive alkalinity.

Whichever mix you use, supplement it with chemical nutrients at regular intervals once the new plant has recovered from the shock of being transplanted. You will find a number of water-soluble chemical fertilizers and encapsulated time-release fertilizers on sale at any garden center or nursery. All fertilizer containers are labeled with three numbers—for example, 20-20-20. These numbers, always listed in a standard order, indicate the percentages of nitrogen, phosphorus and potassium (potash) compounds in the mix. Nitrogen

TOO MUCH OF A GOOD THING

Although plants do not suffer from obesity, they can perish from overfeeding. This can happen if the plant is given too much fertilizer or if it is grown in a potting soil that contains an excess of mineral nutrients. In an analysis of seven brands of potting soil chosen at random, Dr. James W. Boodley of Cornell University found wide variations in nutrient levels. Three were so high they could be fatal to some plants, including such light-garden favorites as African violets and various other gesneriads.

SOMETHING TO GROW ON

makes plants green and lush, stimulating leaf and stem growth. Phosphorus promotes root growth and flower production. Potassium acts as a catalyst for other chemicals, helps a plant resist disease and also contributes to the starch-making process that feeds all parts of the plant. The remainder of the container's contents is an inert material, which reduces the concentration of chemicals and helps distribute them evenly.

Many gardeners tend to overfeed their plants on the theory that if a little fertilizer is good, a lot will be better. But it is hazardous to exceed the application rate recommended on the label. In fact, with the continuous feeding that accompanies gardening in soilless mixes, each application should be reduced far below the amount suggested on the container. For best results, stick to the readily controllable water-soluble fertilizers and follow these rules: if you feed your plants once a week, mix fertilizer at one fourth the recommended strength; if you feed your plants every day as part of a watering regimen, cut the concentration to one tenth. Plants are amazingly efficient users of whatever you feed them and, in a light garden, tall or wide-spreading growth is not the goal; what you are seeking is the small but perfect plant.

ANALYZING NUTRIENTS

No two plants have precisely the same need for nitrogen, phosphorus and potassium any more than any two people metabolize food at the same rate. It is not practical to concoct a chemical for each plant or even for each species, though a specific formula has in fact been developed for the popular African violet—12-36-14. Not every plant you wish to grow will have such precisely prescribed nutritive needs, but from several general formulas you can choose

PULLING IT ALL TOGETHER
Plants of varying sizes and potting-mix needs, but with similar light requirements, can be handsomely and conveniently grouped together to form a single, compact garden. Place the pots in a waterproof box of uncut sphagnum moss, with the rims at a uniform height but hidden in the moss. If clay pots are used, you can reduce the frequency of watering by keeping the moss moist.

one that should prove suitable. Pick a mix with a high first number—30-10-10, for example—to promote leafy growth of acid-loving plants. Pick a balanced formula (20-20-20 or the less concentrated 10-10-10) for most other house plants. For plants that you want to keep in bloom constantly, or for a seasonally flowering plant that is due to set buds, use a mix that is high in the second and third numbers, such as 10-30-20. A compound with a low first number is also a good one to use on mature plants when you want to restrain growth. In each case, it is essential that the fertilizer be a soluble one; these generally come in stiff concentrations, unlike the dry fertilizers that are prepared for outdoor use.

A FISHY FERTILIZER

Many fertilizers also contain trace elements, such as iron, manganese, copper, zinc, molybdenum and boron. Some of these elements are also sold separately; chelated iron, for example, will work wonders on a plant with yellowing leaves caused by iron deficiency. Many light gardeners occasionally switch to fish emulsion, a totally organic fertilizer rich in trace elements. Centuries ago, America's coastal Indians were aware that whole fish, placed in planting holes, would make a crop flourish. Today, fish emulsion, sold in water-soluble concentrates, works the same wonders for garden plants—and without the smell. Fish emulsion is also popular because it is low in the salts that can burn a plant's roots if they are applied in excessive amounts.

Never put a water-soluble fertilizer on dry soil. Always water a plant before you feed it; this will further reduce the concentration of the fertilizer and increase absorption by the plant. Do not fertilize a plant when it has just been transplanted, when it is ailing or when it is dormant. Plants that bloom just once a year should be fed when new growth appears and when buds are forming, but not during the actual blooming period.

Even the most precisely balanced potting mixture should be flushed out about once a month to remove accumulated chemical salts, which can cause root burn. Pour water over the surface of the potting mix until it runs freely out of the hole at the bottom of the pot and let it drain on a rack, repeating the process half an hour later to complete the flushing.

THE ART OF WATERING

Watering plants may seem like the simplest and least controversial task in gardening, but more plants probably succumb to overzealous watering than to all the pests and diseases put together. When a plant is overwatered, the excess moisture prevents air from reaching the roots. Without air, the roots rot. Underwatering is equally hazardous, of course. When roots dry, they are unable to absorb moisture that later becomes available; the plant shrivels and

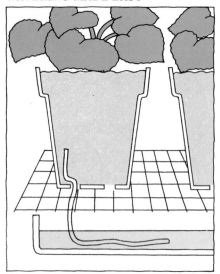

To keep watering from being a chore, equip plants that need constant moisture with fiberglass wicks. When you repot, insert a wick through a hole in the bottom of the pot, extending upward into the mix as shown, or fray the end of the wick and splay it at the bottom of the pot. Cut a grid a bit bigger than the water tray, using ½-inch-mesh wire screening. Set pots on the grid with the wicks extending into the water. Add a water-soluble fertilizer to the tray, diluted to one tenth the strength recommended on the label. Once each month, water the plant from the top of the pot.

dies. There is no simple way to prescribe a universal watering technique for a light garden, since requirements vary depending on the kinds of plants you grow and their distance from the fixture. The best advice is to get to know your plants as individuals. Work at developing a refined sense of touch so that your fingers can tell you when the soil needs water.

Certain species of cacti and other succulents require precise watering. For them, and for less fussy plants, too, you may want to purchase a soil-moisture tester, a relatively inexpensive device that consists of a metal probe topped with a meter. To use the tester, insert the probe one half to two thirds of the soil depth (the probable location of the most concentrated part of the root structure) and note the reading on the meter. By matching the reading with numbers in a watering guide that is supplied with the meter, you will know when to water various kinds of plants. With or without a meter, survey your plants every couple of days. You will find that light-garden plants will need to be watered more often than other house plants because they grow so much faster.

Active, mature plants vary in their water needs. Some fleshy plants, such as dumb cane, most cacti, euonymus and kalanchoe, grow best if they are allowed to become nearly dry before rewatering. Other plants have modest water needs and should be kept evenly moist but never soggy. Among these are African violets, some begonias, coleuses, columneas and peperomias. A few plants, including miniature roses and most ferns, should never be allowed to get dry (though even they must not be overwatered).

Water the soil rather than the leaves, using a long-nosed watering can without a sprinkler head, or a kitchen syringe-type baster. Avoid slopping water onto stems and leaves where it will collect in the crevices between the stems and the leaf petioles, providing a place for rot to start. You also risk spotting leaves on some species such as African violets and episcias if you water indiscriminately. (Such spots are dead cells that have been killed by the shock of cold water.)

Use ordinary tap water, rain water or water collected in a dehumidifier, and use it at room temperature or a bit warmer. Do not use cold water—it will severely set back many plants, especially if it is used in winter.

A number of automatic and semiautomatic watering systems are available to the light gardener—everything from a fiberglass wick that is embedded in soil and draws water from a reservoir *(left)* to Rube Goldberg delivery systems that include thin plastic tubing with pinpoint irrigation holes punched at each plant. Such automatic or partly automatic systems are no match for your own judgment as to when and how much to water, but they are a good backup when you go away on vacation and cannot find a friend to come in and water your plants.

Maintaining the proper temperature for light-garden plants is just as important to their health as is proper watering. The most common light-garden tenants are subtropical and tropical plants that enjoy 70° to 80° days and 60° to 70° nights, the same comfort range that most people enjoy. The day-night differential of 10 to 15 degrees is important, too; after a day of active photosynthesis, light-grown plants need a cooler night to assimilate newly produced starches and sugars.

A maximum-minimum thermometer is a helpful tool in achieving the proper temperature range. It has a U-shaped column of mercury rather than the vertical one found on ordinary thermometers. It records the day's high temperature on one side of the U and the day's low temperature on the other. Be sure to place the thermometer next to your plants so it measures their temperature and not the room's, which may be several degrees cooler. Reset it daily to record the next 24-hour range, and tinker with your thermostat until you and your plants are satisfied.

Maintaining the proper level of humidity is more difficult than controlling your garden's temperature, at least in winter when the humidity in some houses may fall as low as 20 per cent—a near-desert condition. When the atmosphere is that dry, your tropical and semitropical plants may show brown leaf edges, dull foliage and a general limpness that will eventually prove fatal.

The best way to solve the humidity problem is with a mechanical humidifier set to maintain 40 to 50 per cent humidity. It can be added to a warm-air furnace, or it can be an independent unit in your light-garden room. Be careful not to set the device too high. One enthusiast inadvertently set his humidifier at 80 per cent before he went away for the weekend. When he returned, the air in his living room was so moist that water was dripping from the ceiling. The plants loved this impromptu jungle, but it did not help his furnishings or wallpaper.

There are simpler methods than a room humidifier that will supply some extra humidity for your plants. One gardener uses the metal racks from an abandoned refrigerator: she places the racks over a tray about 2 inches deep filled with water, then groups her potted plants on the racks. Set just above the water, the plants catch the moisture evaporating from the tray. If you have no old refrigerator racks, the plastic grids used in fluorescent fixtures make admirable, and handsome, substitutes; the grids can be bought at electric supply or plastic supply stores.

Clustering plants also helps to raise the humidity level around them. Every plant constantly gives off moisture through its leaves. When a number of plants are together they share that moisture and all of them benefit.

You can supplement natural humidity by making three or four daily passes over your light garden with an atomizer filled with lukewarm water. The mist disappears after 15 to 20 minutes of evaporation, but your plants will benefit from even a brief rise in humidity. Avoid misting your garden at night when the lights are out and the temperature has dropped: the dampness clings to the leaves and could invite disease.

Another solution to the humidity problem, the only one that is adequate for plants that require very high humidity, is a terrarium, an enclosed and lighted case in which moisture is constantly recycled. Bowls, bottles and glass boxes large enough to hold several plants all can be adapted to terrarium use. Ready-made rectangular fish tanks of the 10- to 20-gallon sizes, available in pet shops, are usually less costly than the containers that are sold in garden shops, and they are well proportioned to the light-distribution pattern of a pair of 20-watt fluorescent tubes.

For drainage, cover the bottom of your terrarium with a 1-inch layer of clean gravel. Next add a thin layer of crushed (not powdered) charcoal to absorb odors. Then fill the container to a depth of 3 inches with Mix II *(page 45),* thoroughly moistened. Set the terrarium plants directly in this mix. If you prefer, you can set plants in the terrarium in pots; in that case use a layer of gravel or perlite, but omit the charcoal.

Though terrariums traditionally get little or no fresh air, the light gardener must make some adjustments to compensate for the heat emanating from the ballast in the fluorescent fixture. Cover the terrarium with glass or plastic wrap and set it under lights, leaving an inch-wide opening if the sides of the tank become covered with condensed moisture. (Store-bought terrariums may come with covers of glass or wood; if you are converting a fish tank, you can build a cover like the one on the opposite page from a few pieces of lumber, with the light fixture mounted inside the tank.) Check the plants frequently, adjusting the opening until the heat and humidity in the terrarium seem to suit their needs.

One of the more interesting problems in light gardening—either in a terrarium or in an open, many-tiered setup—is dealing with rapid growth. Newcomers to light gardening find that their old

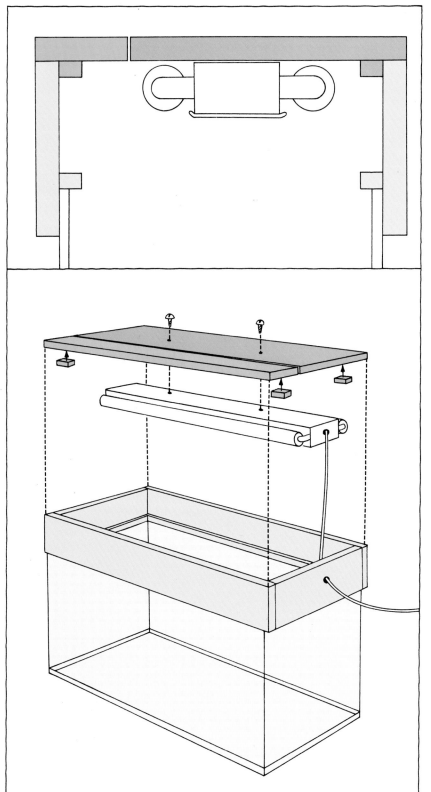

AN AQUARIUM TERRARIUM

An aquarium tank converted into a terrarium can harbor tropical miniatures that require high humidity. Since dimensions of tanks vary, take careful measurements. In addition to a fluorescent lighting fixture that will fit inside the tank, you will need approximately 7 feet of 1-by-6 boards; 7 feet of ½-by-¾-inch molding; a 13-by-26-inch piece of ½-inch-thick exterior-grade plywood; nails 2 inches long and waterproof glue.

First make the top frame (colored tan at left). Cut and nail the 1-by-6 boards to form an open box around the tank. To support this box above the tank, glue strips of molding 1½ inches above the bottom of each inside edge. Drill a hole in the frame for the fixture cord. To make the removable cover, cut the plywood into 3- and 9-inch-wide segments. To hold the cover atop the frame, glue strips of molding 1 inch in from the outside edge of each piece of plywood.

Attach the fixture to the 9-inch part of the cover (green). The 3-inch part of the cover (red) can be tilted or removed to control the humidity. Paint the inside wood white.

notions about when and how often to repot are frequently out of phase with their burgeoning plants. Just as the constant environment of a light garden encourages rapid foliage growth, it also promotes accelerated root growth. Do not be tempted to get ahead of the problem by putting your young plants in oversized pots, because the natural instinct is to water the plant in proportion to the pot size rather than the plant size. In doing so, you end up with potting mix that is almost always wet deep down, even when a touch test on the surface tells you that the plant is dry. And a persistently wet mix is a mix without sufficient air. It is better to pick the smallest-sized pot that will accommodate your plant without crowding its roots. Many gardeners use this literal rule of thumb: a proper-sized pot is one that allows enough room for a thumb's width of mix between the plant's root ball and the pot wall.

THE TIME TO REPOT   If you suspect that a plant has outgrown its pot—perhaps because several roots have strayed out of the hole in the bottom, or the plant has stopped growing during its active period or has wilted slightly within a few hours of watering—it is time to investigate. Water the mix normally and allow it to stand an hour or so. Then place the main stem of the plant between your fingers splayed across the top of the mix, and turn the pot upside down. Tap the rim gently on the edge of a bench and the plant, root ball and all, will slide out neatly into your hand. If it does not, run a kitchen knife carefully around the inside of the pot to loosen the rootlets and try again. If the root mass looks like a tight ball of white string and there is no space left for growth, it is time to repot. But giving such a plant a new pot will not do much good if the roots are wound on themselves to the point of strangulation. Before you repot, take a look at the root development and, if necessary, loosen and spread the outer roots. If the roots resist, soak the root ball in a bucket of water, then pull the ends apart. You may break some of them off, the plant will soon sprout new ones to take their place. With a sharp, clean knife, cut away any roots that appear to be rotted.

In transplanting, move to a pot one size (1 inch in diameter) larger. Pots 1½ to 5 inches in diameter are best suited for the small, compact plants favored for cultivation under fluorescent fixtures; plastic pots are preferred by most light gardeners because they hold moisture longer than do clay pots. One gardener uses transparent plastic pots because she likes to have a window on water and root conditions. Another settles all of his plants in square plastic pots; the square containers nestle snugly together and in a confined space provide room for an extra plant or two in each row. Plastic bulb pans and azalea pots, proportionately shallower than standard pots, also have their adherents. And clay pots, despite their porosity, are useful for certain purposes; their heavy bases keep tall, top-heavy plants from toppling over. It you are using an old pot, scrub it thoroughly with ordinary soap and water to get rid of harmful salt deposits. Washing with one part household bleach to nine parts water will eliminate any disease pathogens or pests that might be lingering. If you are using a clay pot, soak it overnight. The dry walls of an unsoaked pot will steal moisture from the potting mix so it shrinks inward, letting water run down the sides. Before adding the mix, line the bottom of the pot with a small piece of plastic screening; it cuts almost as easily as cloth and will not rust or corrode. The screen will catch soil that might wash through the bottom hole and the next time you need to check roots, all you have to do is push a pencil up through the hole and push the entire plant out.

After the plant has been removed, put some moistened planting mix in its new pot and center the plant within the container so that the juncture of stem and roots is about ½ inch below the lip of the pot. Then spoon in the rest of the potting mix, spreading the roots out as the level rises. Keep pressing the mix inward as you add it to ensure a compact mix. Orchid growers use a potting stick for this chore, but you can perform the same operation with a blunt-tipped table knife. You can tell that the compactness is just about right when water sinks in gradually. If the water drops away instantly or if bubbles rise to the surface, the mix probably needs to be firmed; if water sits on the surface, the mix is too tightly packed.

When you have finished repotting, keep in mind that the plant

REJUVENATING AN AFRICAN VIOLET

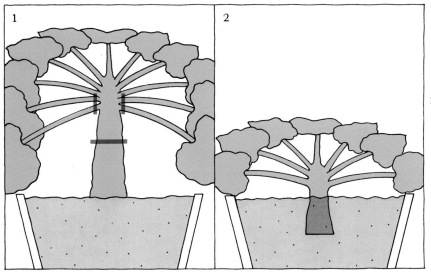

1. After a few years, an African violet often develops an unattractive bare neck. To rejuvenate it, pinch off the blossoms and lower two rows of leaves. Sever the neck 1 ½ inches below the remaining leaves.

2. Dust the base with a rooting powder and insert the neck into barely moist vermiculite so the leaves just clear the vermiculite. Enclose the plant in a clear plastic bag to maintain a high humidity. In a month or so, new roots will be well developed and the plant can be put in a 3-inch pot filled with African violet soil mix.

has suffered a major shock. Water it sparingly and give it at least 10 days rest before resuming feeding.

Well-tended plants in a light garden usually grow like Jack's beanstalk, and if you are new to light gardening you may feel your efforts have been rewarded and want to leave it at that. But plants need to be controlled if they are not to outgrow their garden, their pot and their welcome. Don't wait to be convinced. Begin to pinch off and prune a branching plant while it is still young.

Pinching off can be done any time after the plant has four to six leaves visible on the stem. Simply pinch off the tip of the main stem with your finger and thumb to stop vertical growth; dormant stem buds just below the tip soon break through to produce branches. In the same manner, you can continue to pinch off side shoots to encourage bushier growth and keep your plant in proportion to its limited surroundings.

Pruning is more drastic. It involves cutting off entire branches with a sharp pair of garden scissors or a knife. Weak branches, branches that spoil the overall shape of the plant and branches that look suspiciously unhealthy should go, even if they bear a flower or two. Bigger and better ones will soon pop out elsewhere and the plant will be the stronger for it. One of the glories of light gardening is that you do not have to wait months for the plant to respond. Because growth is continuous, improvement comes quickly.

Cleaning and polishing plant leaves regularly is another important housekeeping chore in your light garden, for dust not only spoils a plant's appearance but chokes the pores through which it breathes and cuts off light as effectively as heavy shade.

RESTRAINING GROWTH

HANGING PLANTS

1. *To suspend plants beneath a ceiling-mounted fluorescent fixture, use link chains and S hooks so that the distance between the light source and the plants is readily adjustable.*

2. *To hang pots directly from a fixture, make certain the fixture is unplugged, then drill two holes ½ inch apart between the tubes. Slip an S hook into the holes in order to hold a chain. To hang a heavy plant from a plaster ceiling, screw a strong hook directly into a ceiling joist beneath the plaster, or use a heavy-duty toggle bolt that will spread out behind the plaster to support the weight safely.*

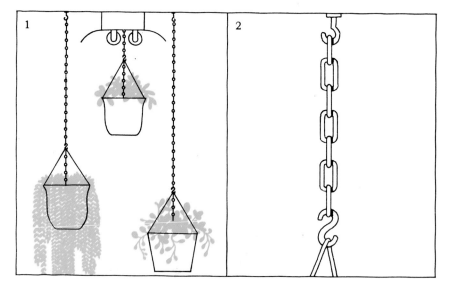

Some experts advocate dusting leaves with a soft brush; with cacti, other succulents and delicate flowering plants, this is the only practical way to keep them clean. But be aware that a brush can pass on a pest or disease from an ailing plant to a healthy one; so wash the brush scrupulously as you move from plant to plant.

For sturdier plants, an actual bath once a month is an additional aid in keeping them clean and healthy. With one hand across the top of the pot to hold the soil ball in place, tip the plant at a 45° angle and run a soft stream of tepid water over and under the leaves. Shake the plant gently to dislodge any excess water before you return it to the light garden.

Scrupulous housekeeping and good cultural practices will help to reduce infestation and infection in your light garden. Every time you clean your plants, take a close look at the leaves—tops, bottoms and stems. If you see any evidence of the presence of mites, mealy bugs, aphids or other pests, try rinsing them away with a stream of water from a faucet or shower.

If you spot scale, tiny brown shell-like insects that gather like so many blisters along the undersides of leaves, scrub them away with a cotton swab dabbed with rubbing alcohol.

If a problem persists, you may decide that a pesticide is the only solution. But never use a spray or aerosol pesticide indoors; children or pets might come in contact with toxic residue. Take the plant outside to spray it.

Some plants, like the African violet, have foliage that is so compact that a spray would only reach the outside leaves. For them, it is best to use a systemic pesticide, so called because the solution is absorbed by the plant through its roots and circulated throughout its vascular system.

If you spot signs of a fungus disease or nematodes, tiny worms that attack roots and leaves, the wisest thing to do is to dispose of the infested plant, along with the potting mix and the pot. Both fungus diseases and nematodes are so destructive that you should not risk allowing them to spread.

Making the transition from gardening by sunlight to gardening by artificial light is mostly a matter of refining the techniques you learned outdoors rather than learning new ones, whether you are watering or treating a mealy-bug infestation. Once you have mastered the nuances of caring for plants grown under artificial light, you are ready to graduate to some of the frontiers of light gardening—propagating new plants, raising hybrids that do particularly well under artificial light and the other multiplication tricks that are discussed in the next chapter.

PEST CONTROLS

Gesneriads: spurred to greater glory

Until African violets like those shown opposite were first grown under fluorescent lights, year-round bloom on a house plant was unknown. People had grown these plants on window sills since late in the last century, but often with disappointing results, especially if a succession of dull and gloomy days occurred.

When the fluorescent tube was introduced in 1938, indoor gardeners quickly discovered that under these lights African violets would produce flowers almost continuously, without dormant periods or ill effects, and without being affected by seasons or weather.

This success created a demand for more continuously blooming flowers and soon other tropical plants were sought out for study. All the plants on the pages that follow are relatives of the African violet, chosen from the plant family called the gesneriads. Many gesneriads do so well under artificial light that they produce more flowers indoors in winter than they ever would in a greenhouse. When commercial growers noted that these plants thrived in an atmosphere comfortable for people, they hybridized hundreds of varieties to get compact form, spectacular color and abundant bloom.

In general, the gesneriads bear their leaves in a rosette, like that of the streptocarpus on pages 58 and 59, but a few, like the columnea on page 60, bear long, heavy strands of waxy leaves that make them unwieldy for light-garden culture unless they are suspended in baskets under lights. The blossoms come in a great range of shapes: the flower may be flat, like that of many episcias, bell-shaped like that of the sinningias, tubular like that of the aeschynanthus known as the lipstick plant, or pouched like the blossom that earned the common name "goldfish plant" for the hypocyrtas.

Most of the lesser known gesneriads will do well wherever the African violet prospers. In fact, most of them can be grown on a window sill, as African violets were for so many years. They may even bloom occasionally in natural light. But only in a light garden do the gesneriads offer the indoor gardener that ultimate reward—a mass of spectacular flowers all year long.

An assortment of African violets includes
(clockwise from top right) Miriam Steel,
Eva, Able White, Violet Trail (center), Edna
Fischer, Red Sparkler and Anna.

Variety among the cousins

Although diverse in appearance, all the plants below and opposite are a single kind of gesneriad. They belong to the genus *Strepto-carpus,* whose approximately 150 species are compact plants prized not only for their constancy in producing flowers but also for their tolerance of a broader range of temperature, humidity and light than the better-known favorites, African violets and florists' gloxinias. Some, like Maasens White *(top, opposite)* bloom profusely as well as continuously, bearing as many as 100 flowers at one time.

A Wiesmoor hybrid's brilliant blossom, up to 3 inches wide, grows among leaves that are up to a foot in length.

A two-toned blossom of a Nymph hybrid, 2 inches wide, rises above the tongue-shaped, crinkled leaves.

Maasens White, closely related to Nymph, produces a radiant nosegay of nearly two dozen flowers.

Hollywood's frilly, trumpet-shaped blossoms rise in a loose cluster from the center of a rosette of leaves.

Saxorum's flower on a threadlike stem seems to defy gravity above a downy cluster of its low-growing, oval leaves.

A plus value in the foliage

Even before fluorescents came into use, several gesneriads were grown in baskets and on window sills for their dramatic foliage. Their tantalizing range of shades of green and variations in sheen and veining are indicated here. Relatives of the episcias *(below and lower left, opposite)* may have dark red or copper-colored leaves. A columnea hybrid *(below, left)* may also have rough, two-toned leaves *(page 63).* There is even one streptocarpus, *S. grandis,* that produces only a single leaf, a monster up to three feet long.

Hanging ropes of glossy, scalelike leaves, 6 to 8 feet long, hold the fiery blossoms of a columnea, Othello.

A single blossom on an episcia, Green Haga, is set like a jewel amid leaves with a pebbly texture and deep veins.

Velvety leaves sharply veined form a compact rosette for the nodding blossom of a sinningia, Florence K.

On this episcia, Moss Agate, thick leaves with lacy veins can grow up to 5 inches long around vivid blossoms.

Aeschynanthus pullobia, the lipstick plant, has foliage as handsome as the tubular flowers it is named for.

Improving on nature

Although gesneriads need a modest amount of light, usually between 250 and 500 foot-candles, these plants rarely produce the rich abundance of vivid flowers shown here unless they are grown under artificial illumination. For the florists' gloxinia of the *Sinningia* genus *(below right, opposite)*, steady, even light from directly overhead produces a symmetrical rosette of foliage. For the *Episcia dianthiflora (below left, opposite)* light can be the deciding factor in having these exquisite flowers or no bloom at all.

Flowers of a Kohleria erianthus hirsuta are clustered among bright-edged leaves on an upright stem.

A nematanthus, Tropicana, which is also called thread flower, bears dangling blossoms on slender stems.

Similar in appearance to its relative at left, a hypocyrta named Rio is distinguished by tube-shaped flowers.

The spreading, stippled blossoms of a
kohleria, Rongo, grow on sturdy,
compact stems less than a foot tall.

Columnea is ablaze with many flaming
flowers through the year; on this
Cornellian they look like flying fish.

Finely fringed blossoms with tinted
throats cascade among Episcia
dianthiflora's velvety leaves.

A florists' gloxinia will soon be
completely enveloped by trumpet-
shaped blossoms 5 inches wide.

Easy multiplication exercises 4

Beverley Nichols, a well-known English gardening writer, was fond of recalling his first experiment in plant propagation. While enjoying a walk on a brisk fall day, he saw a rose geranium growing by the side of the road. Only one pinkish blossom remained, and the forlorn plant looked as though it would soon succumb to frost. Nichols decided the rose geranium deserved a better fate, but uprooting it seemed too drastic a measure. So he decided to try taking a cutting from the stem.

"I had never taken a cutting before," Nichols wrote, "and though I had heard that it could be done, the idea, when one came to put it into practice, seemed so fantastic that it made me tremble with apprehension. It is exactly as though you were to cut off your wife's leg, stick it in the lawn, and be greeted on the following day by an entirely new woman, sprung from the leg."

Gingerly, Nichols severed the end of a branch, carried it home and put it in a pot of soil. His small gesture of compassion paid off handsomely. In less than two weeks the cutting had begun to produce new growth. Within a few years, this parent plant had yielded more than a dozen bushy progeny from additional cuttings.

Nichols' success was not just beginner's luck. Most plants ensure their survival by reproducing in a number of ways. Using a stem cutting is but one of several approaches to vegetative propagation. Plants can also be re-created from roots, runners, bulblets, buds and leaves. And, of course, they also grow from seed.

As a light gardener, you are uniquely able to provide the perfect conditions—controlled temperature, light and moisture—to take the guesswork out of plant propagation and make it one of the special delights of sunless gardening. Indeed, one young Washington, D.C., light gardener gives away all of the plants he thus propagates. The fascination for him lies in watching one of nature's miracles take place in a corner of his bedroom.

Two bumper crops a year of miniature African violets are grown from leaf cuttings under fluorescent lights by Martha Meehan of Wheaton, Maryland. She gives them 16 to 18 hours of light a day.

But most of us have more practical reasons for propagating plants under artificial light. Such plants invariably are healthier, sturdier, more disease resistant, more compact and better acclimated to their environment than plants grown to maturity in a greenhouse, then introduced into a home light garden. One gardener is so wary of greenhouse plants that before he brings a new one into his light garden, he takes several cuttings in case the newcomer fails.

Then, too, there is the matter of cost. In time, most plants grow old, their leaves become thick and lusterless, their stems ungainly. Artificial lights hasten this aging process by encouraging faster growth. Buying new plants to replace those that are past their prime is expensive and unnecessary. Taking cuttings from your own plants will provide vigorous new stock—and may even revitalize the old.

EXPANDING A COLLECTION

Growing new plants from cuttings or seeds is also a way to introduce uncommon varieties into your light garden. Many plant stores sell only standard favorites. But by trading with friends, by ordering from seed catalogues, by joining such groups as the Bromeliad Society, the Gloxinia Society, the Cactus and Succulent Society or the Saintpaulia International Society, and by participating in a chapter of the Light Gardening Society of America, you can obtain unusual seeds and cuttings at little or no cost.

Seeds are typically used to start annuals and vegetables that complete a life cycle in a single season. Since growing from seed is the only kind of sexual plant propagation, the new plants bear characteristics of both parents. In fact, unless they are carefully produced first-generation hybrids from pure stock, the seedlings may revert to traits of more distant, and probably less desirable, ancestors. Or the seeds may not germinate at all. Nevertheless, growing from seed is the easiest and most practical way to start many plants, including coleuses, tuberous-rooted begonias and many cacti.

IDENTICAL OFFSPRING

But vegetative propagation from cuttings, plant divisions or runners is surer than propagation from seeds—a superior plant is inevitably reproduced with no variation whatsoever from the parent. And for the tropical and semitropical plants featured in most light gardens, the results are quicker. Vegetative propagation works because cells of plants can revert to their embryonic stage and reorganize themselves to perform any needed function as parts of leaves, roots or stems. In theory all plant cells can perform all functions, but almost every species has characteristics that make one type of vegetative propagation more successful than another. Sever a branch from the stem that connects it to its roots, and the base of that cut will, under favorable circumstances, redefine itself as roots, in the manner of Beverley Nichols' rose geranium.

In general, the newer, more vigorously growing parts of a plant are more likely to take root as cuttings than older, more woody parts. The most effective propagation techniques for many popular light-garden plants are given in the encyclopedia *(Chapter 5)*.

You do not need specialized equipment or special lights for propagation. Many gardeners use the space below the ends of their fluorescent fixtures where the light levels are slightly lower than directly under the tubes; these locations are well suited to rooting cuttings and starting seeds. But if you want a separate propagation space, a two-tube, 20-watt fixture can handle 35 to 50 cuttings or seedlings at a time. A timing device attached to the fixture, set for a 16-hour cycle, will make the job easier and more efficient.

A PROPAGATING BOX

The container for propagation can be modest or sophisticated, depending on your needs and budget: a plastic margarine tub with plastic wrap across the top, a covered terrarium or a fully equipped miniature greenhouse. A ready-made propagation box with a heating coil, a thermostat, a hygrometer and a timer is a fine device but not necessary for most plants. A transparent sweater box with a rigid lid is nearly as good if you monitor temperature and humidity.

A necessary feature of any propagation container is a transparent, colorless cover that will admit light but hold in moisture and heat. The depth should be at least 3 inches. Unless you place the container and lights in an unheated basement or other cool place, heat from the ballast of a two-tube fixture should keep the temperature near the optimum 70° to 75°. The humidity is even easier to control, since moisture recirculates within the enclosed space. If root cuttings need a boost at night when the thermostat is turned down, you can regulate the temperature with an inexpensive heating cable, a short length of plastic-encased electrical wire that produces heat of around 75°. You simply arrange the cable beneath the box in serpentine coils to distribute the heat evenly.

Once you have selected a propagation box, pour in as much horticultural-grade vermiculite as possible without crowding the cuttings against the lid. Avoid finely pulverized vermiculite that feels greasy or slippery. It will pack too tightly to permit enough air circulation to keep the emerging roots from rotting. Pellets that feel relatively crisp and look like ⅛-inch accordions are best. Moisten and drain the vermiculite until it feels moist but is not soggy; this is a critical step. One cup of tepid water per 10 cups of dry vermiculite is about right. Let the rooting medium stand overnight; by morning there should not be any water left in the bottom of the box. If you are a beginner, you will probably think the vermiculite is too dry, but a just-moist medium works best.

A CASE OF MISTAKEN IDENTITY
The so-called florists' gloxinia, long a light-garden favorite because of its velvety bell-shaped blossoms of white, red, lavender or purple, is not really a gloxinia. It is a sinningia. Discovered in Brazil, it was formally named gloxinia in 1785 for B. P. Gloxin, a German physician and botanist. Nearly 50 years after it was christened, botanists found to their chagrin that another series had been given the same name in the early 1700s. By then, however, florists' gloxinias were so popular that nobody bothered to correct the common name. Gloxinia perennis, the true gloxinia, has bell-shaped flowers similar to those of the florists' gloxinia, but it is too tall for most light gardens.

WELL-ROOTED CUTTINGS

A rooting hormone, which exists naturally in all plants in minute quantities, can speed and strengthen a cutting's rooting ability. These hormones come as powders and are available mixed with a fungicide to inhibit disease. Simply dip the rooting end of the cutting (or edge of a leaf) into the powder and tap lightly to remove excess. Too much hormone rooting powder can injure the cutting.

Stem cuttings are probably the most common means of vegetative propagation. They are easy to obtain and the degree of success is high. You can take a stem cutting from almost any branching plant, including such indoor favorites as Natal plum, crossandra, geranium, fibrous-rooted begonias, impatiens and columnea.

To take a stem cutting, select a healthy new green shoot 3 to 6 inches long—or long enough to have half a dozen leaves. Sever the cutting just below the bottom leaf with a sharp knife or razor blade. Remove any flowers and any leaves that would rot beneath the surface of the vermiculite. At least two leaves should remain to provide the energy, through photosynthesis, for developing roots; an additional two or three leaves may be left on the stem if you wish, but more than a few may tax the water-supplying ability of the rootless stem segment. Dip the bottom of the cutting and the lowest node—the place where a leaf grew—in rooting powder and set the cutting deeply enough in the moist vermiculite so the node is covered and the cutting will stand unsupported.

After you have planted your cuttings, cover the box and place it where the light source is not more than 12 inches away. Remember to keep the light on for 16 hours daily. If the box lid becomes clouded with moisture, open the top slightly to allow some air to circulate to dry the rooting medium a bit. Should the rooting medium become so dry that there is no condensation on the box lid, add a bit of water, using a mister so you will not disturb new roots.

After a week or so, check your cuttings' progress by lifting one tenderly out of the loose vermiculite. If the rootlets are short and few, replace the cutting in the rooting medium. When the rootlets look vigorous and are evenly distributed around the base, it is time to repot the cuttings. Depending upon the species, a cutting will usually grow to transplanting size in one to four weeks. One enthusiast swears he saw a coleus cutting show signs of rooting under artificial light four hours after it was set in vermiculite. Be aware, though, that some cuttings may take a month or more to form roots.

When you move a rooted cutting to an individual pot, use the potting mix favored by that kind of plant *(Chapter 5)*. Watch your cutting closely for the first few hours for signs of wilting. Some will need to be introduced gradually to life outside the propagation box.

If a plant appears to have trouble adjusting, make a small tent of plastic wrap for it, gradually loosening the cover until it has become acclimated to the outside world, a process called hardening off.

In a different kind of vegetative propagation, leaf cuttings from plants with fleshy or hairy leaves are relatively easy to propagate. Among these are African violets, chirita, echeveria, peperomia, gloxinia and streptocarpus. Pick single leaves that are full grown, firm, unblemished and growing toward the outside of the plant, rather than leaves that form part of the center rosette. Snip the leaf from the parent plant so that at least a half inch of the leafstalk remains below the leaf. Dip the leafstalk in hormone powder, tap off the excess and insert the leafstalk into moistened vermiculite with the leaf slightly tilted so its top gets most of the light. The base of the leaf should not touch the surface of the rooting medium.

A leaf cutting will root quickly, but do not move it from the closed propagation box until new leaves growing around its base are approximately one third the size of the parent leaf. (This may take as long as four or five months.) When the new leaves have reached this size, separate the plantlets, pulling them apart carefully so you do not injure the fragile new roots, and put them in separate pots of the soilless mix recommended for that species in the encyclopedia that begins on page 79. If the parent leaf comes from a rare plant and you want to make the most of it, you may be able to repeat the operation a second time. Slice off the rooted end of the parent leafstalk; after you have planted it dip the fresh-cut remainder in rooting powder and return it to the propagation box.

PLANTING A LEAF

RECYCLING THE TRIMMINGS

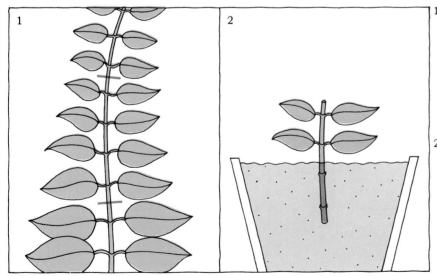

1. Cutting back trailing plants such as columnea and hypocyrta will keep them from outgrowing your light garden and will also yield material for new plants. Trim the plant in four-leaf segments cut from below the growing tip and pinch the two bottom sets of leaves from each cutting.

2. Dust the bottom of each cutting with rooting powder and pot in a moist mixture of equal parts peat moss and vermiculite or perlite. If you want to give the parent plant a bushier look, plant the cutting next to it in the same pot.

If you want to take a leaf cutting from a large-leaved plant, such as a rex begonia or a streptocarpus, you can trim the leaf down to a manageable size. Cut off the outer end so only an arc-shaped segment around the base of the leafstalk is left and plant the leafstalk. Then cut the rest of the leaf into wedges so each piece has a major leaf vein running through it. Apply hormone powder to the lower third of each wedge; set that end in moist vermiculite—about a half inch deep. Cover the box and wait for plantlets to appear.

Plants with large, leathery leaves such as the rex begonia can also be propagated by the slit-leaf method. With a razor blade, make short cuts across the leaf's midrib and other major veins at half-inch intervals, dust the leaf's underside with rooting powder and put it, underside down, on moist vermiculite. Poke the stem into the rooting medium to provide moisture. To keep the leaf in contact with the medium, run hairpins through its edges. After two or three weeks in the covered propagation box, plantlets should develop at the slits. When they are 2 inches high, transplant each one to its own pot. (For other leaf-cutting variations, see pages 75 and 76.)

DIVIDING UP PLANTS

Plants that send up multiple stems, those that produce plantlets naturally around the mother plant and those that send out runners are easily divided into two or more plants. The ubiquitous African violet can be propagated in this fashion from suckers along the center stem, as can some orchids, prayer plants, calatheas, spathiphyllums, streptocarpuses and many others.

Like major surgery on a human, dividing clumps of roots produces a major shock on the newly separated parts, so perform this operation only on plants that are in good health. The best time to

(continued on page 74)

Lilliputians on a liquid diet

The ultimate step in controlling the environment of an indoor light garden has been taken in the terrarium opposite. The glowing miniature gloxinias are not growing in the usual terrarium soil mixture; rather, they are nourished hydroponically by a constantly circulating solution of nutrients. The only support for the plants is provided by live sphagnum moss, which gives the gloxinias' roots something to cling to. The plants receive uniform light for 18 hours a day from three 20-watt fluorescent tubes that have been concealed in the cover of the tank. Temperature and humidity are constant in the draft-free enclosure.

At the back of the terrarium (left in this view), a vertical sheet of cork bark conceals the circulating mechanism. Nutrient solution drips over the cork among the leaves of a creeping fig. The owner adds two drops of liquid fertilizer to the system and replaces any water that has evaporated. New plants for this terrarium are started from cuttings rooted in the terrarium or individual hydroponic pots (overleaf).

Moss-supporting pieces of red shale and a Wanda miniature begonia (center) nestle among trumpet-bearing gloxinias.

Doll Baby (left) and Cindy-Ella (right), two dainty gloxinias, are stars of a garden show 2 feet wide and 16 inches high.

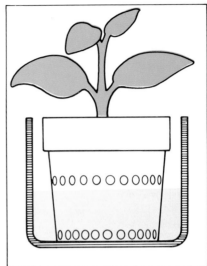

To make a hydroponic pot for a stem cutting, punch two rows of holes in a plastic-foam pot. Fill the bottom half of the pot with gravel, the top half with sphagnum moss, and set in a larger container holding a 5 per cent solution of 10-15-10 fertilizer.

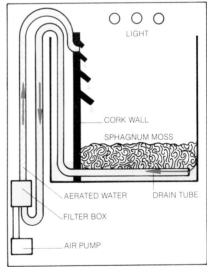

This cross section of the hydroponic light garden shows how the nutrient solution is circulated. An air pump outside the tank aerates the solution. Lightened by air bubbles, the solution rises through the filter box and up the tubing, then trickles down the cork wall into the sphagnum moss. The solution drips through the moss into a drain tube and re-enters the tubing system. The liquid in the tank must cover the open end of the drain tube to maintain the continuous flow of aerated water to the plants.

divide a plant is when it is dormant. If it has no dormant stage, divide it just before or shortly after it flowers.

Before dividing a plant, remove it from its pot and shake off as much potting mix as you can to get a good look at the roots. Separate the roots by hand if there are natural divisions that come apart easily. If necessary, cut the clump apart with a sharp, clean knife. Dust both sides of the wound with a fungicide to forestall infection. Plant the sections in separate pots, making sure each section has leaves and roots. Press the mix down below the wound so the cut is exposed to the air; this too will deter infection by minimizing contamination until healing is under way. Fill in the hole around the wound three or four days later, then treat the plant as you would any other newly potted plant in your light garden.

You can propagate many gesneriads from their rhizomes, the rootlike water and food-storage stems that grow horizontally above or below ground. Achimenes, koellikeria and smithiantha can be grown from their rhizomes, which resemble elongated pine cones. To propagate a rhizomatous plant, remove the parent plant from its pot when the top growth is dormant. Break off a few of the brittle rhizomes and place them in a propagation box with some dry vermiculite. Repot the parent plant. When the rhizomes sprout (which can take several months), put them in individual 1-inch pots and place the pots in your light garden.

To propagate a plant that puts out runners, such as a strawberry geranium or a spider plant, pin a runner—a creeping stem that puts out roots—in a nearby pot. When it starts to develop leaves and its roots become firmly anchored, sever it from the parent plant. This umbilical-cord method is virtually fail safe because the mother plant supplies nutrients while the baby plant is developing.

STARTING WITH SEEDS The final method of starting plants in your light garden is the most natural way—from seeds. If you want to get an early start on your outdoor annuals and vegetables, this is the solution. The technique is similar to that used in starting cuttings. Remember to check the maturation length on the seed packet and plan accordingly before you sow. If you sow too early, your plants may be ready for transplanting weeks before the outdoor weather is ready for them. Coordinate your planting dates with the approximate dates of the last frost in your region. At times you may want to grow plants from seeds just for your light garden. Popular candidates for seed propagation include crossandra, impatiens, rechsteineria and gloxinia.

Almost any viable seed contains an embryonic plant, complete with enough stored food to sustain vigorous growth in the seedling stage. (Orchids are an exception.) Seeds will not produce duplicates of either parent plant, but seeds bought from a supplier who produces them under carefully controlled conditions will breed true with a high degree of regularity. (Growing seeds produced by your own plants is probably not worth the trouble.)

Most flower and vegetable seeds remain viable for at least two years if they are kept cool and dry, though some lose their viability shortly after they mature. The best policy is to follow the instructions given on the seed packet.

If you intend to keep a plant in your light garden instead of moving it outdoors, start the seeds in a propagating box filled with moistened vermiculite. But if you expect to move the plants outdoors, start the seeds in a light, crumbly commercial potting soil. In either case, scatter the seeds on top of the moist seedbed, then press large seeds into the surface; small seeds will sift in unaided. Distribute the seeds sparingly; you will achieve a high percentage of germination under lights, and crowded seedlings compete for light and air with the result that none of them get enough. Next, spread a ⅛-inch layer of dry, finely milled sphagnum moss over the surface of the seedbed to discourage damping-off, a fungus disease that rots seedling stems and can wipe out a whole stand overnight. Some gardeners find the best way to distribute the moss evenly is to press it through a kitchen sieve held over the propagation box.

After seeding, cover the propagation box and place it so the top of the seedbed is within 6 inches of the fluorescent tubes. Check the temperature occasionally: it should be kept between 70° and 75°. If necessary, warm the bottom of the container with a heating cable. The seedbed must be kept moist, but if you have to add water, do so

A QUICKER WAY TO REPRODUCE BEGONIAS

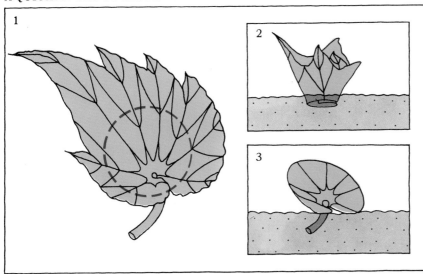

1. A leaf cutting can be used to propagate a rex or rhizomatous begonia in the shortest time, producing two plantlets in less than two months. Snip off a leaf with a 1-inch stem. At the stem, cut a circular piece 1 inch in diameter (dotted line).

2. Roll the outer part of the leaf into a loose cone with the cut edges at the narrow end. Coat lightly with rooting powder and press the cut edge 1 inch into moist vermiculite.

3. Coat the stem lightly with rooting powder, then insert it halfway in moist vermiculite in a container with a transparent lid. Provide end-of-tube light until plantlets appear.

sparingly. Heavy watering will wash the seeds deep into the soil or knock over tender seedlings.

Depending upon the kind of seeds planted, the first green foliage should appear in four days to two weeks. Be patient. The first growth, called seed leaves, are not true leaves, but when they appear, increase the light intensity slightly by moving the propagation box to within 3 inches of the tubes and leave the cover ajar to permit some ventilation. When the first true leaves appear (looking like those of the parent plant) it is time to transplant the seedlings.

To move the young plants, insert a wooden plant label under the roots and lift gently. Hold a leaf if necessary, but do not touch the tender stem: the slightest pressure on it could destroy the seedling. One veteran light gardener wears a magnifying eyepiece

PROPAGATING FROM LEAVES

A long, narrow streptocarpus leaf can be propagated to produce many plantlets. Use a razor blade to cut the leaf lengthwise on both sides of the leafstalk. Discard the leafstalk. Dip the cut edge of each leaf half in rooting powder and press it ½ inch into moist vermiculite in a propagation box with a transparent cover. Under a low level of fluorescent light, plantlets appear in one to two months. Transplant them individually to 3-inch pots containing equal parts of sphagnum peat moss, vermiculite and perlite. Feed weekly.

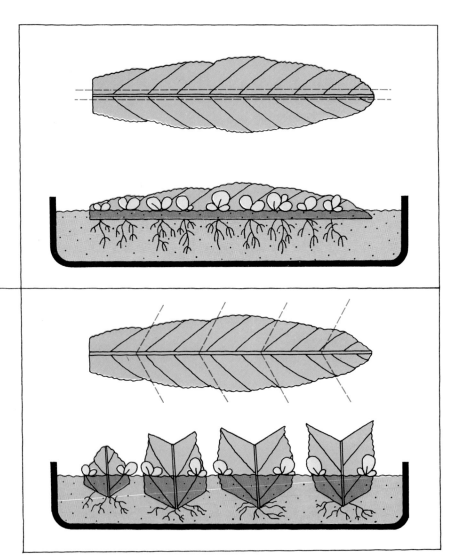

Another method of propagating from a long, narrow leaf is to make V-shaped cuts in the leaf 1½ inches apart. Make sure the cuts point toward the stem end. Dust each point with a hormone rooting powder and insert it about ½ inch deep in the rooting medium. When the plantlets are about 2 inches tall prepare them for the shock of transplanting by leaving the cover off the propagation box for increasing periods of time each day for the first week.

when transplanting seedlings. He says that he feels a little like a watchmaker when he wears it, but he doesn't lose many plants.

Replant seedlings about 2 inches apart in a covered box of potting mix, setting them at exactly the same depth they were growing at initially (you can see the soil line on the stem). Tamp the mix down firmly around each plant with two fingers straddling but not touching the stem. Cover the planting bed and place it within 3 inches of the lights. When the plants resume healthy growth, it is time to acclimate them gradually to the cooler temperatures and lower humidity outside their incubator. This must be done gradually; moving a seedling directly into a light-garden pot or outdoor bed is a bit like expecting a toddler to run before he can walk.

To harden off the seedlings, open the lid of the box a few inches more for a few hours each day for a week until the plants become used to the relatively harsh outside environment. If you intend to move some of the plants outdoors, put them outside for a few hours a day so they can get used to natural light and temperature.

ACCLIMATING SEEDLINGS

You also can lessen the shock of transplanting by cutting the mix in the plant box into squares, much as you might cut a cake, so that each square holds a small plant. The blocks can then go into their new pots or into the ground with a minimum of disturbance.

Artificial-light gardening is still very much in an evolutionary stage. Its potential for enriching lives—and diets—is just beginning to be appreciated. More than two centuries ago, Jonathan Swift's Gulliver traveled to the imaginary land of Laputa, where he found a scientist trying to extract sunbeams from cucumbers. The imaginative fellow had it in mind to store those warm rays in jars and release them in winter when sunshine was in short supply.

Today, real-life experiments with light are of a more practical nature. For instance, if cheaper energy sources can be developed, scientists are ready to supplement the world's food supply with crops grown indoors the year round under artificial light.

Meanwhile, the amateur light gardener can conduct his own research, trying various combinations of light, humidity, temperature and fertilizer. One gardener in Michigan has won many ribbons at flower shows for her miniature gardens of alpine plants that normally grow best in the cool temperatures and bright sunlight of a mountain meadow. Her light garden is near a basement window. A fan brings in cool outside air to simulate the alpine environment. It is this spirit of experimentation that makes light gardening such a continuing pleasure—whether you have only a modest table-lamp arrangement for a few African violets or a whole indoor garden basking under a battery of sophisticated fixtures.

An encyclopedia of plants for light gardens 5

No longer restricted by cloudy skies and seasonal changes in the lengths of days, home gardeners can provide their plants with measured amounts of artificial light at any time they wish. With this control comes the means of growing a tremendous variety of plants indoors, of keeping them growing and blooming throughout the year, of producing vividly colored blooms and foliage, and of performing other feats of horticultural wizardry that can only leave a window-sill gardener filled with envy.

The plants described in the encyclopedia that follows were selected for qualities that make them especially suited to a light garden, such as convenient size, lengthy periods of bloom or strongly patterned leaves. The special effects that can be commanded with artificial light are described, as are the cultural needs of each plant.

The simplest lighting arrangement that will produce successful results is recommended in each case. For most of these plants, the standard is a 4-foot-long fixture with a built-in reflector, holding two 40-watt fluorescent tubes, one cool-white and one warm-white. In some instances a higher foot-candle level is needed to induce bloom or unusually strong leaf markings; this can be achieved with a fixture holding four tubes instead of two. Light gardeners who are tempted to grow such exotic plants as orchids will need to invest in a bank of eight to 10 standard tubes, or six to eight high-output tubes, or four to six very-high-output tubes.

The potting mixes suggested are the soilless type favored by most light gardeners because they weigh little, retain moisture well and are uniform, sterile and porous. But unlike potting soils that contain loam, soilless mixes contain almost no nutrients, so very frequent feeding with very dilute liquid fertilizer is recommended. Uniform light is no substitute for good gardening judgment, of course. As always, the gardener must rely on the appearance of his plants and the feel of the potting mix to tell him how well his garden grows.

A light garden can offer year-round flowers on an African violet (lower left), deepened leaf color in a dracaena (bottom center), prolonged bloom on an achimenes (top right) and exotic flowers on an orchid (center).

MAGIC FLOWER
Achimenes hybrid

DELTA MAIDENHAIR
Adiantum raddianum

A

ACHIMENES

A. hybrids (all called magic flower, nut orchid, widow's-tear)

Like many other gesneriads, achimenes grow and flower abundantly under fluorescent lights. They are valued for the pure colors of their blooms, which they produce continuously during summer months. Achimenes grow 8 to 12 inches tall from scaly underground stems, or rhizomes, that are less than an inch long and resemble small pine cones. Hairy, clustered, 1½- to 3-inch dark green leaves serve as a background for tubular flowers with flat 1- to 2½-inch faces in a variety of colors that includes pink, red, lavender, yellow and white. Among the upright hybrids and species best suited to gardening under lights are Ambroise Verschaffelt, with white flowers tinged with purple; the dwarf *A. andrieuxi,* with violet flowers that have purple-spotted throats; Atropurpurea, with red-to-purple flowers; and the yellow *A. flava.*

HOW TO GROW. Achimenes grow best in medium to bright light, about 500 foot-candles, for 14 to 16 hours daily. Place plants about 3 to 6 inches below a standard two-tube fixture. Night temperatures of 60° to 65°, day temperatures of 70° to 75°, and humidity between 50 and 60 per cent are ideal. In spring, plant three large or six small rhizomes horizontally 1 inch deep in a 5- or 6-inch pot. Use a soilless mixture of equal parts vermiculite, perlite and sphagnum peat moss, adding 1 teaspoon of ground limestone or ¼ cup of crushed eggshells per quart of mix; otherwise, use a packaged soilless mix, adding limestone or eggshells in the same proportions. Water sparingly until growth appears, then keep the soil evenly moist, but not soggy, at all times; if the soil dries, the plant will return to dormancy. Avoid splashing water on the leaves and flowers. Weekly applications of a water-soluble high-phosphorus fertilizer such as 10-30-20, diluted to one fourth the strength recommended on the label, are essential for abundant flowering. Pinch off growth tips to encourage branching and keep the plants compact. When plants stop blooming, water less frequently until the foliage yellows, then store rhizomes in the pot at 50° to 60° and water only enough to keep the soil from drying completely. Rhizomes can also be stored in barely moist vermiculite in a plastic bag that has several ¼-inch holes punched in it. Propagate by dividing rhizomes; by removing and potting the rhizomes that sometimes grow in leaf joints; by rooting tip cuttings in moist vermiculite; or growing from seeds.

ADIANTUM

A. hispidulum (rosy or rough maidenhair); *A. raddianum* (delta maidenhair); *A. tenerum wrightii* (fan maidenhair)

In light gardens, maidenhair ferns grow more luxuriant fronds than they usually have when grown under ordinary house-plant conditions. One of the daintiest and prettiest of all ferns, maidenhairs are admired for their airy, delicate, leafy fronds with wiry, branching stems. Rosy or rough maidenhair forms thick clumps of 8- to 16-inch fronds whose leaflets are rose colored when young. Delta maidenhair is a small species with fringed, triangular leaflets on fronds that are less than 6 inches long. The graceful, arching fronds of the fan maidenhair grow to a length of 20 inches with overlapping, fan-shaped leaflets that turn from pink to light green as they mature.

HOW TO GROW. Maidenhairs grow best when given 12 to 14 hours of medium light, 200 to 500 foot-candles, each day. Place ferns 12 inches below a two-tube fixture. Night temperatures of 50° to 60° suit these plants. Provide humidity as close to 60 per cent as possible by misting plants, resting pots on a moisture tray or growing the ferns in a lighted terrarium. Select a pot only slightly larger than the plant itself and plant in a soilless mixture of 2 parts sphagnum peat moss, 1 part perlite and 1 part vermiculite, adding 1 teaspoon of bone meal per quart of mix; otherwise, use a packaged soilless mix prepared for African violets, adding bone meal in the same proportions. For the lime-loving fan maidenhair, add 1½ teaspoons of ground limestone to each quart of the potting mixture. Feed biweekly during periods of active growth using a high-nitrogen (5-2-2) fertilizer such as fish emulsion, diluted to one fourth the strength recommended on the label. Keep the ferns evenly moist but never soggy. Browned leaf edges indicate that the fern is getting too much light; shriveled young leaves indicate too little humidity. Propagate by dividing and repotting mature plants.

AECHMEA
A. chantinii; A. fasciata (urn plant); *A. miniata discolor*

Symmetrical rosettes of patterned strap-shaped leaves whose bases form cuplike structures characterize aechmeas. The bright flowers and berry-like fruit of these bromeliads, lasting several months, are borne on spikes rising from the cup and appear more frequently on plants grown in light gardens than they do on most window-sill plants. *A. chantinii* has silver bands across its stiff, 1- to 2-foot olive-green leaves; red and yellow flowers emerge among red, petal-like bracts (modified leaves) along a branched spike; the plant's fruit changes from white to blue as it matures. The urn plant has green leaves, 18 inches long and 3 inches wide, that are banded with white, edged with black spines and densely covered with gray scales; it has pink bracts with blue flowers followed by red berries. *A. miniata discolor* has glossy green 1- to 1½-foot leaves that are maroon on the lower side; it bears a branched spike of long-lasting red-orange berries with blue flowers at their tips.

HOW TO GROW. Give aechmeas bright light, 500 to 750 foot-candles, for 12 to 14 hours daily. Place them 6 to 12 inches below a four-tube fixture. Maintain night temperatures of 60° to 65° and day temperatures of 70° or higher. Keep humidity as close to 50 per cent as possible by misting plants and placing pots on a moisture tray. Plant in a 5-inch or smaller pot, using a soilless mix of equal parts sphagnum peat moss, vermiculite and perlite; alternatively, use a packaged soilless mix. Keep the cup in the center of the plant's leaf rosette filled with water; water the soil only when the top layer of the growing medium feels dry when pinched between the fingers. Too much water will rot the base of a bromeliad. Fertilize weekly with a water-soluble, balanced fertilizer, such as 20-20-20 at one fourth the strength recommended on the label. Place mature plants in a plastic bag with a sliced apple for five or six days to encourage flowering. The ethylene gas given off by the fruit will help induce the bromeliad to produce a flower spike about two months later. The mother plant after blooming slowly dies during the first or second year but it produces several offshoots. These can be grown as multiple rosettes or divided with each offshoot being potted individually. Offshoots bloom when they are two years old.

AEONIUM See *Aichryson*

AESCHYNANTHUS, also called TRICHOSPORUM
A. hybrids; A. micranthus; A. obconicus; A. parvifolius, also called *A. lobbianus; A. pulcher; A. tricolor* (all called lipstick plant, basketvine)

Although these gesneriads have trailing or twining stems up to 3 feet long that limit mature plants to spacious light

URN PLANT
Aechmea fasciata

gardens, lipstick plants are prized for their long-lasting red, orange or yellow tubular flowers. Resembling lipsticks in shape, the 1- to 4-inch blooms appear intermittently throughout the year but are most abundant in spring and summer. Glossy oval leaves are paired along the plant's stems and the flowers of most species are clustered at the ends of stems.

Among the hybrids, Black Pagoda is a continuously blooming plant whose orange and yellow flowers, speckled with brown, are set against ornamental foliage that is marbled with red and green underneath. *A. micranthus* and *A. obconicus* both have dark red flowers but those of the former appear all along each woody stem while the slightly larger blooms of the latter are clustered at the tips. *A. parvifolius* and *A. pulcher* both have scarlet flowers with yellow throats but the calyx cups holding the flower petals of *A. parvifolius* are purple, while those of *A. pulcher* are green. The blood-red blossoms of *A. tricolor* have orange throats and are striped with black.

HOW TO GROW. Lipstick plants require a medium amount of light, about 250 to 500 foot-candles, for 14 to 16 hours daily. Place them 6 to 12 inches below a standard two-tube fixture. Night temperatures of 65° to 70° and day temperatures of 75° or higher are ideal. Plant in wide, shallow pots, using a soilless mixture of 2 parts sphagnum peat moss, 1 part vermiculite and 1 part perlite, adding 1 teaspoon of ground limestone or ¼ cup crushed eggshells per quart of mix; otherwise, use a packaged soilless African violet mix adding limestone or eggshells in the same proportions. Feed weekly with a water-soluble high-phosphorus fertilizer such as 10-30-20, diluted to one fourth the strength recommended on the label. Using tepid water, soak the potting mixture thoroughly, then let the top layer dry before watering again. After plants flower, pinch off tips to encourage new growth. Young plants can be trained to climb a low trellis; large plants can be moved to hanging baskets outside the light garden. Propagate by rooting tip cuttings in moist vermiculite or grow plants from seed.

AFRICAN VIOLET See *Saintpaulia*

AGAVE

A. filifera compacta (dwarf thread-bearing century plant, thread agave); *A. striata nana; A. victoriae-reginae* (Queen Victoria century plant) (all called century plant, agave)

Most succulent century plants take 10 to 50 years to mature sufficiently so they will bear flower stalks, but no matter: agaves are grown more for their fleshy foliage than for their blooms. The stiff, sword-shaped leaves in tight rosettes have sharply toothed edges that frequently end in needle-like spines. Leaves are filled with tough, stringy fibers; one large species is the source of the sisal used for making ropes. The dwarf thread-bearing century plant has 4-inch leaves with white, thorny edges that dry and split to release curly filaments; it bears a maroon flower on a 3-foot stalk. The extremely slow-growing *A. striata nana* is a miniature rosette of flat, pale green leaves only 2 to 3 inches long. Leaves are sometimes striped with a darker green; the flowers too are green. The Queen Victoria century plant has deeply furrowed leaves with white edges that end in short spines; green flowers are borne on a 4-foot spike. Agave foliage dies after a plant flowers, but small offshoots are produced for propagation.

HOW TO GROW. Century plants need 1,000 to 1,500 foot-candles of light, achieved by placing them 6 inches or less below a four-tube fixture. Illuminate plants for 14 to 16 hours daily while they are actively growing and gradually

LIPSTICK PLANT
Aeschynanthus hybrid 'Black Pagoda'

reduce this to 10 to 12 hours a day during the winter resting period. Night temperatures as low as 50° and day temperatures of 75° or higher suit them but there should be only a 10° difference between day and night temperatures. These succulents can be maintained in 25 to 30 per cent humidity. Plant in a mixture of 1 part peat moss, 2 parts vermiculite and 2 parts perlite, adding 1 teaspoon of bone meal and either 1 teaspoon of ground limestone or ¼ cup of crushed eggshells per quart of mix; otherwise, use a packaged soilless mix prepared for cacti, adding bone meal and a lime source in the same proportions. From spring to fall, let the mix become moderately dry between waterings.

Feed biweekly after watering with a high-phosphorus fertilizer such as 15-30-15, diluted to one fourth the strength recommended on the label. During the winter resting period, withhold fertilizer and water only enough to keep the leaves from shriveling. The dwarf thread-bearing century plant and the *A. striata nana* can be propagated by removing offsets and planting them in the potting mixture. All three can also be grown from seed.

AGLAONEMA

A. commutatum, also called *A. marantifolium* and *Schismatoglottis commutatum* (Chinese evergreen); *A. costatum* (spotted Chinese evergreen); *A. crispum,* also called *A. roebelinii* and *Schismatoglottis roebelinii* (all called aglaonema)

The decorative variegations found on the durable, leathery leaves of aglaonemas are enhanced when these foliage plants are grown under lights. Mature plants reach 2 to 3 feet in height but aglaonemas grow slowly and young plants will fit in most light gardens. Each species listed produces a white, leaflike spathe that curves back from a nubby yellow flower spike, the spadix; as the flowers fade and the spadix ripens, fleshy red berries develop. The Chinese evergreen has dark green leaves 6 to 9 inches long and 2 to 3 inches wide with pale green veins. The variety White Rajah, sometimes sold as *A. pseudo-bracteatum,* has heavy white markings down the center of its leaves. The spotted Chinese evergreen is a compact species that seldom grows taller than 10 inches. Its heart-shaped, 6-inch green leaves have white veins down the center and spots over the entire surfaces. *A. crispum* has oval, pointed leaves, 10 to 12 inches long, that are gray to green and heavily streaked with silver.

HOW TO GROW. Give aglaonemas low light, 75 to 200 footcandles, for 12 to 14 hours daily by placing them 12 to 18 inches below a two-tube fixture. If leaf markings fade, the light level is too low. Maintain night temperatures of 65° to 70°, day temperatures of 75° to 85°, and 50 per cent humidity. Repot when roots crowd the container, using a soilless mixture of equal parts sphagnum peat moss, perlite and vermiculite, adding either 1 teaspoon of ground limestone or ¼ cup of crushed eggshells per quart of mix; otherwise, use a packaged soilless mix, adding a lime source in the same proportions. Keep the soil barely moist at all times, never letting it get soggy. Feed weekly with a balanced house-plant fertilizer such as 20-20-20, diluted to one fourth the strength recommended on the label. Propagate from stem cuttings rooted in moist vermiculite or by division of the plants. Aglaonema cuttings can also be grown in water with fertilizer added at one tenth the strength recommended on the label.

AICHRYSON, also called AEONIUM

A. bethencourtianum; A. domesticum (youth-and-old-age) (both called aichryson)

Woody, forked stems, each tipped with a rosette of fleshy, spoon-shaped leaves, give succulent aichrysons the appear-

QUEEN VICTORIA CENTURY PLANT
Agave victoriae-reginae

CHINESE EVERGREEN
Aglaonema commutatum

AICHRYSON
Aichryson bethencourtianum

TRUE ALOE
Aloe vera

ance of miniature shrubs. Mature rosettes die after they bloom in late winter or early spring but they are replaced by new offshoots that appear at the base of the plant. *A. bethencourtianum* grows 6 inches tall with ¾-inch-long fuzzy leaves and minute, bell-shaped yellow flowers. *A. domesticum* has darker green leaves ⅔ inch long that grow in rosettes on 1-foot-tall plants; the ½-inch yellow flowers grow in conspicuous clusters.

HOW TO GROW. Aichrysons require 1,000 to 1,500 foot-candles of light, achieved by placing plants 6 inches or less below a four-tube fluorescent fixture. These succulents normally have a period of active growth from fall through spring and a rest period during the summer; grown indoors, however, they may change to a winter resting pattern. Watch for any closing or shrinking of the fleshy rosettes, an indication of dormancy. While plants are actively growing, illuminate them for 14 to 16 hours daily; reduce lighting to 10 to 12 hours daily while plants are resting. Night temperatures of 50° to 55° and day temperatures of 75° or higher are suitable. Humidity of 25 to 30 per cent is adequate. Plants need repotting only every three to five years. Use a soilless mixture of 1 part sphagnum peat moss, 2 parts perlite and 2 parts vermiculite, adding 1 teaspoon of bone meal and either 1 teaspoon of ground limestone or ¼ cup of crushed eggshells to each quart of mix; otherwise, use a packaged soilless mix prepared for cacti, adding bone meal and a lime source in the same proportions. During the growing season, let the soil dry almost completely between thorough waterings and feed the plants biweekly with a high-phosphorus fertilizer such as 15-30-15, diluted to one fourth the recommended strength. While plants are dormant, water only enough to keep them from shriveling and do not feed. Propagate from leaf cuttings or by removing small offshoot rosettes. Let the cut ends of leaves dry 24 hours, then root in moist vermiculite. Plant offshoots in the potting mix. Aichrysons can also be grown from seed.

ALOE
A. brevifolia (short-leaved aloe); *A. haworthiodes; A. humilis* (crocodile jaws); *A. jacunda; A. variegata* (tiger aloe, partridge-breast aloe, pheasant-wing aloe, Kanniedood aloe); *A. vera* (true aloe) (all called aloe)

Aloes are succulent plants that form rosettes of fleshy, stiff leaves. In ancient Rome and in parts of Africa and Asia today the thick sap of true aloe is used to heal sores, and ground leaves serve as a poultice for burns or cuts. Because aloes grow slowly and do not develop a wide leaf span, they are good plants to include in small light gardens where they sometimes bear tubular flowers in several bright shades of yellow, orange or red.

The short-leaved aloe has rows of erect white spines that line the edges of its 3-inch leaves; older plants bear clusters of red flowers on 16-inch flower spikes in summer. The erect, 1- to 2-inch leaves of *A. haworthiodes* bristle with long white spines; the tiny plants bear 6-inch flower spikes with red blossoms in winter. Crocodile jaws is a dwarf species that has white bumps called tubercles running across the backs of its 1- to 2-inch leaves; its flowers are red. *A. jacunda* forms 3-inch rosettes of brown-to-green leaves streaked with pale green or white spots; older plants spread to make foot-wide mats and bear pink flowers on short spikes. Tiger aloe has blue-green leaves with bands of white or pale green spots running across their backs. The edges of the 5- to 6-inch leaves are white and thorny; flowers are red. True aloe is a larger plant with spotted leaves that are 12 to 20 inches long and yellow flowers.

HOW TO GROW. Give aloes 1,000 to 1,500 foot-candles of light by placing them 6 inches or less below a four-tube fixture. Illuminate plants for 14 to 16 hours daily from spring through fall, and for 10 to 12 hours daily during their winter resting period. Temperatures ranging from 50° at night to 75° or higher by day are suitable, but there should be only a 10° difference between day and night temperatures. Humidity of 25 to 30 per cent is adequate.

Pot aloes in a soilless mix of 1 part peat moss, 2 parts perlite and 2 parts vermiculite, adding 1 teaspoon of bone meal and either 1 teaspoon of ground limestone or ¼ cup of crushed eggshells per quart of mix; otherwise, use a packaged soilless mix prepared for cacti, adding bone meal and a lime source in the same proportions. Let the soil become moderately dry between waterings from spring to fall. Feed biweekly with a high-phosphorus fertilizer such as 15-30-15 diluted to one fourth the strength recommended on the label. During the winter resting period, withhold fertilizer and provide just enough water to keep the leaves from shriveling. For additional plants, propagate by cutting off small offshoots that develop alongside the mature plants. Let the juicy cut surfaces form calluses for 24 hours, then set them in moist vermiculite.

ALUMINUM PLANT See *Pilea*

ANANAS
A. comosus (pineapple); *A. comosus variegatus* (variegated pineapple); *A. nanus* (dwarf pineapple)

The pineapple can be grown indoors as a novelty for the miniature fruit it bears. Except in semitropical areas such as Florida, artificial light yields more symmetrical indoor plants with more fully developed color than does natural light coming in a window. *A. comosus,* the commercial species, is the easiest pineapple to grow, if the light garden has enough space for its 2- to 3-foot mature height. On two-year-old plants, a thick, 2- to 4-foot stalk rising from the center of a rosette of 30 to 50 stiff, spiny-edged green leaves bears the pineapple. The variegated pineapple has leaves banded in pink and white; under bright light the center of the rosette turns red. The dwarf pineapple, whose size is better suited to most light gardens, bears 1- to 2-inch fruit above a rosette of 15-inch spiny leaves.

HOW TO GROW. Pineapples require very bright light, about 1,000 foot-candles, for 14 to 16 hours daily. They should be placed about 6 inches below a standard four-tube fixture. Night temperatures of 60° to 65° and day temperatures of 70° or higher are best. Mist plants and use humidity trays to keep the humidity as close to 50 per cent as possible. Pot in a soilless mixture of equal parts perlite, vermiculite and sphagnum peat moss; otherwise, use a prepackaged soilless mix. Water when the top of the mix feels dry to the touch. Feed weekly with a balanced, water-soluble 20-20-20 fertilizer diluted to one fourth the strength recommended on the label. Ethylene gas given off by a ripening apple induces bloom; to encourage flowering on a two-year-old plant, enclose it in a plastic bag with an apple for five or six days. After removal from the bag, a flower stalk should form in six to eight weeks. To propagate, cut off the leafy top of a fruit, wash off any fruit that remains on it, remove enough lower leaves to expose an inch of stalk and root in moist vermiculite. Small plantlets sometimes appear at the bases of mature plants; they can be separated and potted individually.

ANGEL WING BEGONIA See *Begonia*
ANOECTOCHILUS See *Haemaria*

PINEAPPLE PLANT
Ananas comosus

ANTHERICUM See *Chlorophytum*

ANTHURIUM

A. crystallinum (crystal anthurium); *A. scherzerianum* (flamingo flower, pigtail plant)

While window-sill gardeners can enjoy the exotic blooms of tropical anthuriums only in the spring and summer—during months of dependable light—it is possible to have one or two blooms at a time year round in a light garden. The striking flower-like bracts, actually modified leaves, last six or eight weeks on the plant and up to a month as cut flowers. Tiny blossoms crowd a limp spike, or spadix, that hangs from the top of each waxy bract. While crystal anthurium has plain green bracts, the velvety green foliage of the mature plant is silver veined above and pale rose beneath. The broad, oval leaves, 21 inches long and 13 inches wide, grow on stems 6 to 10 inches tall. The flamingo flower grows 8 to 12 inches tall. The 3-inch red bracts with twisted orange spadices rise above 6- to 8-inch green leaves. The hybrid *A. scherzerianum rothschildianum* is white speckled with red.

HOW TO GROW. For best blooms, give anthuriums medium light, 400 to 600 foot-candles, 12 to 14 hours daily. Place them 6 to 12 inches below a two-tube fixture. Temperatures of 60° to 65° at night and 70° or more by day are best. To provide the needed 50 per cent humidity, stand pots on a moisture tray and mist several times daily; dry air causes withered leaves. Plant in osmunda fern fiber or in a mixture of 2 parts fir bark and 1 part coarse peat moss; soak potting medium overnight, then pack tightly around the roots. Plant roots just above the soil line. Keep the medium evenly moist but never soggy.

Feed weekly after watering with a high-nitrogen fertilizer such as 30-10-10 diluted to one fourth the strength recommended on the label. Browned leaf tips and edges indicate underwatering; overwatering causes rot. To propagate additional plants, remove offshoots, with their aerial roots attached, from the parent plant and place them in 3-inch pots filled with moist potting medium. Anthuriums can also be grown from seed sown on moist sphagnum moss and heated from the bottom to 80°; plants that are grown from seed reach blooming size in three to four years.

APHELANDRA

A. squarrosa (zebra plant, aphelandra)

Although the showy flower cones of the zebra plant ordinarily blossom only once a year in the fall, some varieties go through six-week blooming periods twice annually when grown under lights. Conspicuous, waxy 4- to 8-inch flower pyramids bloom on square spikes growing from the top of 12- to 18-inch stems. Spikes may appear singly or in multiples. The pointed oval leaves, 10 to 12 inches long, are dark green, striped with ivory or yellow on top, pale on their undersides; the pink-to-red stems are barely visible under the heavy foliage. Varieties recommended for light gardening include Brockfeld, Dania, Fritz Prinsler and Louisae.

HOW TO GROW. Give zebra plants medium light, 400 to 600 foot-candles, placing them 6 to 12 inches from a two-tube fixture. Illuminate 14 to 16 hours daily for lush, dense foliage; to produce abundant flowers, give the zebra plant 13- to 14-hour nights. Temperatures of 60° to 65° at night and 70° to 75° during the day are ideal with a humidity of about 50 per cent. To maintain humidity, stand pots on a moisture tray and mist plants several times daily. Plant in a soilless mixture of 2 parts sphagnum peat moss, 1 part potting soil and 1 part perlite, adding 1 teaspoon ground limestone or ¼ cup crushed eggshells per quart of mix; you can

FLAMINGO FLOWER
Anthurium scherzerianum

also use a packaged soilless mix for African violets, adding limestone or eggshells in the same proportions. Though soil should never be soggy, keep the mix evenly moist at all times because plants lose their leaves quickly if the moisture level is too low. Feed weekly after watering with a balanced fertilizer such as 20-20-20, diluted to one quarter the rate recommended on the label. Pinch new shoots to keep plants bushy and to encourage multiple flower spikes. Prune the top of the plant severely after the fall blooming period or the plant will become straggly. In early spring, cut the stem back to one or two joints above the old wood and repot in fresh soilless mix. Propagate by rooting tip cuttings in moist vermiculite; enclose cuttings in a plastic bag or box until roots are well formed.

ARABIAN JASMINE See *Jasminum*

ASPARAGUS
A. meyerii, also called *A. densiflorus meyerii* (foxtail asparagus fern); *A. plumosus,* also called *A. setaceus* (asparagus fern)

Members of the lily family, these asparagus ferns are grown for their airy, delicate foliage, though they are not true ferns. Under dependable light, the bright green foliage color intensifies and the plants may bear tiny white flowers along their wiry stems. Asparagus ferns have no true leaves; rather, they have needle-like flattened stems called cladophylls that serve the purpose of the leaves they resemble. These cladophylls grow so densely on the foxtail asparagus fern's 1- to 2-foot stiff stems that the plant resembles a cluster of fluffy plumes. The more common asparagus fern, *A. plumosus,* has lacy, arching 12- to 18-inch prickly stems that will twine around a support.

HOW TO GROW. These plants require 200 to 500 foot-candles of light for 12 to 14 hours daily. Place them 6 to 12 inches below a two-tube fixture. Provide night temperatures of 50° to 55°, day temperatures of 68° to 72°. Maintain humidity as close to 50 per cent as possible by placing the pots on a moisture tray; humidity below 50 per cent may cause the foliage to turn brown. Repot when roots crowd the container, using a soilless mixture of equal parts sphagnum peat moss, perlite and vermiculite, adding either 1 teaspoon of ground limestone or ¼ cup of crushed eggshells per quart of mix; otherwise, use a packaged soilless mix, adding limestone or eggshells in the same proportions. Keep the mix barely moist at all times, never letting it get soggy. Avoid splashing water on the foliage. Feed weekly with a balanced fertilizer such as 20-20-20 diluted to one fourth the strength that is recommended on the label. Propagate by dividing the clumps of thick, fleshy roots of mature plants. Both species of asparagus ferns can also be grown from seed.

ASPARAGUS FERN See *Asparagus*
ASPLENIUM See *Cyrtomium*

B
BABY'S TEARS See *Helxine*
BALL CACTUS See *Notocactus*
BANDED ARROWROOT See *Maranta*
BASKETVINE See *Aeschynanthus*
BAUSE DIEFFENBACHIA See *Dieffenbachia*

BEGONIA
B. hybrid *Argenteo-guttata* (angel wing begonia, trout begonia); *B.* Belva Kusler hybrids; *B. bowerae* (eyelash begonia); *B. cubensis* (holly-leaved begonia); *B.* hybrid 'Duscharff'

ZEBRA PLANT
Aphelandra squarrosa 'Dania'

ASPARAGUS FERN
Asparagus plumosus

ANGEL WING BEGONIA
Begonia hybrid *argenteo-guttata*

HAIRY-LEAVED BEGONIA
Begonia hybrid 'Duscharff'

(hairy-leaved begonia); *B. elatior* hybrids (Rieger begonia); *B. rex* hybrids (rex begonia); *B. semperflorens* (wax begonia)

A genus with hundreds of species and thousands of hybrids, begonias have captivated light gardeners just as they have appealed to generations of outdoor and indoor gardeners. Several of the species are remarkably generous with their blooms, giving every gardener the sweet taste of success. Leaves have a great array of sizes, textures and shapes. Even beginning begonia growers can easily multiply plants from cuttings and leaves. While light gardeners should avoid the taller begonias, especially cane types with stems jointed like bamboo, there are enough compact and dwarf varieties to satisfy any collector.

Begonias are classified by root systems. There are begonias with threadlike fibrous roots, others that grow from thickened horizontal underground stems called rhizomes, and still others that emerge from plump, upright underground stems called tubers. Within these three categories, begonias are further subdivided by leaf and stem characteristics. The eight begonias listed above are representative of the variations in flower and leaf types available for beginning, intermediate and advanced begonia growers.

Only young angel wing begonias will fit in most light gardens—the mature height is 2 to 4 feet. But while most begonias have either interesting leaves or flowers, this plant has both. The jagged 4- to 6-inch leaves with irregularly toothed edges are green dotted with silver on top, red underneath. Unlike other begonias, angel-wing leaves are horizontal, hence the name. Clusters of salmon, coral or white flowers hang from leaf joints.

Belva Kusler is an American begonia fancier who developed more than two dozen hybrids that bear her name. Most are fibrous-rooted, cane-stemmed types but Lenore Oliver is a bushy, compact Kusler hybrid that grows only a foot tall. The 6-inch leaves, red when young, are dark green with silver spots when mature. Pink flower clusters start to appear when plants are only 5 inches tall.

Size is no problem with the very compact eyelash begonia, often grown in terrariums. This rhizomatous begonia's waxy leaves are sometimes variegated in two shades of green, marbled with red or marked with black. Erect hairs line the leaf edges and stems, giving the plant its name. Leaves are its most interesting feature, but it also bears flowers that are a delicate shade of pink.

The holly-leaved begonia is another dwarf. Growing up to a foot tall, this fibrous-rooted begonia has crinkled, glossy green leaves that sometimes have a metallic red cast. The stems are streaked with red and green and flowers are white.

Grown mainly for foliage, hairy-leaved begonias are blanketed with white or brown hairs. Resembling angel wings, these fibrous-rooted begonias vary in size from the dwarf San Miguel, which is less than a foot tall, to the Duscharff, which grows to a height of 2 feet or more and bears small white or pink flowers.

Wax begonias, also fibrous-rooted, are the beginner's delight. Low, compact and easily shaped by pinching off tips, the plants grow 6 to 14 inches tall with waxy green or red leaves up to 4 inches long. The plants bloom almost continuously, bearing single, double or semidouble flowers in colors of white to pink, red, coral, salmon and combinations of these hues. This species has many varieties and hybrids ranging from the familiar bedding begonias to such exotic types as Geneva Scarlet Beauty that has orange-to-red blooms so crowded with petals they resemble chrysanthemums.

Rex begonias are rhizomatous plants that have spectacular leaves in a myriad of textures, shapes and color patterns.

Most of them are very hairy. Some leaves are vivid green with glossy silver centers, others are red with white bars paralleling their edges. Commercial growers offer silver-to-white leaves that are veined with green, lustrous purple foliage blotched with bronze, and other varicolored mixtures. Rex begonias grow up to 15 inches tall but tend to spread horizontally. The inconspicuous flowers hidden beneath the leaves are pink or white.

The Rieger hybrids are tuberous plants that go through periodic dormancy. Growing 12 to 18 inches, some are upright and others trail. Begonia fanciers prize their large 2- to 3-inch red, pink, rose, yellow or orange flowers, often with ruffled edges and double sets of petals that give blooms the look of a rose or chrysanthemum. Shiny, jagged leaves vary from yellow-green through deep green or blue-green.

HOW TO GROW. Give begonias medium light, 400 to 600 foot-candles, by placing them 6 to 12 inches below a two-tube fixture. Illuminate fibrous-rooted and tuberous begonias for 16 to 18 hours daily. Rhizomatous begonias will bloom well if the gardener simulates a change from winter to spring by providing two weeks of 15-hour nights, followed by two weeks of 14-hour nights, then two weeks of 13-hour nights and finally 12-hour nights during the blooming and subsequent dormant periods. All begonias grow best when temperatures range from 65° at night to as high as 85° by day. The humidity should be at least 50 per cent; place pots on moisture trays and mist the plants daily. The hairy-leaved, fibrous-rooted species and the rhizomatous begonias need 65 to 70 per cent humidity; they should be planted in a covered terrarium if a room humidifier is not used.

Plant fibrous-rooted or tuberous begonias in a soilless mixture of 2 parts sphagnum peat moss, 1 part vermiculite and 1 part perlite or use a packaged soilless mix for African violets. Grow rhizomatous begonias in a faster-draining soilless mixture of equal parts sphagnum peat moss, perlite and vermiculite or use a packaged regular soilless mix. Whatever the growing medium, add 1 teaspoon ground limestone or ¼ cup crushed eggshells per quart of mix. Keep fibrous-rooted begonias evenly moist but never soggy; allow rhizomatous and tuberous begonias to dry slightly between waterings. Fertilize all types of begonias biweekly after watering with a balanced fertilizer such as 20-20-20 diluted to one fourth the strength suggested on the label. Fibrous-rooted begonias will grow and bloom year round. Rhizomatous begonias go through semidormant periods when growth slows and blooming stops; give them less water and withhold fertilizer until the new growth begins. Tuberous begonias become dormant once a year; keep them under lights after blooming stops until foliage fades, then store the tubers in their pots or remove and store them in dry peat moss for several months before repotting for a new growth cycle. Fibrous-rooted begonias are easily grown from seed and can be propagated by rooting stem cuttings in moist vermiculite. Rhizomatous begonias can be grown from seed or propagated by division of their rhizomes; thick-leaved rhizomatous species such as rex begonias can also be propagated either by slitting leaves and pinning them on top of moist vermiculite or by placing leaf wedges containing a portion of a large vein ½ inch deep in moist vermiculite. Tuberous begonias can be propagated by separating the tubers or by growing plants from seed.

BILLBERGIA

B. nutans (queen's tears); *B. saundersii* (both called billbergia)

Hardly cause for weeping, the brilliantly multicolored blossoms of queen's tears are not named for their effect on

REX BEGONIA
Begonia rex 'Silver Queen'

WAX BEGONIA
Begonia semperflorens 'Geneva Scarlet Beauty'

QUEEN'S TEARS
Billbergia nutans

SPIDER ORCHID
Brassia lanceana

monarchy but for the drops of sticky, pollen-trapping liquid on the stigmas in the flower centers. These tubular flowers, like those of all the billbergias, are encircled by colorful ribbon-like bracts, which are actually modified leaves. The flower stalks arch from a cuplike structure in the center of the plant. This cup is formed by tall rosettes of leaves that are spotted, marbled or banded with silver. Queen's tears has pink-to-red bracts and yellow-to-green flowers edged with blue; its sword-shaped, 8- to 12-inch green leaves turn red after extended exposure to bright light. *B. saundersii* is a smaller plant growing 8 to 12 inches high with stiff green to bronze leaves that are spotted with ivory and tinged with pink; it has red bracts and blue flowers.

HOW TO GROW. Give billbergias medium to bright light, about 500 to 700 foot-candles, for 12 to 14 hours daily to get the most pronounced color in their foliage. Billbergias usually bloom in late fall to early winter; for later blooms, give them only 10 to 12 hours of illumination during fall and early winter. Adjust a two-tube fixture so it is 6 inches or less above the plant. Maintain night temperatures of 60° to 65° and day temperatures of 70° or higher. Keep humidity as close to 50 per cent as possible by misting plants and setting pots on a moisture tray.

Plant in a soilless mix of equal parts sphagnum peat moss, vermiculite and perlite; do not add lime. Alternatively, use a packaged soilless mix. Keep the cup in the center of the plant's leaf rosette filled with water, but add water to the mix only when the top of it feels dry when pinched between the fingers. Saturating it with water will rot the base of a bromeliad. Fertilize weekly with a water-soluble, balanced fertilizer such as 20-20-20 at one fourth the strength recommended on the label. Place a mature plant in a plastic bag with a sliced ripe apple for five or six days to encourage flowering; the ethylene gas given off by the apple will help induce the bromeliad to produce a flower spike in about two months. Plants produce numerous offshoots, which can be removed and potted in individual containers. Offshoots bloom when two years old. Billbergias can also be grown from seed to blooming plants in three years.

BLOOD LILY See *Haemanthus*
BLUE CHALK STICKS See *Kleinia*

BRASSIA

B. caudata; B. lanceana; B. maculata (all called spider orchid)

Most window-sill gardens lack the year-round strong light needed to bring a spider orchid into bloom. Under lights, however, each of the plant's 3- to 6-inch swollen stems, called pseudobulbs, annually produces one to three leaves and a single 15- to 18-inch flower stalk that bears six to 15 waxy flowers. Each flower is composed of elongated outer petal-like sepals that resemble the legs of a spider and give the orchid its name, plus smaller inner petals and a conspicuous lower petal called the lip.

Sometime in the fall, *B. caudata* sends up an arching flower spike amid its 7- to 12-inch leaves; the 6-inch sepals and smaller petals are green to yellow and barred with brown, while the broad, pointed lip is yellow spotted with green and brown. *B. lanceana* is a summer-blooming orchid with more fragrance than other spider-orchid species. Each plant has a single, tapered 9- to 12-inch leaf; the vivid yellow 2½-inch sepals and 1½-inch petals are blotched with brown and red; the wavy lip is yellow flecked with brown. The smaller *B. maculata* has 6- to 8-inch leaves; the 3-inch sepals and the 1½-inch petals are green to yellow and spotted with brown; the wavy white lip is mottled with brown and purple. This species blooms from spring to early summer.

HOW TO GROW. To produce bloom, a brassia needs 750 to 1,000 foot-candles of light. Place the orchid 6 to 12 inches below a four-tube fixture, or 6 inches or less below a two-tube fixture, lowering the plant as flower spikes grow. Illuminate the plant for 14 to 16 hours daily. Provide temperatures of 55° to 60° at night and from 65° to 70° by day; a 10° difference between day and night temperatures is essential for blooming. A brassia grows best when the humidity is 50 to 75 per cent. Stand the pot on a moisture tray, mist twice daily, and use a room humidifier to achieve high humidity. Since fungus diseases flourish in moist but stagnant air, provide good air circulation around the plants but do not let them stand in cold drafts. Grow a brassia in a soilless mixture of 2 parts fir bark or shredded tree-fern fiber and 1 part coarse peat moss; a plant can also be fastened to a hanging slab of tree fern. Orchids require an acid planting mix; do not add lime. Repot when the plant and its aerial roots grow over the edges of the pot. Allow the soil to dry slightly between waterings and feed biweekly with a fertilizer formulated for orchids such as 30-10-10 or 18-18-18, diluted to one fourth the strength recommended on the label. Do not fertilize during the dormant or resting period. Propagate additional spider orchids when repotting by dividing a plant, leaving three or four pseudobulbs per division.

BRAZILIAN EDELWEISS See *Rechsteineria*
BUNNY EARS See *Opuntia*
BUSH BASIL See *Ocimum*
BUTTERFLY ORCHID See *Epidendrum*
BUTTON FERN See *Pellaea*

C

CACTUS, BALL See *Notocactus*
CACTUS, CHIN See *Gymnocalycium*
CACTUS, COB See *Lobivia*
CACTUS, CROWN See *Rebutia*
CACTUS, FIRE CROWN See *Rebutia*
CACTUS, FLAPJACK See *Opuntia*
CACTUS, GOLDEN BARREL See *Echinocactus*
CACTUS, GOLDEN LACE See *Mammillaria*
CACTUS, GOLDEN STAR See *Mammillaria*
CACTUS, ORANGE COB See *Lobivia*
CACTUS, PLAID See *Gymnocalycium*
CACTUS, POWDER PUFF See *Mammillaria*
CACTUS, RED CROWN See *Rebutia*
CACTUS, SCARLET BALL See *Notocactus*

CALADIUM

C. hortulanum (fancy-leaved caladium)

The many combinations of red, pink, silver, white and green markings on the arrowhead-shaped leaves of caladiums are greatly intensified in a light garden. The 4- to 7-inch leaves, paper-thin and almost translucent, are carried on slender stalks up to 2 feet tall. In a light garden, flowers consisting of a nubby tube called a spadix, partially surrounded by a pink leaflike structure called a spathe, often appear. Caladiums grow from a tuber, bulbous tissue 1½ to 2½ inches across. While these tubers can be planted and grown at any time of the year under lights, they all undergo annual dormancy.

HOW TO GROW. To develop the best colors, caladiums require 750 to 1,000 foot-candles of light for 12 to 14 hours daily and should be placed 6 inches or less below a two-tube fixture or 6 to 12 inches below a four-tube fixture. Night

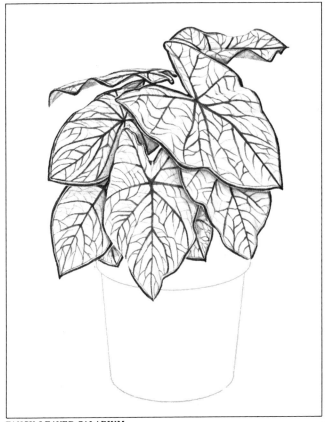

FANCY-LEAVED CALADIUM
Caladium hortulanum 'Candidum'

temperatures of 65° to 70°, day temperatures of 75° to 85° and humidity as close to 50 per cent as possible are best. To raise the humidity level, place the pots on a moisture tray. Pot tubers individually, indented side up, 2 inches below the surface in a 5- to 7-inch pot. Use a soilless mixture of equal parts sphagnum peat moss, perlite and vermiculite, adding either 1 teaspoon of ground limestone or ¼ cup of crushed eggshells per quart of mix; otherwise, use a packaged soilless mix and add lime in the same proportions.

Keep newly planted tubers in a warm place, 70° or higher. While tubers are actively growing, keep the soil barely moist, never letting it get soggy. Feed weekly with a balanced house-plant fertilizer such as 20-20-20 diluted to one fourth the strength recommended on the label. For best foliage growth and tuber development, pinch off any flowers that appear. When leaves begin to wither, seven or eight months after the tubers were planted, water less frequently until the leaves turn completely yellow. Remove all top growth, let the soil dry, then remove the tubers and store them in dry peat moss or vermiculite at 55° to 60° for four or five months. Repot in fresh potting mix to begin a new growth cycle. Propagate by dividing large tubers or grow caladiums from seed.

CANTERBURY BELLS See *Gloxinia*
CAPE JASMINE See *Gardenia*
CAPE PRIMROSE See *Streptocarpus*

CAPSICUM
C. annuum (ornamental pepper)

White flower stems tinged with green or violet followed by fruit as brightly colored as a string of Christmas bulbs are a double incentive for growing ornamental peppers. The foot-tall plants are covered with 2- to 3-inch peppers, actually many-seeded berries, growing upright above 2- to 3-inch deep-green oval foliage. The glossy, juiceless peppers are edible, but only if you like them hot—they are related to chilies. *C. annuum conoides* may have cone-shaped green, white, yellow, red and purple peppers on the same plant simultaneously, depending on how ripe each one is. The slim, pointed peppers of the Fiesta variety are yellow when immature, changing to orange, then red as they grow.

HOW TO GROW. Since ornamental peppers need medium light, 400 to 600 foot-candles, set them 6 inches beneath a two-tube fixture or 6 to 12 inches below a four-tube fixture for 14 to 16 hours daily. Keep temperatures between 60° and 65° at night, 70° to 75° during the day. Humidity between 30 and 40 per cent is adequate for good growth; stand pots on a moisture tray to raise humidity. Start young plants or seeds in a 3-inch pot and increase pot size as the plant matures. Use a soilless mixture of 2 parts sphagnum peat moss, 1 part perlite and 1 part vermiculite, adding 1 teaspoon ground limestone or ¼ cup of crushed eggshells per quart of mix; otherwise, use a packaged soilless mix for African violets, adding a lime source in the same proportions. Feed weekly after watering with a balanced 20-20-20 fertilizer diluted to one-quarter strength. Keep the soil evenly moist; soggy or dry soil causes leaf and flower drop. Sow seeds on moist peat moss. Seedlings can be potted in three weeks; plants bear fruit when six to eight months old.

CARDINAL FLOWER See *Rechsteineria*

CATTLEYA
C. luteola; C. hybrids (cattleya orchid)

Beginning orchid growers favor cattleyas because they

ORNAMENTAL PEPPER
Capsicum annuum 'Fiesta'

have a reputation for durability and because cattleya hybrids offer an immense choice of exotic color combinations and shapes. Cattleyas grow from swollen stems called pseudobulbs. Their flowers grow singly or in clusters along an arching flower stalk up to 18 inches long; this stalk grows from a single leaf or a pair of leaves. Large blooms appear at various times of the year, depending on the species or hybrid. Since many cattleya species are tall, light gardeners favor miniatures like the dainty *C. luteola* or hybrids developed by crossing *Cattleya* with a dwarf genus. *C. luteola* has 3- to 4-inch leaves and yellow flowers only 2 inches across with tubular white lower petals, the lips, velvety inside and sometimes streaked with purple on the outside. Two *Cattleya* hybrids suited to light gardens are *Laeliocattleya,* a cross between *Cattleya* and *Laelia,* and *Sophrolaeliocattleya,* a multiple cross of the dwarf *Sophronitis* with *Laelia* and *Cattleya.* Both of these hybrid orchids bear large flowers on small plants. Ivory, white, lilac and rose appear in various combinations in the flowers, which frequently have yellow throats. Many *Sophrolaeliocattleyas* in shades of red have been developed in the search for a pure-red orchid.

HOW TO GROW. Cattleyas require 1,500 to 2,000 footcandles of light to produce bloom, achieved by growing them under a bank of six 4-foot cool- and warm-white fluorescent tubes, or four 4-foot very-high-output tubes. Place the plants as close to the lights as possible without letting them touch the tubes, lowering the plants as flower spikes grow and illuminating them for 14 to 16 hours daily. Temperatures of 55° to 60° at night and 65° to 70° by day are best; orchids require a 10° temperature drop at night in order to bloom. Humidity of 50 to 60 per cent is necessary; place pots on a moisture tray, mist plants twice daily and use a room humidifier to keep humidity high. Since fungus diseases spread in humid, stagnant air, be sure to provide good air circulation around the plants.

Orchids need repotting every two or three years when plants and their aerial roots grow over the edges of pots. Use a soilless mixture of 2 parts fir bark or shredded tree-fern fiber, 1 part perlite and 1 part coarse peat moss; an acid soil is essential, so add no lime. Cattleyas can also be fastened to a hanging slab of tree fern. Let the soil dry slightly between waterings; water standing around the roots will quickly rot cattleyas. Feed biweekly with a fertilizer formulated for orchids such as 30-10-10 or 18-18-18, diluted to one fourth the strength recommended on the label. Do not fertilize during dormancy. Propagate by dividing plants that have bloomed, keeping a clump of four or five pseudobulbs in each division.

CHAMAEDOREA

C. elegans, also called *C. pulchella* and *Neanthe bella* (parlor palm, Neanthe palm)

For a touch of tropical foliage, light gardeners can cultivate the graceful parlor palm. This miniature palm can be grown in a terrarium when it is young; mature potted plants seldom become more than 18 inches tall; they bear featherlike, 9- to 12-inch fronds of narrow, leathery leaflets.

HOW TO GROW. Parlor palms need low to medium light, about 200 foot-candles, for 10 to 12 hours daily and grow well when placed 12 inches below a two-tube fixture. Because of their low light requirements, you can set them in the lower light intensity near the ends of the tubes. Give them night temperatures of 65° to 70° and day temperatures of 75° to 85°, maintaining the humidity as close to 50 per cent as possible by growing young plants in a terrarium and by placing mature potted plants on a moisture tray. Parlor palms grow best when their roots are crowded in their con-

MINIATURE CATTLEYA ORCHID
Cattleya luteola

PARLOR PALM
Chamaedorea elegans

CHIRITA
Chirita sinensis

MANDA'S SPIDER PLANT
Chlorophytum comosum mandaianum

tainers. When repotting is necessary, use a soilless mixture of equal parts of sphagnum peat moss, perlite and vermiculite, adding 1 teaspoon of bone meal and either 1 teaspoon of ground limestone or ¼ cup of crushed eggshells per quart of mix; otherwise, use a packaged soilless mix, adding bone meal and a lime source in the same proportions. Keep the soil moist but never soggy. Feed every other week from spring through fall with a balanced house-plant fertilizer such as 20-20-20 diluted to one fourth the strength recommended on the label; do not fertilize during the winter when the palm is dormant. Parlor palms are usually grown from seed.

CHARMING DIEFFENBACHIA See *Dieffenbachia*
CHIN CACTUS See *Gymnocalycium*
CHINESE EVERGREEN See *Aglaonema*
CHINESE RUBBER PLANT See *Crassula*

CHIRITA
C. sinensis (chirita)

Compact growth makes the chirita a good choice for a light garden. This gesneriad is grown for its tight rosettes of bright green, hairy oval leaves, which are occasionally variegated with spectacular silver markings. Growing conditions must be ideal, however, for chirita plants to bear their bell-shaped, 1-inch lilac flowers.

HOW TO GROW. Give chiritas medium to bright light, about 500 foot-candles, for 14 to 16 hours daily. Place plants about 6 inches below a standard two-tube fixture. Maintain temperatures of 55° to 65° at night, 70° to 75° by day, using a humidity tray to keep the humidity as close to 50 per cent as possible. Use a soilless mixture of equal parts sphagnum peat moss, perlite and vermiculite, adding 1 teaspoon of ground limestone or ¼ cup of crushed eggshells per quart of mix; otherwise, use a packaged soilless mix, adding limestone or eggshells in the same proportions. Fertilize weekly with a high-phosphorus fertilizer such as 10-30-20, diluted to one fourth the strength recommended on the label. Allow the top of the mix to dry slightly between waterings; avoid splashing because water may spot the foliage. Browned leaf edges indicate the plant is getting too much water. Propagate with stem cuttings, taken at any time, or grow from seed.

CHLOROPHYTUM
C. comosum, also called *Anthericum comosum* and *A. sternbergianum* (spider plant, ribbon plant, bracket plant)

A graceful member of the lily family, the spider plant has arching rosettes of narrow 4- to 6-inch leaves that are green striped with white or yellow. A mature plant produces arching runners up to 2 feet long; plants grown under fluorescent lights are especially prolific in this regard. The tiny white flowers that grow at the tips of these runners are followed by small plantlets with aerial roots that can be left on the parent plant to increase its fullness or cut off for propagation of new plants. *C. comosum mandaianum* is a compact variety with green leaves that have a white or yellow stripe down their centers; leaves are 4 to 6 inches long and ½ inch wide. *C. comosum variegatum,* the most common spider plant, has white-edged green leaves 10 to 16 inches long and about an inch wide. *C. comosum vittatum* has white bands down the centers of its leaves, 4 to 8 inches long and ½ inch wide.

HOW TO GROW. Spider plants grow best when given medium light, 400 to 650 foot-candles, for 12 to 14 hours daily. Place plants 6 to 12 inches below a two-tube fixture. Provide night temperatures of 50° to 55° and day temperatures of 68° to 72°, keeping the humidity as close to 50 per cent as possible. To raise the humidity, place pots on a moisture tray. Spider plants grow so quickly under lights that roots quickly fill their containers, so plants need frequent repotting. Use a soilless mixture of equal parts sphagnum peat moss, perlite and vermiculite, adding either 1 teaspoon of ground limestone or ¼ cup of crushed eggshells per quart of mix; alternatively, use a packaged soilless mix, adding a lime source in the same proportions. Keep the soil evenly moist but not soggy. When the soil is repeatedly allowed to dry and is then resoaked, leaf tips may turn brown; a soil that is too acid can also cause leaf-tip browning. Fertilize weekly, using a balanced house-plant formula such as 20-20-20 diluted to one fourth the strength recommended on the label. Propagate by cutting off the plantlets that appear along the runners, rooting them in moist vermiculite, then potting them in growing medium. Plants can also be propagated by dividing the fleshy roots.

CISSUS
C. antarctica, also called *C. glandulosa* and *Vitis antarctica* (kangaroo ivy); *C. discolor,* also called *C. velutina* (trailing begonia); *C. quadrangularis; C. rhombifolia*, also called *Vitis rhombifolia* (grape ivy); *C. striata* (dwarf grape vine)

Ivies of the *Cissus* genus include many climbing plants cultivated for their colorful foliage. Most have tendrils along their stems by which they will attach themselves to a trellis, bark pole or other support. Their soft stems will also cascade from hanging baskets; frequent pinching off of new growth keeps plants bushy. The leaf coloring of plants grown under fluorescent lights is superior to that of window-sill plants. Although these ivies tolerate neglect, with good care they reward the gardener with lush, abundant growth.

Kangaroo ivy has hairy branches that bear shiny 4- to 6-inch oval green leaves with toothed edges. A dwarf variety of kangaroo ivy, *C. antarctica minima,* has leaves only 3 inches long. Trailing begonia is an especially vivid species with red stems; the velvety, quiltlike oblong leaves, 3 to 4 inches long, are silver, green and violet above, maroon underneath. *C. quadrangularis* has 2-inch leaves that fork into three narrow segments; these leaves grow from joints along thick, cactus-like four-sided stems that appear to have corners that are pinched into thin segments called wings. Grape ivy has hairy brown stems and three-lobed leaves 4 inches long and 3 to 4 inches wide; young growth is covered with downy white hairs and turns from bronze to green as it matures. Five-lobed leaves, 1½ inches wide, grow so densely on the dwarf grape vine that they hide its thin stems.

HOW TO GROW. Give *Cissus* species medium light, 200 to 500 foot-candles, for 10 to 12 hours daily; they grow best when placed 6 to 12 inches below a two-tube fixture. Night temperatures of 50° to 55°, day temperatures of 68° to 72°, and 30 to 40 per cent humidity are best for all but the trailing begonia; it needs night temperatures of 65° to 70°, day temperatures of 75° to 85°, and humidity as close to 50 per cent as possible. Place pots of trailing begonia on a moisture tray to raise the humidity level. For all species, when roots crowd a container, repot in a soilless mixture of equal parts sphagnum peat moss, perlite and vermiculite adding either 1 teaspoon of ground limestone or ¼ cup crushed eggshells per quart of mix; otherwise, use a packaged soilless mix, adding a lime source in the same proportions. Let the soil dry slightly between waterings and feed weekly with a balanced house-plant fertilizer such as 20-20-20 diluted to one fourth the recommended strength. Propagate by rooting stem cuttings in moist vermiculite.

CLAMSHELL ORCHID See *Epidendrum*

GRAPE IVY
Cissus rhombifolia

CROTON
Codiaeum variegatum pictum

COMMON COLEUS
Coleus blumei hybrid

COB CACTUS See *Lobivia*

CODIAEUM
C. variegatum pictum (croton)

Although these fast-growing tropical shrubs may crowd other plants, light gardeners give space to crotons for the shapes and colors of their leaves, which reach a decorative peak under strong, dependable light. The leaves, 3 to 18 inches long and 1 to 6 inches wide, can be straplike, oval, lobed or spiraled. Leaf colors encompass a wide spectrum from yellow to green, purple, red and orange, as well as shades of white and ivory. As many as five colors may appear on one plant. Foliage often changes color as a plant matures. Light gardeners with limited space can grow young plants limited to 2 or 3 feet in height by frequent pruning.

HOW TO GROW. To develop the best color, crotons need very bright light, 1,000 to 1,500 foot-candles, for 12 to 14 hours daily. Grow them 6 inches below a four-tube fixture. Provide night temperatures of 65° to 70°, day temperatures of 75° to 85°, and humidity as close to 50 per cent as possible. Stand pots on a moisture tray to raise the humidity level. Avoid drafts, which may cause leaves to fall off. When roots fill a container, repot in a soilless mixture of equal parts sphagnum peat moss, perlite and vermiculite, adding either 1 teaspoon of ground limestone or ¼ cup of crushed eggshells per quart of mix; otherwise, use a packaged soilless mix, adding limestone or eggshells in the same proportions. Let the soil dry slightly between waterings and feed weekly with a balanced house-plant fertilizer such as 20-20-20, diluted to one fourth the strength recommended on the label. Propagate plants by rooting tip cuttings in moist vermiculite.

COLEUS
C. blumei hybrids (common coleus)

Fast-growing plants of remarkably easy culture, the coleuses are members of the mint family. Their beautifully patterned and brilliantly colored oval leaves, 2 to 6 inches long, are borne in pairs along succulent square stems, combining many shades of pink, red, orange, yellow, deep purple and green. Under fluorescent lights, these rich foliage colors are brought to a peak on plants that tend to grow compactly. Insignificant blue-to-lilac flowers grow on spikes from the tips of branches. Although a coleus can grow to 2½ feet, pruning can keep it under a foot in height and diameter.

HOW TO GROW. Coleus plants need medium to bright light, 500 to 1,000 foot-candles, for 12 to 14 hours daily. Place plants 6 inches or less below a two-tube fixture, or 6 to 12 inches below a four-tube fixture. Night temperatures of 65° to 70°, day temperatures of 75° to 85°, and 30 to 40 per cent humidity are best. When roots become crowded in a container, repot in a soilless mixture of 2 parts sphagnum peat moss, 1 part perlite and 1 part vermiculite, adding either 1 teaspoon of ground limestone or ¼ cup of crushed eggshells per quart of mix; otherwise, use a packaged soilless mix prepared for African violets, adding a lime source in the same proportions. Keep the soil evenly moist at all times but never soggy; letting the soil dry causes heavy leaf drop. Feed weekly with a balanced house-plant fertilizer such as 20-20-20, diluted to one fourth the strength recommended on the label. Prune by cutting off portions of the stems, making each cut just above a pair of leaves. These stem cuttings can be rooted in moist vermiculite or water to produce new plants. Coleus also can be easily grown from seed germinated in moist vermiculite.

COLOMBIA BUTTERCUP See *Oncidium*

COLUMNEA
C. hybrids (columnea)

When grown under lights, columneas almost continuously produce spectacular yellow, orange, red or pink flowers shaped like goldfish. The long-lasting, 3-inch flowers of this gesneriad are borne singly or in clusters. The leaves of different hybrids vary from smooth and glossy to soft and hairy; some are variegated. The upright, compact varieties are ideal for the light garden; two suitable varieties are Robin, which has large, bright-red flowers and small dark leaves, and the Chanticleer, orange flowered. Larger trailing varieties are better suited for hanging baskets.

HOW TO GROW. Columneas need only low light, about 150 to 250 foot-candles, for 14 to 16 hours daily and grow best if positioned about 12 inches from a standard two-tube fixture. Day temperatures of 70° to 75° and night temperatures of 60° to 65° are ideal except in winter, when night temperatures of 50° to 60° are needed for flowering. Maintain humidity as high as possible (60 per cent is ideal) by misting plants frequently and by placing pots on humidity trays. When potting, use a soilless mixture of equal parts perlite, vermiculite and sphagnum peat moss, adding either 1 teaspoon of ground limestone or ¼ cup of crushed eggshells per quart; otherwise, use a packaged soilless mix, incorporating eggshells or limestone in the same proportions. Keep the mix evenly moist; withered flower buds indicate too much water and yellowed leaves signal too little water. Fertilize weekly with a water-soluble high-phosphorus fertilizer such as 10-30-20 diluted to one fourth the strength recommended on the label. Propagate from stem cuttings rooted in moist vermiculite, or grow from seed.

COMPARETTIA
C. falcata; C. macroplectron (both called comparettia orchid)

Dwarf orchids suited to the limited space of a light garden, comparettias grow from clumps of thickened stems called pseudobulbs. Each pseudobulb annually produces a single leaf followed by a drooping 15- to 30-inch flower stalk in summer. Up to 15 brightly colored flowers grow along this stalk, each with small petal-like outer sepals, equally small inner petals, a large lower petal (the lip) and a pointed hollow spur projecting from the back of the flower. *C. falcata* has ½-inch rose-to-purple sepals, petals and spurs; the prominent lip is veined in a darker shade of the same colors. Each 6-inch leaf is green on top, purple below. *C. macroplectron* has 20-inch flower stalks lined with 2-inch white or pale rose flowers with 2-inch spurs. The broad lip is white spotted with red or purple and the 2- to 5-inch leaves are green streaked underneath with rust and yellow.

HOW TO GROW. Comparettias need 1,200 to 2,400 foot-candles of light in order to bloom well. This can be achieved by growing them under a bank of eight to 10 4-foot cool- and warm-white fluorescent tubes, or six to eight 4-foot high-output tubes, or four to six 4-foot very-high-output tubes. Illuminate the plants for 14 to 16 hours daily, placing them as close to the fixture as possible without touching the tubes. Gradually lower the plants as flower spikes grow. If leaves turn a very dark green, the plants are getting too little light; yellowed leaves indicate too much light. Provide temperatures of 55° to 60° at night and from 65° to 70° by day; orchids require a 10° temperature drop at night in order to bloom. Humidity of 50 to 75 per cent is best; mist the plants twice daily, place pots on a moisture tray and use a room humidifier to raise the humidity to this high level. Since stagnant, humid air encourages fungus disease, allow enough space around plants to permit good ventilation.

COLUMNEA
Columnea hybrid 'Robin'

COMPARETTIA ORCHID
Comparettia falcata

Repot a comparettia when the plant and its aerial roots grow over the edge of the pot. Use an acid mixture of 2 parts fir bark or shredded tree-fern fiber and 1 part coarse peat moss; a comparettia can also be attached to a suspended slab of tree fern. Allow the potting mix to dry slightly between waterings; any water standing around the roots quickly rots an orchid. Feed weekly with a fertilizer formulated for orchids, such as 30-10-10 or 18-18-18, diluted to one fourth the strength recommended on the label. Propagate when repotting by dividing the clumps of pseudobulbs, keeping four or five pseudobulbs in each division.

CORAL ORCHID See *Rodriguezia*

CRASSULA

C. argentea, also called *C. portulacea* (jade plant, Chinese rubber plant); *C. falcata* (scarlet paint brush, propeller plant); *C. lycopodiodes* (rattail crassula); *C. perforata* (necklace vine, string of buttons); *C. schmidtii* (red-flowering crassula)

Window-sill gardeners often grow the popular jade plant and its relatives as foliage plants, but light gardeners can bring mature, pot-bound crassulas into bloom under fluorescents. While the various succulents in this large genus differ dramatically in foliage sizes, shapes and colors, all have thick, fleshy, smooth leaves and tiny, delicate five-petaled flowers. The jade plant's 1- to 2-inch oval leaves grow on thick stems that branch frequently until the plant resembles a miniature tree. Leaf edges take on a red tinge when the plant receives bright light. Growing very slowly to an average of 15 to 20 inches in height, a mature plant sometimes bears clusters of pale pink to white starlike flowers. The scarlet paint brush has scythe-shaped 3- to 4-inch leaves growing in a whorl up a central stem that can reach 10 inches in height; older plants bear flat clusters of bright red flowers on stalks rising from their tops.

Rattail crassula is a creeping plant whose 6- to 8-inch semierect stems are sheathed with tiny scalelike pointed leaves; minute white flowers appear between leaves. The necklace vine has pointed oval leaves only an inch long ascending 2-foot-tall erect stems; the fleshy leaves are sometimes spotted with gray and the yellow flowers appear in clusters at the tips of branches. Red flowering crassula is a miniature succulent with needle-like 1- to 2-inch leaves on 3- to 6-inch stems; the erect foliage is edged with white hairs and the red flowers are borne in clusters at stem tips.

HOW TO GROW. Crassulas grow best when they receive 1,000 to 1,500 foot-candles, achieved by placing them 6 inches or less below a four-tube fixture, for 14 to 16 hours daily while they are actively growing from spring through fall, and for 10 to 12 hours during their winter resting period. Night temperatures of 50° to 55° and day temperatures between 68° and 72° are ideal, although crassulas will grow at temperatures both higher and lower than this range. Humidity of 25 to 30 per cent is adequate. Plants grow slowly and need to be repotted only every three to five years when roots fill their containers; root-bound plants bloom best.

When repotting, use a soilless mixture of 1 part sphagnum peat moss, 2 parts perlite and 2 parts vermiculite, adding 1 teaspoon of bone meal and either 1 teaspoon of ground limestone or ¼ cup of crushed eggshells per quart of mix; otherwise, use a packaged soilless mix prepared for cacti, adding bone meal and a lime source in the same proportions. From spring to fall, allow the soil to become nearly dry between waterings and feed weekly with a high-phosphorus fertilizer such as 15-30-15 diluted to one fourth the recommended strength. During winter, withhold fertilizer; water

SCARLET PAINT BRUSH
Crassula falcata

just enough to keep the leaves from shriveling. Propagate from stem or leaf cuttings, allowing the juicy cuts to dry 24 hours before inserting cuttings into moist vermiculite.

CREEPING FIG See *Ficus*
CROCODILE JAWS See *Aloe*

CROSSANDRA
C. infundibuliformis, also called *C. undulaefolia* (firecracker flower)

Long, dependable periods of bright light and a high level of humidity will keep firecracker flowers blooming year round. But these shrubby plants can become 3 feet tall, unless they are vigilantly pruned to keep them small enough to prosper under lights. Even then, allow abundant head room; the thick, square flower spikes encircled by red or orange flowers rise above whorls of 3- to 5-inch evergreen leaves. Each spike has 20 to 30 vivid flowers with inch-long curved petals. The vigorous flowers last as long as a month.

HOW TO GROW. Firecracker flowers bloom continuously 6 inches or less below a two-tube fixture or 6 to 12 inches below a four-tube fixture; they need bright light, 500 to 1,000 foot-candles. Illuminate the plants 14 to 16 hours daily. Temperatures of 60° to 65° at night and 70° or higher during the day are best. High humidity—65 to 70 per cent—is needed to achieve the best blooms; supplement room humidity with a humidifier. Provide good ventilation but avoid placing plants in drafts.

Start the plants in 2-inch pots, using a soilless mix of 2 parts sphagnum peat moss, 1 part perlite and 1 part vermiculite, adding 1 teaspoon of ground limestone or ¼ cup of crushed eggshells per quart of mix; otherwise, use a packaged soilless mix, adding a lime source in the same proportions. Gradually move plants into 4- or 5-inch pots; keep the roots crowded in their pots to help restrict plant size. Keep the potting mix evenly moist but never soggy. Feed weekly after watering with a balanced fertilizer such as 20-20-20, diluted to one fourth the strength recommended on the label. To keep plants blooming, remove faded flowers before seeds form. Propagate by rooting cuttings in moist vermiculite; enclose cuttings in a plastic box or bag to ensure high humidity while the roots form. Firecracker flowers can also be grown from seed to blooming size in nine months but germination is erratic.

CROTON See *Codiaeum*
CROWN CACTUS See *Rebutia*
CROWN OF THORNS See *Euphorbia*

CRYPTANTHUS
C. bivittatus, also called *C. rosea picta; C.* hybrid 'It'; *C. zonatus zebrinus* (all called earth star)

Earth stars are bromeliads grown for and named for their flat starlike rosettes of colorful striped leaves. *C. bivittatus* has wavy, green, spiny-edged leaves, 6 inches long, with white or pink stripes. The hybrid It has 18-inch copper-to-green leaves with ivory stripes and red edges. *C. zonatus zebrinus* has 6- to 9-inch wavy bronze leaves zigzagged with silver bands. All of these species have intensified leaf colors when they are grown under lights.

HOW TO GROW. Although cryptanthus will grow in lower light, it develops its best leaf color in bright light, about 500 to 750 foot-candles, for 12 to 14 hours daily. Adjust a two-tube 48-inch fixture so it is about 6 inches above the plant. Night temperatures of 60° to 65° and day temperatures of 70° or higher are ideal. Keep humidity as close to 50 per

FIRECRACKER FLOWER
Crossandra infundibuliformis

EARTH STAR
Cryptanthus bivittatus

ELFIN HERB
Cuphea hyssopifolia

PUSSY EARS
Cyanotis somaliensis

cent as possible by misting plants and setting pots on a moisture tray. Pot in a soilless mix of equal parts sphagnum peat moss, vermiculite and perlite; do not add lime; otherwise, use a packaged soilless mix. Mist the plant frequently but water the mix only when the top layer feels dry when pinched between the fingers. Saturating the mix will rot the base of a bromeliad. Feed earth stars weekly with a water-soluble, balanced fertilizer such as 20-20-20 at one fourth the strength recommended on the label. After bearing insignificant flowers, the mother plant will slowly die during the next several years, but it produces offshoots; these should be removed and potted individually.

CRYSTAL ANTHURIUM See *Anthurium*

CUPHEA

C. hyssopifolia (elfin herb)

Unlike flowering plants that balk when light, temperature and humidity are not precisely to their liking, the neatly shaped elfin herb blooms on and on in a light garden, content with little attention. Its blossoms are not showy, but they can be counted on. Pairs of needle-like ½-inch leaves crowd the wiry branches. Tiny violet, pink or white flowers appear like minute stars in the joints between the leaves and the stems. The symmetrical plants grow 6 to 10 inches tall and 1 to 2 feet across. They can be kept smaller by pruning.

HOW TO GROW. Elfin herbs will flourish under medium light, 200 to 500 foot-candles, achieved by placing them 12 inches below a two-tube fixture and illuminating them for 12 to 16 hours a day. If they are placed closer to the fluorescent tubes their leaf tips develop a red tinge. Temperatures can range from 50° at night to 75° or higher during the day. These plants are all but indifferent to the humidity level, growing equally well in a moist terrarium or in the low humidity found in most homes during the winter. Move plants gradually from 2-inch to 6-inch pots as they mature, using a soilless mixture composed of equal parts sphagnum peat moss, vermiculite and perlite, adding 1 teaspoon of ground limestone or ¼ cup of crushed eggshells per quart of mix; otherwise, use a packaged soilless mix, adding a lime source in the same proportions. Keep the mixture evenly moist but never let it become soggy.

Feed weekly after watering with a balanced fertilizer such as 20-20-20 diluted to one fourth the strength suggested on the label. Propagate additional plants by rooting cuttings of new growth in moist vermiculite. Elfin herbs can also be grown from seed, developing into blooming plants in about four or five months.

CYANOTIS

C. kewensis (teddy-bear vine); *C. somaliensis* (pussy ears, fuzzy ears) (both called cyanotis)

The woolly hair that blankets the fleshy leaves of cyanotis plants reminds gardeners of furry animals. This unique foliage and the feathery flowers that appear throughout the growing season make these plants unusual among succulents. The leaves grow in whorls on branching stems that creep along the surface. Flowers appear on straight stems growing from leaf bases. The teddy-bear vine has inch-long leaves matted with brown fuzz and its ⅓-inch flowers are red with blue tufts called beards. Pussy ears has pointed leaves, 1½ inches long, that are covered with soft white hairs; its ⅓-inch flowers are blue.

HOW TO GROW. Give cyanotis 1,000 to 1,500 foot-candles of light by placing plants 6 inches or less below a four-tube fixture. Plants normally have an active growing period from spring through fall and a rest period during the winter. Light them for 14 to 16 hours while they are actively growing and for 10 to 12 hours during dormancy. Provide temperatures of 65° at night and 75° or higher by day, with 25 to 30 per cent humidity. Plants grow slowly and need repotting only every three to five years. Plant in a soilless mixture of 1 part sphagnum peat moss, 2 parts perlite and 2 parts vermiculite, adding 1 teaspoon of bone meal and either 1 teaspoon of ground limestone or ¼ cup of crushed eggshells per quart of mix; otherwise use a packaged soilless mix prepared for cacti, adding bone meal and a lime source in the same proportions. While they are actively growing, allow the soil around the plants to dry slightly between waterings and feed biweekly with a high-phosphorus fertilizer such as 15-30-15 diluted to one fourth the strength recommended on the label. During dormancy, allow the soil to dry almost completely between waterings and withhold fertilizer. Propagate from leaf or stem cuttings, allowing the juicy, cut surfaces to dry 24 hours before inserting them in moist vermiculite.

CYMBALARIA

C. muralis, also called *Linaria cymbalaria* (Kenilworth ivy, mother-of-thousands)

Kenilworth ivy is deceptive: despite the dainty, waxy look of its leaves and its delicate violet flowers, this perennial vine is such a tough, persistent plant that many gardeners consider it a weed. The wiry stems root at every joint that touches soil and the flowers produce such quantities of seed that the ivy jumps into every nearby pot. Still, Kenilworth ivy is a good choice for a light gardener who wants a plant that flowers freely and is not fussy about constant attention. The plant's stems trail gracefully over the sides of pots, can be trained to grow on a small trellis or will quickly carpet a terrarium. Yellow-throated, ½-inch flowers develop spurs. The round or kidney-shaped ⅝-inch-wide leaves are usually green above, purple below. The upper leaf surfaces of *C. muralis variegata,* variegated Kenilworth ivy, are shaded with green and ivory or two tones of green.

HOW TO GROW. Kenilworth ivy is not demanding about growing conditions but will flower best if it receives bright light, 500 to 1,000 foot-candles, for 12 to 14 hours daily. To achieve this light, place the plant 6 inches or less below a two-tube fixture or 6 to 12 inches below a four-tube fixture. Provide temperatures ranging from 60° at night to 75° by day for optimum growth. Plant in a soilless mixture of 2 parts peat moss, 1 part perlite and 1 part vermiculite, adding 1 teaspoon of ground limestone or ¼ cup of crushed eggshells per quart of mix; otherwise, use a packaged soilless mix prepared for African violets, adding a lime source in the same proportions. Keep the soil evenly moist but never soggy. Feed weekly after watering with a balanced fertilizer such as 20-20-20 diluted to one fourth the strength recommended on the label. Propagate by severing and potting rooted sections of stem.

CYMBIDIUM

C. miniature hybrids (miniature cymbidium orchid)

Popular in corsages, miniature cymbidium orchids bear long-lasting sprays of flowers from fall to early spring on plants only 12 to 15 inches tall. The orchids grow from fleshy stems called pseudobulbs; each sends out leathery, straplike leaves and an erect flower stalk. Each bloom lasts up to three months on the plant and is composed of a ring of long, pointed petal-like outer sepals, a set of small inner petals and a large lower petal, the lip, frequently lobed and ridged. Colors range from mahogany and bronze through purple,

VARIEGATED KENILWORTH IVY
Cymbalaria muralis variegata

MINIATURE CYMBIDIUM ORCHID
Cymbidium hybrid 'Flirtation'

pink, yellow and ivory. Often several colors appear in one flower and the petals and lip are spotted or streaked. The cymbidium Flirtation blooms twice a year, unusual among orchids, bearing 2-inch-wide pink-to-ivory flowers with petals shaded with light purple and white lips blotched with maroon. Peter Pan has blossoms 2½ inches across with green petals and lips freckled with red or brown.

HOW TO GROW. Miniature cymbidium orchids need 1,200 to 2,400 or more foot-candles, achieved by growing them under a bank of eight to 10 4-foot cool- and warm-white fluorescent tubes, or six to eight 4-foot high-output tubes, or four to six very-high-output tubes. Place the orchids as close to the tubes as possible without touching them and illuminate plants for 14 to 16 hours daily. Standard cymbidiums require cool temperatures but miniatures do best when night temperatures are 55° to 60° and day temperatures range from 65° to 70°; a 10° drop in temperature at night is necessary for blooming. Humidity of 50 to 60 per cent is best; place pots on a moisture tray, mist twice daily and use a room humidifier to raise the humidity. But since high humidity and stagnant air can promote fungus growth, also provide good air circulation around the plants.

Grow miniature cymbidiums in 4- to 6-inch pots in a mixture of 2 parts fir bark or shredded tree-fern fiber and 1 part coarse peat moss. Keep the soil evenly moist but never soggy; orchids rot quickly if water stands around their roots. Feed each week with a fertilizer formulated for orchids such as 30-10-10 or 18-18-18, diluted to one fourth the strength recommended on the label. Repot plants every two to four years when plants and their aerial roots begin creeping over the edges of the containers. Propagate by dividing pseudobulb clumps when repotting, keeping at least five or six pseudobulbs in each division.

CYPERUS

C. alternifolius gracilis (slender umbrella plant); *C. diffusus,* also called *C. laxus* (dwarf umbrella plant); *C. haspan viviparus* (pygmy papyrus)

These moisture-loving species of the *Cyperus* genus have tall, slender stems called culms bearing graceful tufts of about 20 grasslike leaves radiating from their tips. Tiny flowers are borne on spikes above the foliage. The slender umbrella plant is a compact variety with 12- to 18-inch culms topped with 4- to 8-inch leaves. The dwarf umbrella plant has stems only 12 inches tall but its leaves vary from 4 to 15 inches long; the plant also has coarse leaves at its base that produce runners. The pygmy papyrus has 18-inch stems and stiff, upright 2- to 3-inch leaves.

HOW TO GROW. *Cyperus* species grow best when they receive bright light, 500 to 1,000 foot-candles, achieved by placing them 6 inches or less below a two-tube fixture or 6 to 12 inches below a four-tube fixture. Illuminate plants for 12 to 14 hours daily. Provide night temperatures of 50° to 55°, a day range of 68° to 72°, and humidity as close to 50 per cent as possible. When potting, use a soilless mixture of equal parts sphagnum peat moss, perlite and vermiculite; otherwise, use a packaged soilless mix. To each quart of either medium add approximately 1 teaspoon of ground limestone or ¼ cup of crushed eggshells. Since these plants grow best when their soil is wet, keep their pots standing in a saucer or tray of water. Feed weekly with a balanced house-plant fertilizer such as 20-20-20, diluted to one fourth the strength recommended on the label. To flush out fertilizer salts that might reach toxic levels, periodically pour fresh water on the growing medium until it runs out the drainage holes. Plants can be propagated either by dividing their roots or by

DWARF UMBRELLA PLANT
Cyperus diffusus

cutting off a culm, trimming its leaves to ½-inch length, then standing the culm leaf side down in water to root. Plants can also be grown from seed.

CYRTOMIUM
C. falcatum (holly fern, Japanese holly fern)

Under artificial light, holly ferns develop thicker clumps of fronds and grow faster than they do under ordinary house-plant conditions. As their name implies, the leaflets resemble those of a holly tree. The leathery evergreen leaflets, 3 to 5 inches long, are paired along gracefully arching fronds up to 30 inches long. The robust variety *rochefordianum* has wavy, saw-toothed edges on 2-inch-wide fronds.

HOW TO GROW. Holly fern should receive 14 hours of low- to medium-intensity light (150 to 400 foot-candles) each day. Place plants so the top of the fern is about 12 inches below a two-tube fixture. Night temperatures of 50° to 60°, daytime temperatures of 70° to 80° and humidity as close to 60 per cent as possible are best. To help achieve higher humidity, mist plants and place pots on a moisture tray. Plant in a pot whose diameter measures one third the plant's height. Use a soilless mixture of 2 parts sphagnum peat moss, 1 part perlite and 1 part vermiculite, adding 1 teaspoon of bone meal per quart of mix; otherwise, use a packaged soilless mix prepared for African violets, adding bone meal in the same proportion. Feed every two weeks during periods of active growth, using a high-nitrogen (5-2-2) fertilizer such as fish emulsion diluted to one fourth the strength recommended on the label. Soil should be barely moist at all times. Brown leaves indicate that the fern is too close to the fluorescent tubes. Propagate by dividing mature plants.

D

DANCING LADY ORCHIDS See *Oncidium*
DELTA MAIDENHAIR FERN See *Adiantum*

DIEFFENBACHIA
D. amoena (charming dieffenbachia); *D. bausei* (Bause dieffenbachia); *D. exotica*, also called *D. arvida* (exotic dieffenbachia); *D. picta*, also called *D. brasiliensis* (variable dieffenbachia) (all called dieffenbachia or dumb cane)

The handsome patterns of color on the oval leaves of dieffenbachias are intensified when they are grown under fluorescent lights. Although the plants can become 4 to 5 feet tall, young plants with graceful tufts of leaves are suited to a light garden. As plants mature, lower leaves wither and stems elongate. Charming dieffenbachia has leathery 12- to 18-inch green leaves marked with cream along their veins. Bause dieffenbachia, a more compact species, has 6- to 18-inch yellow-to-green leaves spotted with white and both spotted and edged with dark green. The low-growing exotic dieffenbachia has 8- to 10-inch green leaves that are heavily splotched with brilliant markings. Variable dieffenbachia has glossy green 10-inch leaves, marbled and splotched with white; its leaf stalks are spotted with pale green. The name dumb cane was given to dieffenbachia because both stems and leaves contain a harmful sap that causes skin pain and swelling; if tasted, the poison in the sap, calcium oxalate, causes temporary speechlessness.

HOW TO GROW. Dieffenbachias need low to medium light, 250 to 500 foot-candles, for 12 to 14 hours daily; place them 12 inches below a two-tube fixture. A night temperature range of 65° to 70°, a day range of 75° to 85° and humidity as close to 50 per cent as possible are best. Place pots on a moisture tray to raise the humidity level. When roots crowd their container, repot in a soilless mixture of equal parts

ROCHEFORD'S HOLLY FERN
Cyrtomium falcatum rochefordianum

EXOTIC DIEFFENBACHIA
Dieffenbachia exotica

SANDER'S DRACAENA
Dracaena sanderiana

PAINTED LADY
Echeveria derenbergii

sphagnum peat moss, perlite and vermiculite, adding either 1 teaspoon of ground limestone or ¼ cup of crushed eggshells per quart of mix; otherwise, use a packaged soilless mix, adding the same amounts of a lime source to each quart. Allow the soil to dry slightly between waterings. Feed weekly with a balanced house-plant fertilizer such as 20-20-20, diluted to one fourth the strength recommended on the label. Plants can be propagated by cutting a stem into 2-inch pieces, letting the cut ends dry for 24 hours, then laying them horizontally in moist peat moss to root. If suckers or small new plants appear at the bases of older plants, they may be cut off and potted individually.

DRACAENA
D. godseffiana (gold-dust dracaena); *D. sanderiana* (Sander's dracaena)

Fluorescent lights bring out the best in the decoratively patterned leaves of dracaenas. These easily cultivated plants have such a wide variety of leaf shapes and sizes that it is surprising to find the plants are related. The two species listed are relatively small, hence are suited to the limited space of a light garden. The gold-dust dracaena has multiple stems that can reach 2½ feet in height. Its 5-inch oval dark-green leaves, irregularly spotted with gold markings that turn white as leaves mature, grow along the stems in whorls of three. The plants bear green-to-yellow flowers followed by red berries. The variety known as Florida Beauty grows very slowly and is heavily blotched with color. Sander's dracaena has leathery leaves that are 7 to 10 inches long and an inch wide, growing from slender erect stems; the strap-shaped leaves are dark green with broad white margins.

HOW TO GROW. Dracaenas need medium light, 400 to 650 foot-candles, for 12 to 14 hours daily. Place plants 6 to 12 inches below a two-tube fixture. Provide night temperatures of 65° to 70°, a range of 75° to 85° by day, and humidity as close to 50 per cent as possible. Standing pots on a moisture tray helps raise the humidity. When roots become crowded in the container, repot in a soilless mixture of 2 parts sphagnum peat moss, 1 part perlite and 1 part vermiculite, adding either 1 teaspoon of ground limestone or ¼ cup of crushed eggshells per quart of mix; otherwise, use a packaged soilless mix adding a lime source in the same proportions. Allow the soil to dry slightly between waterings and feed weekly with a balanced house-plant formula such as 20-20-20, diluted to one fourth the strength recommended on the label. Propagate by rooting stem cuttings in moist vermiculite.

DWARF CLUB MOSS See *Selaginella*
DWARF CROWN OF THORNS See *Euphorbia*
DWARF GRAPE IVY See *Cissus*
DWARF PINEAPPLE See *Ananas*
DWARF POMEGRANATE See *Punica*
DWARF THREAD-BEARING CENTURY PLANT See
   Agave
DWARF UMBRELLA PLANT See *Cyperus*

E
EARTH STARS See *Cryptanthus*

ECHEVERIA
E. derenbergii (painted lady); *E. elegans,* also called *Cotyledon elegans* (Mexican snowball); *E. pulvinata* (plush plant) (all called echeveria)

The ground-hugging rosettes of the fleshy leaves of the echeverias grow slowly to become 2 to 4 inches across, making these succulent plants ideal for light gardens with limited space. Under steady, dependable bright light, echeverias also bloom, sending up flower stalks with clusters of white, yellow, pink, orange or red flowers during late winter or early spring. Painted lady forms a 2-inch rosette of green leaves edged in red; orange blossoms appear on stalks that emerge from between the leaves. The Mexican snowball grows 2 to 4 inches across with pale blue-green leaves, which have a waxy white coating that rubs off if the leaves are handled roughly. The plush plant's 2- to 3-inch rosette of gray-green leaves is carried on a stout red-brown stem. A thick coating of white hairs gives the leaves a velvety appearance; under lights, the thick foliage takes on a pink-to-red tinge. The plants bear red or yellow flowers. When plants mature, they develop branching stems, each topped by a new rosette.

HOW TO GROW. Give echeverias 600 to 1,000 foot-candles of light, achieved by placing them 6 to 12 inches below a four-tube fixture for 14 to 16 hours daily from spring through fall and for 10 to 12 hours daily during the winter while plants are at rest. Temperatures can range from 50° at night to 75° or more during the day; there should be a 10° difference between day and night temperatures for optimum growth. Humidity of 20 to 30 per cent is adequate. A plant can remain in one pot for three to five years. When roots fill the container, repot in a soilless mixture of 1 part sphagnum peat moss, 2 parts perlite and 2 parts vermiculite, adding 1 teaspoon of bone meal and either 1 teaspoon of ground limestone or ¼ cup of crushed eggshells per quart of mix; otherwise, use a packaged soilless mix prepared for cacti, adding bone meal and a lime source in the same proportions.

While plants are actively growing, allow the soil to become almost dry between waterings and feed biweekly with a high-phosphorus fertilizer such as 15-30-15 diluted to one fourth the strength recommended on the label. During the plants' winter resting period, withhold fertilizer; water just enough to keep leaves from shriveling. Propagate plants from leaf cuttings or by removing offshoots that grow alongside the plants or, in the case of the plush plant, at the tips of branched stems. Allow juicy cut surfaces to dry 24 hours before inserting the cuttings in moist vermiculite.

ECHINOCACTUS
E. grusonii (golden barrel cactus)

Resembling a spiny, ribbed ball, the golden barrel cactus grows slowly until it become 3 feet wide and almost as tall. A young plant has many small bumps—the tubercles—that begin to merge into solid vertical ribs when the plant is between six and 12 years old. As the plant grows, the number of ribs increases and tufts of long, yellow spines begin to line the ribs. When the plant reaches about 12 inches in diameter, it produces a ring of bright yellow flowers at the top during the summer.

HOW TO GROW. Golden barrel cacti are not difficult to grow under lights, but they grow very slowly. Give them very bright light, 1,000 to 1,500 foot-candles, the amount available 6 inches or less below a four-tube fixture. Illuminate the plants for 14 to 16 hours daily during their active growing period from spring through fall, then gradually reduce the amount of light to 10 to 12 hours per day during the winter resting period. To encourage mature plants to bloom, keep temperatures during the growing season at 50° to 55° at night and 75° or higher during the day; drop to 40° to 45° at night and 65° during the day through the winter.

Plants can remain in the same containers for many years before roots become crowded. Repot in a soilless mixture of 1 part sphagnum peat moss, 2 parts perlite and 2 parts vermiculite, adding 1 teaspoon of bone meal and either 1

GOLDEN BARREL CACTUS
Echinocactus grusonii

teaspoon of ground limestone or ¼ cup of crushed eggshells per quart of mix; otherwise, use a packaged soilless mix prepared for cacti, adding bone meal and a lime source in the same proportions. When repotting, wear heavy gloves and use rolled newspapers as tongs to handle the spiny cactus. Allow the soil to become nearly dry between waterings during the growing season and fertilize biweekly with a high-phosphorus fertilizer such as 15-30-15 diluted to one fourth the recommended strength. During the resting period, water just enough to keep the cactus from shriveling and withhold fertilizer. Golden barrel cacti are usually grown from seed.

ELFIN HERB See *Cuphea*
ENGLISH IVY See *Hedera*

EPIDENDRUM

E. anceps; E. ciliare; E. cochleatum (clamshell orchid); *E. tampense* (butterfly orchid) (all called epidendrum orchid)

The epidendrum orchids form an extremely large genus offering a wide choice of flower shapes and colors. Epidendrums have two or three leathery, strap-shaped leaves and erect flower stalks up to 3 feet tall. These grow from clusters of fleshy stems called pseudobulbs or from reedlike, segmented stems. In the wild, most epidendrums are epiphytes, plants that use aerial roots to cling to trees and to provide nourishment. The waxy flowers, borne singly or in clusters at the tips of flower stalks, are composed of an outer ring of narrow petal-like sepals, smaller inner petals and large lower petals called lips. All of the species listed here can bloom at various times of the year or even year round.

E. anceps, a reed-type epidendrum, has a tight cluster of flowers atop its flower stalk. The ½-inch petals and sepals are brown to green or yellow while the white lip is spotted with yellow and has fringed edges. *E. ciliare* has narrow, pointed sepals and yellow-to-green petals; its white fringed lip is spotted with yellow. The unusual clamshell orchid carries its flowers upside down. Its thin, spidery, twisted sepals are white to green and the shell-shaped lip on top is dark purple to black, striped with yellow veins. The dwarf butterfly orchid produces clusters of inch-wide flowers with yellow-to-green sepals tinged with brown, inner petals almost completely brown and a white lip striped with purple.

HOW TO GROW. Epidendrum orchids need 1,200 to 2,400 or more foot-candles to bloom. This can be achieved by growing them under a bank of eight to 10 4-foot cool- and warm-white fluorescent tubes, six to eight 4-foot high-output tubes, or four to six 4-foot very-high-output tubes. Place plants as close to the fixture as possible without touching the tubes; illuminate them for 14 to 16 hours daily. Yellowed leaves indicate too much light and intensely green foliage indicates too little light. Temperatures of 55° to 60° at night and from 65° to 70° by day are best; orchids need a temperature drop of 10° at night if they are to bloom well. Humidity of 50 to 75 per cent can be provided by misting the plants twice daily, placing the pots on a moisture tray and using a room humidifier. Since humid, stagnant air encourages fungus growth, maintain good air circulation around the plants.

Grow epidendrums in a mixture of 2 parts fir bark or shredded tree-fern fiber, 1 part perlite and 1 part coarse peat moss. Plants can also be fastened to a suspended slab of tree fern. Allow the potting mix to dry slightly between waterings; water standing around roots quickly rots orchids. Feed weekly with a fertilizer formulated for orchids such as 30-10-10 or 18-18-18, diluted to one fourth the strength recommended on the label. Repot when plant and aerial roots creep over the edge of the container, about every two to four

CLAMSHELL ORCHID
Epidendrum cochleatum

years. Propagate when repotting by dividing the clumps of stems, keeping five or six stems per division.

EPISCIA
E. hybrids (all called episcia, flame violet)

Trailing members of the gesneriad family, the episcias are prized for their plush rosettes of 2- to 5-inch leaves in shades of green, rose, copper or silver. Under lights, these shimmering colors seem to glow. Delicate ½- to 1½-inch tubular flowers, contrasting spectacularly with the foliage, appear year round. When small, episcias are good light garden or terrarium plants. Later, they produce runners with whorls of leaves at the tips, making them suitable for hanging baskets when they have outgrown the light garden. The hybrid Pink Brocade has pink-to-red leaves with white and green markings; flowers are red. It is sensitive to drafts and requires the protection of a terrarium. Moss Agate is a freely blooming variety with corrugated dark green leaves overlaid with silver; the red flowers are larger than average. Cygnet is a hybrid with scalloped gray-green leaves and white fringed flowers, faintly spotted with purple.

HOW TO GROW. Episcias require medium to bright light, about 500 foot-candles, for 14 to 16 hours daily. They grow best when placed about 6 inches below a standard two-tube fixture. Night temperatures of 65° and day temperatures of 70° to 75° are ideal. Use humidity trays or plant in a terrarium to maintain high humidity, as close to 60 per cent as possible; dry air causes leaf edges to brown and curl. Repot when roots fill the container, using a soilless mixture of 1 part perlite, 1 part vermiculite and 2 parts sphagnum peat moss, plus either 1 teaspoon of ground limestone or ¼ cup of crushed eggshells per quart; otherwise, use a packaged soilless mix for African violets, adding limestone or eggshells in the proportions given. Keep the mix evenly moist and avoid splashing cold water on the foliage. Feed weekly with a water-soluble high-phosphorus fertilizer such as 10-30-20, at one fourth the recommended strength. Remove runners to get more blooms, new growth and a more compact shape. Propagate additional plants from tips of runners rooted in moist vermiculite.

EUONYMUS
E. japonicus (evergreen euonymus)

Like other foliage plants with colored leaf markings, euonymus is at its best when it is grown under strong, dependable fluorescent light. Unpruned, an evergreen euonymus can become a 3-foot shrub with 1-inch shiny oval leaves on upright branches. But light gardeners can grow young plants and prune them often to keep them compact. The species has several variegated varieties. Yellow Queen euonymus, *E. japonicus aureo-variegatus,* has leaves with broad yellow edges. The Silver Queen euonymus, *E. japonicus argenteo-variegatus,* has leaves edged in white.

HOW TO GROW. Euonymus grows best when it receives medium light, 400 to 650 foot-candles, for 12 to 14 hours daily. Place plants 6 to 12 inches below a two-tube fixture. Provide night temperatures of 40° to 55°, day temperatures of 65° to 75°, and humidity as close to 50 per cent as possible. Place pots on a moisture tray to raise the humidity. Good air circulation is essential, however, as euonymus is subject to mildew attacks. When roots become crowded in their container, repot in a soilless mixture of 2 parts sphagnum peat moss, 1 part perlite and 1 part vermiculite, adding either 1 teaspoon of ground limestone or ¼ cup of crushed eggshells per quart of mix; otherwise, use a packaged soilless mix, adding a lime source in the same proportions. Allow the

FLAME VIOLET
Episcia hybrid 'Pink Brocade'

YELLOW QUEEN EUONYMUS
Euonymus japonicus aureo-variegatus

DWARF CROWN OF THORNS
Euphorbia splendens 'Bojeri'

ARABIAN VIOLET
Exacum affine

soil to dry slightly between waterings and feed each week with a balanced house-plant fertilizer such as 20-20-20, diluted to one fourth the strength recommended on the label. Propagate by rooting tip cuttings in moist vermiculite.

EUPHORBIA

E. splendens, also called *E. milii splendens* (crown of thorns)

The crown of thorns is a plant species that has markedly better blooming and growing habits under lights. While most cactus-like succulents need a period of dormancy in dry soil before they will rebloom, and sometimes respond to moisture by rotting, the crown of thorns will bloom all year under lights if the potting mix remains constantly moist. A member of a diverse genus that ranges from tiny dwarfs to tree-sized plants and includes the familiar Christmas poinsettia, this branching shrub's stems are lined with sharp spines and have pear-shaped leaves clustered at the tip of each branch below small flowers with kidney-shaped, petal-like red bracts. While crown of thorns grows 2 to 3 feet tall, light gardeners have found that the dwarf crown of thorns, *E. splendens* Bojeri, grows only 12 inches tall and blooms profusely under lights with ½-inch red bracts above 1½-inch leaves. The hybrid Keysii also fits well in light gardens; it is similar to the dwarf crown of thorns except that its leaves grow 2 inches long. Both are easily shaped and pruned to fit available space, but take care to wash your hands to remove any of the milky sap that oozes from cut branches; it can produce a severe skin reaction similar to that caused by poison ivy.

HOW TO GROW. Provide euphorbias with 1,000 to 1,500 foot-candles of light by placing them 6 inches or less below a four-tube fixture for 14 to 16 hours daily year round. Maintain temperatures of 55° to 65° at night and 75° or higher by day, with 30 to 40 per cent humidity. Repot when the roots fill the pot, using a soilless mixture of 1 part sphagnum peat moss, 2 parts perlite and 2 parts vermiculite, adding 1 teaspoon of bone meal and either 1 teaspoon of ground limestone or ¼ cup of crushed eggshells per quart of mix; otherwise, use a packaged soilless mix prepared for cactus, adding bone meal and a lime source in the same proportions. For the best bloom, keep the mix barely moist at all times. If the plant becomes dry it will drop its leaves and become dormant. If this happens, give it additional warmth and resume normal watering to bring it back to active growth. Feed weekly with a high-phosphorus fertilizer such as 15-30-15 diluted to one fourth the strength recommended on the label. Propagate at any time from stem cuttings, briefly holding a lighted match to the cut surface to seal it and stop the flow of sap before inserting it in moist vermiculite to root.

EVERGREEN EUONYMUS See *Euonymus*

EXACUM

Exacum affine (Arabian violet)

While the Arabian violet ordinarily remains in bloom for only four months as a house plant, it will bloom for six months or more under lights. New plants begin to bloom when they are only 2 inches tall. Masses of fragrant lavender, blue or white blossoms, star shaped and about ½ inch wide, cover the mature plant. It grows 6 to 10 inches high, bushy and compact, with closely packed bright green leaves. Blithe Spirit has white flowers; Midget is a variety that grows 8 inches tall and produces blue flowers.

HOW TO GROW. Place Arabian violets so they will receive low to medium light, 200 to 500 foot-candles, for 14 to 16 hours daily. To get the higher intensity, place the plants 6 inches below a standard two-tube fixture. Maintain night temperatures of 60° to 65°, day temperatures of 70° to 85° and high humidity, 50 to 60 per cent, using humidity trays and frequent misting. Start seedlings in a 3-inch pot containing a soilless mixture of 2 parts sphagnum peat moss, 1 part vermiculite and 1 part perlite; add 1 teaspoon of ground limestone or ¼ cup of crushed eggshells per quart of mix. Keep the growing medium moist but not soggy. Feed weekly after watering with a water-soluble fertilizer, such as 10-30-20, at one fourth the strength recommended on the label. Arabian violets can be grown from seed. Seeds germinate in two weeks and reach blooming size in six months.

EXOTIC DIEFFENBACHIA See *Dieffenbachia*
EYELASH BEGONIA See *Begonia*

F

FAN MAIDENHAIR FERN See *Adiantum*
FANCY-LEAVED CALADIUM See *Caladium*

FAUCARIA
F. tigrina (tiger's jaws)

As fierce in appearance as its name implies, tiger's jaws has succulent, boat-shaped, gray-green leaves 1 to 2 inches long. Leaf edges bear thick soft spines. The low-growing leaf clusters are spotted with a paler shade of green. Grown under continuous strong light, tiger's jaws bears 1½- to 2½-inch yellow flowers in autumn.

HOW TO GROW. Unlike many succulents, tiger's jaws grows actively from fall through winter and rests during the summer. Watch the plant carefully, however, since it may gradually shift to a winter resting pattern under cultivation. It grows best when it receives 1,000 to 1,500 foot-candles of light for 14 to 16 hours daily while growing actively and for 10 to 12 hours daily during the rest period. Position plants 6 inches or less below a four-tube fixture. Temperatures between 50° and 55° at night, and 75° or higher during the day are required; 30 per cent humidity is adequate.

Plants grow very slowly and need repotting only when roots become crowded, every three to five years. Use a soilless mixture of 1 part sphagnum peat moss, 2 parts perlite and 2 parts vermiculite, adding 1 teaspoon of bone meal and either 1 teaspoon of ground limestone or ¼ cup of crushed eggshells per quart of mix. Allow the soil to become almost dry between waterings during the growing season and feed biweekly with a high-phosphorus fertilizer such as 15-30-15, diluted to one fourth the strength suggested on the label. During the rest period, water the plants only enough to keep the fleshy leaves from shriveling and do not feed them. Propagate tiger's jaws from leaf cuttings, letting the juicy edges dry 24 hours before inserting the cuttings in moist vermiculite, or grow new plants from seeds.

FERN, BUTTON See *Pellaea*
FERN, DELTA MAIDENHAIR See *Adiantum*
FERN, FAN MAIDENHAIR See *Adiantum*
FERN, HOLLY See *Cyrtomium*
FERN, ROUGH MAIDENHAIR See *Adiantum*

FICUS
F. diversifolia, also called *F. lutescens* (mistletoe fig); *F. pumila*, also called *F. repens* (creeping climbing fig)

The *Ficus* genus has 800 species that range from tall woody plants to little vines; they all bear berries or fruits. The species most commonly grown indoors is the rubber plant, but its unbranching stem quickly outgrows a light garden and may reach the ceiling. The relatives listed above

TIGER'S JAWS
Faucaria tigrina

VARIEGATED CREEPING FIG
Ficus pumila variegata

RED-NERVED FITTONIA
Fittonia verschaffeltii

are slow-growing plants with dense foliage. The branching mistletoe fig grows very slowly and ultimately becomes a woody 3-foot shrub. Its dark green 1- to 3-inch leaves, oval to round, are speckled with tiny brown spots. Its small berries are yellow to red. The creeping fig has 1-inch leaves on wiry, trailing stems with small roots that will attach themselves to supports. A mature, unrestricted plant sometimes produces fruiting branches with 4-inch leaves and inedible heart-shaped, brown-to-purple figs. *F. pumila minima* is a small-leaved dwarf variety of the creeping fig, while *F. pumila quercifolia,* the oak-leaved creeping fig, has leathery, dark green leaves lobed like those of an oak tree but less than an inch long. Another variety, *F. pumila variegata,* has streaks of white in its leaves.

HOW TO GROW. Figs grow best when they are placed 6 to 12 inches below a two-tube fixture where they will receive a medium amount of light, 200 to 500 foot-candles. Light them for 12 to 14 hours daily. Temperatures of 65° to 70° at night, 75° to 85° during the day, and humidity as close to 50 per cent as possible are best. To raise the humidity around plants, place pots on a moisture tray. Figs need repotting only when roots become crowded. Use a soilless mixture of 2 parts sphagnum peat moss, 1 part perlite and 1 part vermiculite, adding 1 teaspoon of ground limestone or ¼ cup of crushed eggshells per quart of mix; otherwise, use a packaged soilless mix prepared for African violets, adding a lime source in the same proportions. Keep the soil barely moist at all times; never let it get soggy. *Ficus* species will quickly rot if their roots are too wet. Feed weekly with a balanced house-plant fertilizer such as 20-20-20, diluted to one fourth the strength recommended on the label. Propagate by rooting stem cuttings in moist vermiculite.

FIRECRACKER FLOWER See *Crossandra*
FIRE CROWN CACTUS See *Rebutia*
FIREFERN See *Oxalis*

FITTONIA
F. argyroneura (silver-nerved fittonia, mosaic plant); *F. verschaffeltii* (red-nerved fittonia)

On a window sill, fittonias tend to space out leaves along lax, branching stems, but under dependable, year-round light the papery-thin oval leaves hug their pots to form compact bushy plants. The 2- to 3-inch green leaves of silver-nerved fittonia are laced with white, while the 3- to 4-inch leaves of red-nerved fittonia are deeply lined with red veins. Both species can grow 8 to 10 inches tall but under lights they tend to spread sideways rather than grow upward. In high humidity, they bear tiny yellow flowers tinged with green.

HOW TO GROW. Fittonias grow most compactly when they are placed 12 inches below a two-tube fixture where they will receive 200 to 400 foot-candles of light for 12 to 14 hours daily. Night temperatures of 65° to 70° and day temperatures of 75° to 85° are best. They thrive in the humid atmosphere of a closed terrarium. On a shelf, place pots on a moisture tray to keep the humidity as close to 50 per cent as possible. Repot a plant when roots crowd its container, using a soilless mixture of 2 parts sphagnum peat moss, 1 part perlite and 1 part vermiculite, adding either 1 teaspoon of ground limestone or ¼ cup of crushed eggshells per quart of mix; otherwise, use a packaged mix prepared for African violets, adding lime in the same proportions. Keep the mix barely moist, never letting it get wet or soggy. Feed weekly with a balanced house-plant fertilizer such as 20-20-20, diluted to one fourth the strength suggested on the label. Propagate by rooting stem cuttings in moist vermiculite.

FLAME VIOLET See *Episcia*
FLAMING SWORD See *Vriesia*
FLAMINGO FLOWER See *Anthurium*
FLAPJACK CACTUS See *Opuntia*
FLORIDA BEAUTY DRACAENA See *Dracaena*
FOXTAIL ASPARAGUS FERN See *Asparagus*
FRECKLE-FACE PLANT See *Hypoestes*
FRINGED LAVENDER See *Lavandula*

G

GARDENIA

G. jasminoides veitchii (gardenia, Cape jasmine); *G. jasminoides radicans* (miniature gardenia)

A difficult plant to grow because of its exacting requirements, the gardenia repays the effort that is expended on it with richly fragrant, jasmine-scented blossoms. *G. jasminoides veitchii* is the gardenia variety most successfully grown under fluorescent lights. Waxy 3-inch, snow-white flowers bloom intermittently year round among attractive 4- to 6-inch shiny evergreen leaves, on a bush that grows 1 to 3 feet tall. *G. jasminoides radicans* is a miniature gardenia variety from Japan that grows only about 10 inches tall. Its 1- to 2-inch flowers, which are often double petaled, appear on spreading branches among the 2- to 3-inch narrow, pointed leaves. This dwarf evergreen also blooms year round, but most of the blossoms appear in summer.

HOW TO GROW. Gardenias require bright light, 750 to 1,000 foot-candles, for 16 hours daily. Place them 6 inches or less below a four-tube fixture. Night temperatures of at least 60° but no higher than 65° are required if the plants are to form buds; day temperatures of 68° to 72° are best. Humidity of at least 50 per cent is essential; mist leaves frequently and set pots on a moisture tray. Pot in a mixture of 2 parts sphagnum peat moss, 1 part vermiculite and 1 part perlite; otherwise use a packaged soilless mix prepared for African violets. Do not add lime. Feed weekly with a fertilizer formulated for acid-loving plants diluted to one fourth the strength recommended on the label. Keep the mix moist at all times; never let it get soggy because wet soil will cause the buds to drop off. Avoid drafts, which also cause buds to drop. Prune off faded blossoms. Propagate additional gardenia plants by rooting cuttings of new growth taken from branch tips, putting them in moist peat moss or vermiculite. Place the potted cuttings in clear plastic bags or a terrarium until roots form in about two months.

GARDEN SAGE See *Salvia*

GASTERIA

G. liliputana (Lilliput gasteria); *G. maculata* (spotted gasteria); *G. verrucosa* (ox-tongue gasteria, wart gasteria) (all called gasteria)

Fans of fleshy, straplike leaves, frequently marked with bumps called tubercles, give gasterias an unusual combination of form and texture among succulents. New leaf fans appear beside older ones to slowly cover the surface of their planting mix. Lilliput gasteria rarely exceeds 2 inches in height. Its dark green leaves are liberally spotted and edged with white markings. It bears 5/8-inch bell-shaped red flowers on slender stems that rise from the center of older fans. Spotted gasterias have 8-inch leaves 2 inches wide and speckled with white; they bear red flowers on stalks up to 4 feet tall. Ox-tongue gasteria has raised tubercles that resemble warts on its 6-inch leaves.

HOW TO GROW. The gasterias grow actively from spring through fall, then they rest during the winter. Give them

GARDENIA
Gardenia jasminoides veitchii

SPOTTED GASTERIA
Gasteria maculata

GESNERIA
Gesneria hybrid 'Lemon Drop'

bright light, 600 to 800 foot-candles, for 14 to 16 hours daily while they are growing, and for 10 to 12 hours daily while they are resting. Place plants 6 to 12 inches below a four-tube fixture, increasing the distance as necessary to accommodate flower stalks. Temperatures between 50° and 55° at night and 75° or higher during the day are needed; humidity of 25 to 30 per cent is adequate. Plants grow slowly and need repotting only when roots become crowded, approximately every three to five years.

Plant in a soilless mixture of 1 part sphagnum peat moss, 2 parts perlite and 2 parts vermiculite, adding 1 teaspoon of bone meal and either 1 teaspoon of ground limestone or ¼ cup of crushed eggshells to each quart of the mixture; otherwise use a packaged soilless mix prepared for cacti, adding bone meal and lime in the same proportions. During active growth, let the soil dry almost completely between waterings and feed biweekly with a high-phosphorus fertilizer such as 15-30-15, diluted to one fourth the strength suggested on the label. While the plant is resting, withhold fertilizer and water just enough to keep the fleshy leaves from shriveling. Propagate by dividing multiple fans or by starting leaf cuttings; let the juicy cut surfaces dry 24 hours before inserting cuttings in moist vermiculite.

GERANIUM, LEMON-SCENTED See *Pelargonium*
GERANIUM, STRAWBERRY See *Saxifraga*

GESNERIA
G. citrina; G. christii; G. cuneifolia

Low-growing and shrubby, most gesnerias bloom almost continuously in a light garden with little attention. The exception is *G. citrina,* a temperamental species that bears its ¾-inch tubular yellow flowers only in the winter. Light gardeners tolerate this idiosyncracy, however, because this slow-growing plant with tiny, ½-inch toothed leaves eventually resembles a 6- to 8-inch dwarf tree. The other species listed are very different, with elongated 6-inch glossy leaves that are wrinkled or quiltlike. *G. cuneifolia* produces 1-inch red flowers continuously, whereas *G. cuneifolia quebradillas* has orange-tipped yellow flowers. *G. christii* bears tubular red flowers, and a sterile hybrid, Lemon Drop, a cross between *G. cuneifolia* and *G. citrina,* produces clear yellow flowers.

HOW TO GROW. Gesnerias require medium light, about 200 to 500 foot-candles, for 12 to 14 hours daily. They do best 12 inches below a standard two-tube fixture. Night temperatures should not dip below 65°; day temperatures should rise to 75° to 80°. *G. cuneifolia quebradillas* and Lemon Drop can be grown on an open shelf if the humidity is kept as close to 50 per cent as possible with the use of moisture trays and frequent misting. The other gesnerias, however, require 70 to 80 per cent humidity, which can only be provided by growing them in a terrarium.

Plant in a soilless mix consisting of 2 parts sphagnum moss, 1 part vermiculite and 1 part perlite, adding 1 teaspoon of ground limestone or ¼ cup of crushed eggshells per quart of mix; otherwise, use a packaged soilless African violet mix, adding limestone or eggshells in the same proportions. Feed weekly after watering with a water-soluble high-phosphorus fertilizer such as 10-30-20 at one fourth the strength recommended on the label. Keep the growing medium wet but never soggy except for *G. citrina,* which grows best when the growing medium is kept barely moist. Small plantlets that appear near the base can be separated and potted individually. Leaf cuttings will root in about two months in moist vermiculite; small plants grow from seed in three months and begin blooming when they only have a few leaves.

GIANT WHITE INCH PLANT See *Tradescantia*
GLOXINIA See *Sinningia*

GLOXINIA
G. perennis (Canterbury bells gloxinia, perennial gloxinia)

To a casual plant grower the word gloxinia conjures up an image of a dark green rosette topped by enormous velvety flowers. The gesneriad grower, however, knows that florists' gloxinias botanically are *Sinningia speciosa,* while the plants of *Gloxinia* genus resemble the perennial Canterbury bells. These Canterbury bells gloxinias have 5-inch quilted, heart-shaped leaves growing along red-spotted stems up to 2 feet tall. Fragrant blue-to-lilac, bell-shaped 1½-inch flowers are clustered near the top of the plant. Like many gesneriads, the plant grows from a scaly underground stem, the rhizome.

HOW TO GROW. Canterbury bells gloxinias need bright light, 500 foot-candles or more, for 12 to 14 hours daily. Keep the tallest part of the plant 6 inches below a standard two-tube fixture. Temperatures of 65° at night and 70° to 85° during the day are best. To provide humidity as close to 50 per cent as possible, use a humidity tray to supplement atmospheric moisture. Plant rhizomes individually just below the surface in a 4-inch pot, using a soilless mixture consisting of equal parts sphagnum peat moss, vermiculite and perlite with 1 teaspoon of ground limestone or ¼ cup of crushed eggshells added to each quart of mix. Water sparingly until growth appears, then keep barely moist, watering when the mix feels dry. Feed every week with a water-soluble, high-phosphorus fertilizer such as 10-30-20 at one fourth the strength recommended on the label. Rhizomes planted in early spring will bloom the following summer. Pinch back early growth to keep plants compact. After the flowers have faded, gradually reduce watering until the foliage yellows. Cut off dead foliage and store the rhizomes in their pots for five months at about 60°, watering only enough to keep the growing medium from drying completely. Propagate by dividing rhizomes, or grow from seeds.

GLOXINIA, VIOLET SLIPPER See *Sinningia*
GOLD-DUST DRACAENA See *Dracaena*
GOLDEN BABY'S TEARS See *Helxine*
GOLDEN BARREL CACTUS See *Echinocactus*
GOLDEN LACE CACTUS See *Mammillaria*
GOLDEN LEMON THYME See *Thymus*
GOLDEN STAR CACTUS See *Mammillaria*
GOLDFISH PLANT See *Hypocyrta*

GUZMANIA
G. lingulata; G. monostachya, also called *G. tricolor* (both called guzmania)

Easily grown and popular bromeliads, guzmanias have rosettes of leathery leaves that develop varicolored pin striping and cross-banding when grown under reliable light conditions. Longer lasting than most bromeliad blooms, their flower spikes bear brightly colored modified leaves and white, yellow or red flowers. Each rosette blooms but once in its lifetime. *G. lingulata* has 12- to 16-inch straplike leaves marked at their bases with violet stripes. The short flower stalk bears white flowers above orange-to-red bracts. The larger *G. lingulata cardinalis* has similarly colored leaves but brighter red bracts topped by yellow-to-white flowers. *G. lingulata minor* is a small variety with narrow, 1-foot yellow-green leaves penciled with thin purple lines that start at the leaf base and fade toward the tip. The bracts are yellow to red; the small flowers are pale yellow. *G. monostachya* has 1-foot green leaves and a 5-inch flower spike that rises from

CANTERBURY BELLS GLOXINIA
Gloxinia perennis

the center of its leaf rosette and bears salmon-to-red bracts striped with brown and topped by white-petaled flowers.

HOW TO GROW. Give guzmanias a medium amount of light, about 250 to 500 foot-candles, for 12 to 14 hours daily. Adjust a two-tube fixture so it is 6 to 12 inches above the plant. Maintain night temperatures of 60° to 65° and day temperatures of 70° or higher. Keep humidity as close to 50 per cent as possible by misting plants and setting pots on a moisture tray. Grow them in a soilless mix of equal parts sphagnum peat moss, vermiculite and perlite; do not add lime. Alternatively, use a packaged soilless mix. Keep the cup in the center of the plant's leaf rosette filled with water; allow the mix to dry slightly between waterings. Saturating the mix may rot the base of the plant.

Feed weekly with a water-soluble balanced fertilizer such as 20-20-20 at one fourth the recommended strength. A mature plant that seems reluctant to flower can be placed in a plastic bag with a sliced apple for five or six days; the ethylene gas given off by the ripening fruit helps induce the guzmania to produce a flower spike in about two months. Although the mother plant will slowly die one to two years after flowering, it will produce offshoots that should be potted individually. Offshoots bloom when two years old.

GYMNOCALYCIUM
G. mihanovichii (plaid cactus, chin cactus)

One of the easiest cacti to bring into bloom under lights is the plaid cactus. It grows as a gray-green globe with spiny vertical ribs and shorter horizontal ribs that divide the plant into a cross-hatched, plaidlike pattern. The rib edges of the species are faintly red and the cactus bears a 1- to 2-inch pink-tinged yellow-green flower. The variety *G. mihanovichii friedrichiae* has ribs banded with cream edges. In the 1940s, Japanese growers found a genetic mutation of a variegated form of this variety that lacked chlorophyll and was completely red. Since chlorophyll is essential for photosynthesis, they grafted this mutant onto another cactus to give it a food supply. The original mutant in turn produced yellow, pink and orange spots. These colorful globes are sold as grafted cacti under names like Oriental Doll and Red, Orange, Pink or Yellow Cap.

HOW TO GROW. Give a plaid cactus, either the species or the grafted form, 800 to 1,000 foot-candles of light by placing it 6 inches below a four-tube fixture. The cactus grows actively from spring through fall, then rests during winter. While it is growing, illuminate the plant for 14 to 16 hours daily, then gradually reduce the time to 10 to 12 hours daily during the period of dormancy. Provide night temperatures of 50° to 55°, day temperatures of 75° or higher and 25 to 30 per cent humidity. Since the cactus grows slowly, repotting is necessary only every three to five years when roots begin to crowd the container. Wear heavy gloves to protect your hands and use rolled newspapers as tongs when you handle the spiny cactus. Plant in a soilless mixture of 1 part sphagnum peat moss, 2 parts perlite and 2 parts vermiculite, adding 1 teaspoon of bone meal and either 1 teaspoon of ground limestone or ¼ cup of crushed eggshells to each quart of mix; or use a packaged soilless mix for cacti and add bone meal and a lime source in the same proportions.

During the growing season, let the cactus dry almost completely between deep waterings and feed biweekly with a high-phosphorus fertilizer such as 15-30-15 diluted to one fourth the recommended strength. While the cactus is resting, water only enough to keep it from shriveling and do not feed. The plaid cactus is usually grown from seed. A grafted cactus sometimes develops small plantlets or offshoot plants

GUZMANIA
Guzmania lingulata cardinalis

beside the colored globes; these can be removed and grafted to a green cactus such as *Myrtillocactus* or *Hylocereus*.

GYNURA

G. aurantiaca (Java, purple or royal velvet plant); *G. sarmentosa* (purple passion vine) (both called gynura)

Unusual among foliage plants, the iridescent purple color of the Java velvet plant and the purple passion vine becomes deeper and more vivid when they receive steady bright light. Fully as exotic as the names suggest, the jagged-edged green leaves are blanketed with purple plush so dense on new foliage that the green below is barely perceptible. The Java velvet plant is a trailing species with 1½- to 2-inch leaves; although it can grow 2 feet tall, most light gardeners keep it pruned to a smaller size. The purple passion vine has 2-foot twining or trailing stems with 3- to 4-inch leaves. Deep yellow to bright orange flowers sometimes grow on both species but they have an unpleasant odor and are usually plucked off as they appear; if left on the plants, they are followed by silver, bell-shaped seed capsules.

HOW TO GROW. To develop the most brilliant color, grow gynuras where they will receive bright light, 600 to 800 foot-candles, for 14 to 16 hours daily. Place them 6 inches or less below a two-tube fixture or 12 inches below a four-tube fixture. Night temperatures of 65° to 70°, day temperatures of 75° to 85° and humidity as close to 50 per cent as possible are best. Stand pots on a moisture tray to raise the humidity. When roots become crowded in a container, repot the plant, using a soilless mixture of 2 parts sphagnum peat moss, 1 part perlite and 1 part vermiculite, adding either 1 teaspoon of ground limestone or ¼ cup of crushed eggshells per quart of mix; otherwise, use a mix prepared for African violets, adding a lime source in the same proportions. Keep the mix barely moist, never letting it get soggy. Feed weekly with a balanced house-plant fertilizer such as 20-20-20 diluted to one fourth the strength recommended on the label. Prune plants to shape them to the space available in the light garden. Tip cuttings root easily in moist vermiculite.

H

HAEMANTHUS

H. coccineus; H. katherinae; H. multiflorus; H. puniceus (all called blood lily)

The dramatic blood lilies are named for the intense red color of the flowers of some species. Grown under lights, these enormous bulbs bloom earlier and have lusher foliage and brighter blooms than they do as window-sill pot plants. The 6- to 18-inch fleshy, red-spotted flower stalk usually emerges before the plant's leaves, which grow 10 to 20 inches long and 6 to 8 inches wide. The single stalk bears a cluster of up to a hundred 1- to 2½-inch thin tubular flowers tightly encased in erect bracts, modified leaves that gradually open to let the flowers expand into feathery spheres 3 to 9 inches across. The pollen-bearing stamens that protrude from each flower add color and interest. These enormous flower heads open over a period of six weeks and last as long as one to two weeks. Under ideal conditions, they are followed by scarlet berries. *H. coccineus* bears red flowers with orange stamens in fall; *H. katherinae* puts forth a salmon flower globe with coral-to-red stamens any time from spring to fall; the summer-blooming *H. multiflorus* has coral, pink or red flowers with yellow-tipped stamens; *H. puniceus* blooms in summer with a pale red-to-white flower cluster.

HOW TO GROW. During their season of active growth, give blood lilies 16 to 18 hours of bright light, 500 to 1,000 foot-candles, by keeping the tops of the plants 6 inches or less

PLAID CACTUS
Gymnocalycium mihanovichii friedrichiae 'Red Cap'

PURPLE PASSION VINE
Gynura sarmentosa

BLOOD LILY
Haemanthus katherinae

JEWEL ORCHID
Haemaria discolor dawsonianus

below a two-tube fixture or 6 inches below a four-tube fixture. Place plants under lights as soon as dormant bulbs show signs of growth. After flower stalks wither, leave the plants under lights until the foliage browns and the bulbs become dormant. Temperatures of 55° to 60° at night and 68° to 72° during the day are best while flowers are developing; after flowers open, cooler temperatures will prolong their life. Humidity of 30 to 40 per cent is adequate. Plant the 2- to 4-inch bulbs in pots 1 inch larger in diameter than the bulbs, using a soilless mix composed of 2 parts sphagnum peat moss, 1 part perlite and 1 part vermiculite, adding either 1 teaspoon of ground limestone or ¼ cup of crushed eggshells to each quart of mix; otherwise, use a packaged soilless mix prepared for African violets, adding limestone or eggshells in the same proportions.

Keep the mix evenly moist but not soggy while plants are growing and blooming. During this period, feed weekly after watering with a balanced fertilizer such as 20-20-20, diluted to one fourth the strength recommended on the label. When foliage fades, remove the plant from the light garden and store bulbs in their pots until new growth appears. Keep the mix barely moist, to prevent the bulb from drying out completely. Since bulbs bloom best when roots crowd the pots, they can remain in the same pots for several years. Propagate from the small bulbs that grow beside older bulbs.

HAEMARIA

H. discolor dawsonianus, also called *Ludisia discolor dawsonianus* and *Anoectochilus discolor dawsonianus* (jewel orchid)

An orchid grown for its foliage rather than its flowers, the 2-inch-tall jewel orchid produces tufts of three to six short, gemlike leaves, velvety black to dark purple or dark green with metallic red veins. This glowing foliage grows along a creeping ground stem. Under lights, these tiny orchids may produce 6-inch flower spikes in fall or winter, bearing flowers that are ½ to ¾ inch long with yellow throats.

HOW TO GROW. Jewel orchids require 1,500 to 2,400 foot-candles of light. This can be achieved with a bank of eight to 10 4-foot cool- and warm-white fluorescent tubes, or six to eight 4-foot high-output tubes, or four to six 4-foot very-high-output tubes. Place plants 6 inches from the light source and illuminate them for 14 to 16 hours daily. Provide night temperatures of 60° to 65°, day temperatures of 70° to 75° and humidity of 50 to 75 per cent. To achieve this humidity, grow plants in a terrarium or place potted plants on a moisture tray, mist twice daily and use a room humidifier. Provide good ventilation to prevent fungus disease. Plant in a mixture of 2 parts fir bark or shredded tree-fern fiber, 1 part perlite and 1 part coarse peat moss. Keep the potting mix evenly moist but never soggy; water standing around the roots will quickly rot orchids. Feed each week with a fertilizer formulated for orchids such as 30-10-10 or 18-18-18, diluted to one fourth the strength recommended on the label. Propagate by dividing the creeping rhizome.

HAIRY-LEAVED BEGONIA See *Begonia*

HAWORTHIA

H. fasciata (zebra haworthia); *H. margaritifera* (pearly haworthia); *H. reinwardtii* (wart plant); *H. tenera, H. truncata* (window plant); *H. turgida pallidifolia* (all called haworthia)

Easy to grow as foliage plants on a window sill, haworthias prosper and bloom under lights, bearing tiny white or green flowers. These succulents grow as stemless rosettes of pointed fleshy leaves. Most have bumps called tubercles patterned across their exposed backs. The zebra haworthia's 2- to 3-inch dark green leaves are striped with bands of tubercles. Pearly haworthia has white bumps sprinkled on the leaves of its 3-inch rosettes. The wart plant has similar markings on 2-inch leaves. *H. tenera* has inch-long leaves tipped with gray bristles and edged with teeth. The tip of each leaf on the window plant is blunt, as if it were cut off with a knife. These blunt tips have translucent surfaces that admit light to the plant's interior; in the wild, these haworthias may be buried in sand with only these windows visible. Similarly, the inch-long leaves of *H. turgida pallidifolia* have translucent spots; their upper leaf surfaces have lines of paler green and each leaf ends in a bristly tip.

HOW TO GROW. Haworthias grow best in medium light, 400 to 600 foot-candles, for 12 hours daily. Place them 6 to 8 inches below a two-tube fixture or 12 to 18 inches below a four-tube fixture. Their foliage reacts to brighter light by taking on a red tinge. Maintain temperatures of 50° to 55° at night, up to 75° by day, and 25 to 30 per cent humidity. Plants grow slowly and need repotting infrequently, usually every three to five years. Use a soilless mixture of 1 part sphagnum peat moss, 2 parts perlite and 2 parts vermiculite, adding 1 teaspoon of bone meal and either 1 teaspoon of ground limestone or ¼ cup of crushed eggshells per quart of mix; otherwise, use a packaged soilless mix, adding bone meal and a lime source in the same proportions.

While the plants are actively growing, from spring through fall, allow the soil to become moderately dry between waterings and feed biweekly with a high-phosphorus fertilizer such as 15-30-15, diluted to one fourth the strength recommended on the label. During the winter resting period, water only enough to keep the leaves from shriveling and do not feed. Propagate from leaf cuttings or from small new rosettes that form at the bases of mature ones. Allow juicy cut ends of leaves to dry 24 hours before inserting them in moist vermiculite; plant offshoots in potting mix. Haworthias can also be grown from seed.

HEDERA
H. helix (English ivy)

Indoor gardeners enticed by the rich variety of leaf forms and colors available in English ivies will find that the color variegations become more intense when the vines are grown under lights. The plants will trail from hanging baskets or twine around supports; they can be trained to cover wire shapes stuffed with uncut sphagnum moss. The tiny aerial rootlets along the vines' stems will cling to almost any surface. If new growth on young plants is continually cut back and shoots are unable to find support, the ivies change their growth habits dramatically, becoming semierect plants instead of trailing or climbing. Even the leaves are affected, tending to become oval rather than lobed.

Good varieties for light gardens include the fast-growing Chicago, an English ivy with green 1½- to 2-inch leaves that have the three- to five-lobed shape that most gardeners associate with English ivy. Light, bright green veins stand out against the deeper green of the leaf surface. Glacier's triangular leaves are also 1½ to 2 inches long but more colorful. Several shades of green blend in the leaf centers, and white edges are tinged with pink when grown under bright light. Mamorata's 2-inch leaves are green, marbled with cream and silver.

HOW TO GROW. Although English ivies will grow at low light levels, the best markings are produced under bright light, 600 to 800 foot-candles, supplied for 14 to 16 hours daily. Place plants 6 or less inches below a two-tube fixture

PEARLY HAWORTHIA
Haworthia margaritifera

ENGLISH IVY
Hedera helix varieties (left to right) 'Chicago,' 'Glacier,' 'Mamorata'

GOLDEN BABY'S TEARS
Helxine soleirolii aurea

or 12 inches below a four-tube fixture. Night temperatures of 50° to 55°, day temperatures of 68° to 72°, and humidity between 30 and 40 per cent are desirable. When roots fill a container, repot in a soilless mixture of 2 parts sphagnum peat moss, 1 part perlite and 1 part vermiculite, adding 1 teaspoon of ground limestone or ¼ cup of crushed eggshells per quart of mix; otherwise, use a mix prepared for African violets, adding a lime source in the same proportions. Keep the mix barely moist at all times, never letting it get soggy. Plants should not stand in water, nor should water be left in pot saucers. Feed weekly with a balanced house-plant fertilizer such as 20-20-20, diluted to one fourth the strength recommended on the label. Propagate from tip cuttings rooted in moist vermiculite.

HELXINE
H. soleirolii (baby's tears)

The tiny ¼-inch round leaves of baby's tears will quickly carpet a pot and spill over the edges like froth. In fact, the cushiony mounds engulf a pot or blanket a terrarium so rapidly that some gardeners regard the plant as a weed. When grown under lights, baby's tears may produce minute white flowers at the bases of its leaves. *H. soleirolii aurea*, golden baby's tears, is a variety with white-to-yellow leaves that are slightly larger than the green leaves of the species.

HOW TO GROW. Baby's tears grow in low levels of light, 75 to 200 foot-candles. Place them 12 to 18 inches below a two-tube fixture and illuminate plants for 14 to 16 hours daily. For bloom and lushest growth, provide light levels at the higher end of the range. Temperatures of 50° to 55° at night and 65° to 70° during the day and humidity as close to 50 per cent as possible are best. Place pots on a moisture tray or grow baby's tears in a terrarium to provide extra humidity. When plants become crowded, repot in a soilless mixture of 2 parts sphagnum peat moss, 1 part perlite and 1 part vermiculite, adding either 1 teaspoon of ground limestone or ¼ cup of crushed eggshells per quart of mix; otherwise, use a packaged soilless mix prepared for African violets, adding a lime source in the same proportions. Keep the mix barely moist at all times, never letting it get soggy; do not let water stand in saucers under the pots. Feed weekly with a balanced house-plant fertilizer such as 20-20-20, diluted to one fourth the amount recommended on the label. Propagate by dividing plants.

HOLLY FERN See *Cyrtomium*
HOLLY-LEAVED BEGONIA See *Begonia*
HOLLY MALPIGHIA See *Malpighia*

HOYA
H. bella, also called *H. paxtonii* (miniature wax plant)

Although the miniature wax plant usually blooms only once a year as a house plant, light gardeners can enjoy its fragrant star-shaped flowers several times a year. A slow-growing vine with thick, succulent, glossy leaves, this wax plant bears 2- to 3-inch clusters of white flowers with red-to-purple centers on short stalks. These grow in the joints between 1½-inch pointed leaves and 1- to 2-foot stems. New blossoms appear on stalks where flowers previously grew. *H. bella* is the species preferred for light gardening because it can be pinched and shaped to grow more like a shrub than a vine. *H. bella minima* is a dwarf variety that forms plants only 10 inches tall and 15 inches across. It has stiffer, more wiry stems and smaller flower clusters than *H. bella*.

HOW TO GROW. Give miniature wax plants bright light, 500 to 750 foot-candles, for 14 hours daily. Place them 6 inches below a two-tube fixture. Night temperatures of 60° to 65° and day temperatures of 70° or higher are best. Humidity of 30 to 40 per cent is adequate for good growth. Since plants bloom best when pot bound, keep roots crowded by growing the plants in 3-inch pots. Use equal parts of sphagnum peat moss, vermiculite and perlite; otherwise, use a packaged soilless mix. Do not add lime. Allow the mix to dry slightly between waterings while the plant is in bloom, and water even less during the rest period that follows. Never let the mix become soggy. When plants are blooming, feed weekly after watering with a high-nitrogen fertilizer such as 30-10-10 applied at one fourth the recommended strength; do not fertilize during the rest period. Pinch off tips of new growth to achieve bushiness, taking care to leave old flower stalks. Propagate by rooting stem cuttings in moist vermiculite.

HYPOCYRTA, also called NEMATANTHUS
H. perianthomega; H. strigillosa; H. wettsteinii (all called goldfish plant)

Easy-to-cultivate hypocyrtas are gesneriad shrubs that reward the light gardener with an almost constant succession of 1-inch flowers with inflated pouches, growing along creeping or semiupright stems. *H. perianthomega* has stiff woody branches, pointed 4½-inch leaves and yellow flowers striped with maroon. *H. strigillosa* is a spreading plant that has hairy, dark green 2½-inch leaves and crimson flowers edged in yellow. *H. wettsteinii*, the species that blooms most abundantly, has ¾-inch glossy green, oval leaves and orange flowers tipped with yellow. The hybrid Tropicana forms a compact mound of glossy green leaves interspersed with yellow flowers that are striped with maroon.

HOW TO GROW. Hypocyrtas grow best in low to medium light, about 250 foot-candles, for 14 to 16 hours daily. They should be placed about 12 inches below a standard two-tube fixture. Maintain night temperatures of 65° to 70° and day temperatures of 75° to 80°. Use a humidity tray to maintain humidity as close to 50 per cent as possible. Pot in a soilless mixture of 2 parts sphagnum peat moss, 1 part vermiculite and 1 part perlite. Add 1 teaspoon of ground limestone or ¼ cup of crushed eggshells per quart of mix. Feed weekly after watering with a water-soluble high-phosphorus fertilizer such as 10-30-20 at one fourth the recommended strength. All species have semidormant periods when fertilizer should be withheld. Cut off dead parts to stimulate new growth. Propagate by rooting stem cuttings in moist vermiculite.

HYPOESTES
H. sanguinolenta, also called *H. phyllostashya* or *Eranthemum sanguinolentum* (freckle-face plant, pink-polka-dot plant)

Fluorescent lighting dramatizes the bright pink splotches on the downy 1½- to 2½-inch leaves of freckle-face plants. The varieties Splash and Pink Brocade have more leaf color than the parent species. These fast-growing shrubs can become 2 feet tall but they are easily pinched back and pruned to keep them in the 6- to 12-inch range, a size more suitable for light gardens.

HOW TO GROW. For best color, give freckle-face plants a medium amount of light, 200 to 500 foot-candles, by placing them 12 inches below a two-tube fixture. Illuminate plants for 14 to 16 hours daily. Night temperatures of 65° to 70°, day temperatures of 75° to 85°, and humidity as close to 50 per cent as possible are best. To raise the humidity level, place pots on a moisture tray. When roots fill a container, repot the plant in a soilless mixture of 2 parts sphagnum peat moss, 1 part perlite and 1 part vermiculite, adding either 1

WAX PLANT
Hoya bella

GOLDFISH PLANT
Hypocyrta hybrid 'Tropicana'

FRECKLE-FACE PLANT
Hypoestes sanguinolenta 'Splash'

PATIENT LUCY
Impatiens wallerana 'Orange Baby'

teaspoon of ground limestone or ¼ cup of crushed eggshells per quart of mix; otherwise, use a packaged soilless mix prepared for African violets, adding a lime source in the same proportions. Keep the mix barely moist at all times, never letting it become wet, and do not let water stand in pot saucers. Feed weekly with a balanced house-plant fertilizer such as 20-20-20, diluted to one fourth the recommended strength. Older plants become straggly but new ones are easily started by rooting stem cuttings in moist vermiculite.

I

IMPATIENS
I. wallerana, also called *I. holstii, I. sultani* (impatiens, patient Lucy, busy Lizzie, patience)

Even with haphazard care, impatiens provides rewarding quantities of delicate, flat flowers year round in the light garden. The 1- to 2-inch blooms have a wide range of colors including coral, gold, orange, pink, purple, salmon, red and white. The pointed oval green leaves are frequently variegated with maroon, and some stems are striped with red. Impatiens is usually grown as a compact, bushy plant about a foot high, kept to that size by pinching back new growth. Some dwarf varieties such as Orange Baby grow naturally to a height of only 6 to 10 inches.

HOW TO GROW. For maximum bloom, provide impatiens with medium to bright light, 500 to 750 foot-candles, for 14 to 16 hours daily. To attain this level, position plants 6 to 12 inches below a two-tube fixture or 12 inches below a four-tube fixture. Long days of bright light stimulate colorful foliage on most species. Maintain night temperatures above 60° and day temperatures around 70°. Impatiens blooms best when the relative humidity is 40 per cent or more. Mist plants or use a moisture tray to keep the humidity level high. Pot seedlings in a soilless mix of 2 parts sphagnum peat moss, 1 part vermiculite and 1 part perlite, adding 1 teaspoon of ground limestone or ¼ cup of crushed eggshells per quart of mix; otherwise, use a packaged soilless mix, adding limestone or eggshells in the same proportions. Keep the mix evenly moist but not soggy.

Feed weekly after watering with a balanced water-soluble fertilizer such as 20-20-20 at one fourth the recommended strength. For better bloom and more compact plants, remove faded blossoms and pinch back stems. Propagate from 6-inch stem cuttings rooted in moist vermiculite, or from seed. Under lights, with temperatures of 65° to 70°, seed sown in sphagnum peat moss germinates in about three weeks.

IVY, ENGLISH See *Hedera*
IVY, KENILWORTH See *Cymbalaria*
IVY, VARIEGATED KENILWORTH See *Cymbalaria*
IVY, SWEDISH See *Plectranthus*
IVY, WHITE-EDGED SWEDISH See *Plectranthus*

J

JADE PLANT See *Crassula*
JAPANESE HOLLY FERN See *Cyrtomium*
JASMINE, ARABIAN See *Jasminum*
JASMINE, CAPE See *Gardenia*

JASMINUM
J. sambac (Arabian jasmine)

Light gardeners appreciate Arabian jasmine for the spicy fragrance of its delicate flowers. The perfume will fill a room. The 1-inch white flower rosettes turn purple as they fade; they are tucked among shiny dark green leaves. Maid of Orleans, the evergreen variety that is most often grown under lights, bears semidouble flowers; although it grows to a height of 5 feet, it can be pruned and kept to a height of 1 foot. The Grand Duke of Tuscany is a shrubby variety, bearing double flowers whose petals are sometimes dried and brewed for use as a tea.

HOW TO GROW. Give Arabian jasmine medium to bright light, 400 to 750 foot-candles, for 14 to 16 hours daily. Place the plant 6 inches below the center of a two-tube fixture. Maintain night temperatures of 60° to 65° and day temperatures of 72° or higher or the jasmine will not bloom. Mist daily and set pots on a moisture tray to provide humidity as close to 60 per cent as possible. Pot in a soilless mix of 2 parts sphagnum peat moss, 1 part vermiculite and 1 part perlite; otherwise, use a packaged soilless mix. Do not add lime. Fertilize weekly after watering with a high-nitrogen water-soluble fertilizer such as 30-10-10 at one fourth the strength recommended on the label. Propagate jasmine from stem cuttings rooted in sphagnum peat moss.

JAVA PLANT See *Gynura*
JEW, FOUR-COLOR WANDERING See *Zebrina*
JEW, TWO-COLOR WANDERING See *Zebrina*
JEW, VARIEGATED WANDERING See *Tradescantia*
JEW, WANDERING See *Zebrina*
JEW, WHITE VELVET WANDERING See *Tradescantia*
JEWEL ORCHID See *Haemaria*

K

KANGAROO VINE See *Cissus*
KANNIEDOOD ALOE See *Aloe*
KENILWORTH IVY See *Cymbalaria*

KLEINIA, also called SENECIO

K. repens, also called *Senecio serpens* (blue chalk sticks)

Grown indoors for its unusual form and color, blue chalk sticks is a succulent that will bear flat, white daisy-like flowers in a light garden in spring and summer. The branching, 8- to 12-inch fleshy plant has shallowly grooved 5-inch cylindrical blue leaves.

HOW TO GROW. Blue chalk sticks grows well when placed 6 inches or less below a four-tube fixture, where it will receive 1,000 to 1,500 foot-candles of light. Give the plant 14- to 16-hour days while it is growing actively from spring through fall, and gradually reduce this to eight- to 12-hour days during the winter resting period. Maintain temperatures of 50° to 55° at night and 75° or higher during the day, with 25 to 30 per cent humidity. Blue chalk sticks grows slowly and needs repotting only when its roots fill their container, every three to five years.

Plant in a soilless mixture of 1 part sphagnum peat moss, 2 parts perlite and 2 parts vermiculite, adding 1 teaspoon of bone meal and either 1 teaspoon of ground limestone or ¼ cup of crushed eggshells per quart of mix; otherwise, use a packaged soilless mix prepared for cacti, adding bone meal and a lime source in the same proportions. During periods of active growth, let the soil dry almost completely between waterings and feed biweekly with a high-phosphorus fertilizer such as 10-15-10 diluted to one fourth the recommended strength. During winter dormancy, water just enough to keep the fleshy leaves from shriveling and do not feed. Propagate from leaf cuttings, letting the juicy cut ends dry 24 hours before inserting them in moist vermiculite to root.

KOELLIKERIA

K. erinoides (koellikeria)

The compact growth of the koellikeria and its long-lasting

ARABIAN JASMINE
Jasminum sambac 'Grand Duke of Tuscany'

BLUE CHALK STICKS
Kleinia repens

KOELLIKERIA
Koellikeria erinoides

KOHLERIA
Kohleria bogotensis

flowers borne on 9- to 12-inch spikes make this an attractive flower for terrarium light gardens. Indeed, strong and dependable light and high humidity are necessary to bring this small gesneriad into bloom. Its sprays of tiny open-faced, tubular red-and-white blossoms rise above 1- to 4-inch oval green leaves that are shiny with silver dots. Koellikerias grow from 1-inch underground stems—rhizomes—that resemble tiny pine cones.

HOW TO GROW. To bring koellikerias into bloom, provide bright light, 500 foot-candles or more, for 14 to 16 hours a day. Place plants 6 inches below a standard two-tube fixture until the flower spikes rise. Night temperatures should not go below 65°; day temperatures of 70° to 75° or higher are best. Since humidity of 60 per cent or more is essential for bloom, koellikerias should be grown inside a lighted terrarium. Plant rhizomes horizontally ½ inch deep in a soilless mixture of 2 parts sphagnum peat moss, 1 part vermiculite and 1 part perlite, adding 1 teaspoon of ground limestone or ¼ cup of crushed eggshells per quart of mix. Water sparingly until growth is visible.

Feed after watering with a high-phosphorus water-soluble fertilizer such as 10-30-20 at one fourth the strength recommended on the label. During the growing season keep the soilless mix barely moist, watering only when the top feels dry. When the plant stops flowering, gradually withhold water until the foliage yellows completely, then cut off all of the top growth. Leave the rhizomes in the terrarium during the dormant period, watering only enough to keep the mix from drying completely. Propagate by dividing rhizomes or from stem cuttings rooted in moist vermiculite.

KOHLERIA

K. amabilis; K. bogotensis; K. eriantha; K. hybrids (kohleria)

Light gardeners prize kohlerias for the brightly colored funnel-shaped flowers and the long periods of bloom that these gesneriads have. The three species listed here bloom for six months or more between short periods of semidormancy; the hybrids flower year round. *K. amabilis* is a trailing species with 1-inch pink flowers spotted with purple among fuzzy, broad 4-inch leaves veined with brown. The stems reach 2 feet in length. The red-and-yellow 1-inch flowers of *K. bogotensis* are set against hairy, mottled green-and-brown leaves. This upright species grows up to 2 feet tall. Unless *K. eriantha* is confined to a small pot, it can attain a height of 4 feet. The plant's 5-inch hairy green leaves are edged in red and the 2-inch orange blossoms are spotted with yellow. Three everblooming hybrids, all about a foot tall, are Carnival, with yellow-spotted red flowers; Longwood, with white flowers that have red throats and spots; and Rongo, with pink-to-white flowers spotted with purple. Like many gesneriads, kohlerias grow from thick underground stems, the rhizomes.

HOW TO GROW. Give kohlerias bright light, about 500 foot-candles, for 14 to 16 hours daily. Place plants 6 inches below a standard two-tube fixture. *K. eriantha* blooms best when nearly mature plants are given 13 to 14 hours of darkness for six weeks. All kohlerias need a 10° difference between day and night temperature if they are to bloom well; night temperatures of 60° to 65° and day temperatures of 70° to 80° are best. They thrive in 45 to 60 per cent humidity; supplement existing humidity by using moisture trays below the plants. Plants may drop their buds if the humidity is too low. Plant individual rhizomes 1 inch deep in 4-inch pots containing a soilless mix of equal parts sphagnum peat moss, vermiculite and perlite. Add 1 teaspoon of ground limestone or ¼ cup of crushed eggshells to each quart of mix. Water sparingly until growth appears, then keep the soil evenly moist but never soggy. If the mix dries, buds may drop and plants may become dormant.

Fertilize weekly after watering with a high-phosphorus water-soluble fertilizer such as 10-30-20 at one fourth the strength recommended on the label. After the plants finish blooming, cut off any yellowed stems, water sparingly and withhold fertilizer until new growth begins again. To control plant size and assure a constant supply of blooming plants, pinch off growing tips frequently; you can root the tips in moist vermiculite. Kohlerias can also be propagated by dividing rhizomes or planting tiny rhizomes that sometimes grow in leaf joints on mature plants.

L

LADY'S-SLIPPER ORCHID See *Paphiopedilum*

LAELIA

L. lundii, also called *L. regnellii; L. pumila* (both called laelia orchid)

Small size and brilliant colors recommend these two laelias to light gardeners interested in orchid culture. Closely resembling cattleya orchids, laelias are often crossed with that genus to obtain plants with the cattleya's size and the laelia's colors. These two dwarf laelias grow from clumps of fleshy stems called pseudobulbs. They are epiphytes, plants that send out aerial roots to obtain food and to cling to trees or rocks where they grow wild. *L. lundii* has a 4- to 5-inch flower stalk bearing one or two 1½-inch lavender-to-pink flowers with broad lower petals, the lips, veined with red or purple and very ruffled. This orchid blooms in midwinter before the plant's small leaves develop. The fall-blooming *L. pumila* grows only 3 inches tall and bears a single rose-to-purple flower, 2½ to 3 inches wide, with a yellow-throated red-to-purple lip.

HOW TO GROW. In order to bloom, laelias need 1,500 to 2,400 foot-candles of light, achieved by growing them beneath a bank of eight to 10 4-foot warm- and cool-white fluorescent tubes, or six to eight 4-foot high-output tubes, or four to six 4-foot very-high-output tubes. Set plants as close to the tubes as possible without touching them, lowering plants as flower spikes grow, and use the lights 14 to 16 hours daily. Temperatures ranging from 55° to 60° at night and from 65° to 70° by day are best; orchids require a 10° drop in temperature at night to flower. Maintain 50 to 75 per cent humidity by misting the plants twice daily, placing pots on a moisture tray and using a room humidifier. To prevent fungus disease, provide good air circulation around plants.

Grow laelias in a mixture of 2 parts fir bark or shredded tree-fern fiber, 1 part perlite and 1 part coarse peat moss. They can also be fastened with nylon thread to a suspended slab of tree fern. Allow the potting mix to dry slightly between waterings since any standing water around roots will quickly rot an orchid. Feed weekly with a fertilizer formulated for orchids such as 30-10-10 or 18-18-18, diluted to one fourth the recommended strength. Repot every two to four years when plants and their aerial roots push over the container edge. Propagate by dividing the clumps of pseudobulbs, keeping five or six pseudobulbs per division.

LAGERSTROEMIA

L. indica 'Crape Myrtlette' (crape myrtlette)

Light gardeners who enjoy the ruffled, papery clusters of flowers on crape myrtlette can satisfy themselves year round by growing the dwarf hybrids of these shrubs. While the parent species can grow 20 to 30 feet tall, the dwarfs reach

LAELIA ORCHID
Laelia pumila

CRAPE MYRTLETTE
Lagerstroemia indica 'Crape Myrtlette'

1½ to 4 feet and are easily pruned to half this height when grown indoors. The thin branches bow under the weight of inch-long oval leaves and 2-inch flower clusters in shades of pink, rose, purple or white.

HOW TO GROW. Crape myrtlette blooms best under bright light, 500 to 1,000 foot-candles, achieved by setting the tops of the plants 6 inches or less below the center of a two-tube fixture or 6 inches below a four-tube fixture. Illuminate for 14 to 16 hours daily. Temperatures of 65° to 70° at night and 70° to 75° during the day and humidity as close to 50 per cent as possible are desirable. To increase humidity, place pots on a moisture tray and mist the plants frequently. Start small plants in 3-inch pots and gradually move them into 6-inch pots, planting in a mixture of 2 parts sphagnum peat moss, 1 part vermiculite and 1 part perlite, adding 1 teaspoon of ground limestone or ¼ cup of crushed eggshells per quart of mix; otherwise, use a packaged soilless mix prepared for African violets, adding limestone or eggshells in the same proportions. Keep the soil evenly moist but not soggy.

Feed weekly after watering with a fertilizer that is high in phosphorus and potash such as 10-20-20, diluted to one fourth the recommended strength. To encourage branching of young plants, remove the first crop of flower buds. Since flowers appear on new growth, pruning older plants encourages branching and blooms. Propagate by rooting stem cuttings or sowing seeds in moist vermiculite. Warm a seed bed to 65° or higher with a heating cable under the container.

LAVANDULA
L. dentata (fringed lavender)

Light gardeners enamoured of this fragrant perennial herb can have compact, symmetrical plants that continue to grow all year. Both flowers and leaves have a sweet aroma but colors and leaf shapes vary. Fringed lavender, recommended for indoor light culture, has dark green, 1- to 1½-inch leaves divided into rounded teeth; the flower spikes borne at the tip of each stem are blue. Most lavenders must be crushed to release their odor, but fringed lavender gives off its sweet fragrance when the plant is barely touched.

HOW TO GROW. Lavender will grow well with only a medium amount of light, 200 to 500 foot-candles, which can be achieved by placing the plants 12 inches below a two-tube fluorescent fixture for 14 to 16 hours daily. Night temperatures of 55° to 60° and daytime temperatures of 70° or more promote best growth. The humidity of 40 per cent or less that exists in most homes is sufficient. Place plants in a pot 1 inch larger than the plant's root ball, using a soilless mix of 2 parts sphagnum peat moss, 1 part vermiculite and 1 part perlite, adding 1 teaspoon of ground limestone or ¼ cup crushed eggshells per quart of mix; otherwise, use a packaged soilless mix for African violets adding limestone or eggshells in the same proportions. Allow soil to dry between waterings and avoid soaking plants. Feed weekly after watering with a balanced fertilizer such as 20-20-20 at one quarter of the strength recommended on the label. Propagate by rooting stem cuttings in moist vermiculite, keeping them enclosed in a plastic bag or box until sturdy roots form.

LAVENDER, FRINGED See *Lavandula*
LEMON-SCENTED GERANIUM See *Pelargonium*
LILLIPUT GASTERIA See *Gasteria*
LIPSTICK PLANT See *Aeschynanthus*

LOBIVIA
L. famatimensis, also called *Echinocactus famatimensis* (orange cob cactus); *L. paucartambensis* (both called cob cactus)

FRINGED LAVENDER
Lavandula dentata

Enormous, dahlia-like blooms on diminutive plants make cob cacti a rare find for a light garden, where space is at a premium. The 3- to 6-inch cylindrical cacti, ribbed like corncobs, bear flowers almost as large as the plants themselves in clear, bright shades of red, yellow, pink, orange or purple. Although the blooms last only a few days, they appear continuously during the cacti's season of active growth in late spring and early summer. The orange cob cactus bears red-to-orange 2-inch flowers while the cactus itself has a red-to-purple cast. *L. paucartambensis* bears red flowers from the top to the bottom of the plant. Both species produce small plants as offsets at the base.

HOW TO GROW. Cob cacti require 1,000 to 1,500 foot-candles of light, achieved by placing them 6 inches or less below a four-tube fixture. Illuminate the plants for 14 to 16 hours daily during the growing season and for 10 to 12 hours a day during their winter resting period. A spring-through-fall temperature range of from 65° at night up to 85° or higher during the day and a winter range of 40° at night to 65° by day are best for stimulating good bloom. Humidity of 25 to 30 per cent is adequate.

Cob cacti grow slowly and need repotting only every three to five years when plants and their offsets crowd the containers. Wear heavy gloves as protection from the sharp spines and use rolled newspapers as tongs to repot the cacti in a soilless mixture of 1 part sphagnum peat moss, 2 parts perlite and 2 parts vermiculite, adding 1 teaspoon of bone meal and either 1 teaspoon of ground limestone or ¼ cup of crushed eggshells per quart of mix; otherwise, use a packaged soilless mix prepared for cacti, adding bone meal and a source of lime in the same proportions. During the growing season, allow the soil to dry almost completely between thorough waterings and feed biweekly with a high-phosphorus fertilizer such as 15-30-15 diluted to one fourth the strength recommended on the label. During dormancy, water only enough to keep the cacti from shriveling and do not feed. Cob cacti can be grown from seed to blooming size in three to four years. They can also be propagated by removing the offsets, which form at the bases, letting the juicy cut ends dry for 24 hours, then inserting them in moist vermiculite.

LOBSTER CLAWS See *Vriesia*

M

MAGIC FLOWER See *Achimenes*

MALPIGHIA
Malpighia coccigera (holly malpighia)

A compact, 1-foot-tall plant at maturity, the holly malpighia is an interesting and decorative shrub for light gardens. Flat pink flowers ½ inch wide formed by five round fringed petals bloom in summer among ¾-inch glossy, spiny-edged leaves. The leaves are nearly oval on young plants but become shaped like holly leaves as the plants mature.

HOW TO GROW. Holly malpighia requires bright light, 500 to 750 foot-candles, for 14 to 16 hours daily. Place the tops of plants 6 inches below a two-tube fixture. Maintain night temperatures of 55° to 60° and day temperatures of 68° to 72°. Humidity of 30 to 35 per cent is adequate. Plant in a soilless mix of 2 parts sphagnum peat moss, 1 part vermiculite and 1 part perlite; otherwise, use a packaged soilless mix. Do not add lime. Allow the mix to dry slightly between waterings. Feed young, nonblooming plants weekly after watering with a water-soluble balanced fertilizer such as 10-10-10 diluted to one fourth the strength recommended on the label; feed mature, blooming plants weekly with a high-

ORANGE COB CACTUS
Lobivia famatimensis

HOLLY MALPIGHIA
Malpighia coccigera

POWDER PUFF CACTUS
Mammillaria bocasana

RABBIT'S TRACKS
Maranta leuconeura kerchoveana

phosphorus fertilizer such as 10-30-20 at the same rate. Holly malpighia goes through a period of winter dormancy; withhold fertilizer and water sparingly until spring. To maintain a compact shape and to encourage more blooms, prune the stems as they become straggly. Propagate from stem cuttings rooted in moist vermiculite; the new plants will grow to blooming size in six months to a year. Plants can also be grown from seed to blooming size in a year.

MAMMILLARIA

M. bocasana (powder-puff cactus); *M. bombycina; M. elongata* (golden-star cactus, golden-lace cactus) (all called pincushion cactus, mammillaria)

Growing as small globes or cylinders with bumps spiraling up their surfaces, pincushion cacti are frequently covered with white woolly hair that hides hooked spines. Each globe or finger of these popular plants is usually only an inch or two thick, but they produce offsets so readily they rapidly expand into clusters a foot across. The flowers that appear during the spring-through-fall growing season characteristically grow in a ring at the top of the cluster. Brown spines on the powder puff's 2-inch globes are obscured by a thick coating of wool; ¾-inch yellow flowers are followed by red seed pods that protrude an inch from the plant. *M. bombycina* is both woollier and larger, with fingers 2½ inches thick and up to 8 inches long; its ½-inch flowers are deep pink. The golden-star cactus has fingers an inch in diameter and 4 to 6 inches tall with star bursts of yellow spines at the top of each surface bump; its ½-inch flowers are yellow.

HOW TO GROW. Pincushion cacti require 1,000 to 1,500 foot-candles of light and should be grown 6 inches or less below a four-tube fixture. During their active growing season, provide 14 to 16 hours of illumination daily, reducing this to 10 to 12 hours during the winter resting period. From spring through fall, a temperature range from 65° at night up to 85° during the day is recommended; for best blossoms the following year, maintain winter temperatures from 40° at night up to 65° during the day. Humidity of 25 to 30 per cent is adequate.

Plants grow slowly and need repotting only once every three to five years. Protect your hands with heavy gloves and use rolled newspapers as tongs to handle the spiny cacti. Use a soilless mixture of 1 part sphagnum peat moss, 2 parts perlite and 2 parts vermiculite, adding 1 teaspoon of bone meal and either 1 teaspoon of ground limestone or ¼ cup of crushed eggshells per quart of mix; otherwise, use a packaged soilless mix prepared for cacti, adding bone meal and a lime source in the same proportions.

While plants are actively growing, water them thoroughly, then let the soil become nearly dry before watering again; feed biweekly with a high-phosphorus fertilizer such as 15-30-15 diluted to one fourth the recommended strength. During winter dormancy, water just enough to keep the cacti from shriveling and do not feed. Of the species listed here, *M. bombycina* is most susceptible to rot caused by too much water. Propagate by cutting off the small new plants that develop alongside older cacti; let the juicy cut surface dry for 24 hours before inserting it in moist vermiculite.

MARANTA

M. leuconeura (prayer plant, banded arrowroot)

When day becomes night as the fluorescent sun in the light garden goes off, the varicolored leaves of the prayer plant turn upward like folded hands. Held horizontally during the day, these oval leaves display two shades of green or green and brown, veined with gray or red on top and red or purple underneath. Growing up to 6 inches long and 3 inches wide, the leaves are carried on 6- to 8-inch stems that rise from fleshy roots. The variety *M. leuconeura kerchoveana,* called rabbit's tracks, has brown spots resembling paw prints paralleling the middle rib of each leaf. These blotches, red on the underside of the leaf, turn dark green as the leaf matures.

HOW TO GROW. Provide prayer plants with medium light, 200 to 500 foot-candles, for 14 to 16 hours daily. Place plants 12 inches below a two-tube fixture. Temperatures of 65° to 70° at night, 75° to 85° during the day, and humidity as close to 50 per cent as possible are best. To raise the humidity level, place pots on a moisture tray. Prayer plants grow through the year under lights. Repot when roots become crowded in the container, using a shallow pot one size larger than the last. Plant in a soilless mixture of 2 parts sphagnum peat moss, 1 part perlite and 1 part vermiculite, adding either 1 teaspoon of ground limestone or ¼ cup of crushed eggshells per quart of mix; otherwise, use a packaged soilless mix, adding a lime source in the same proportions. Keep the mix moist at all times. Feed weekly, using a balanced house-plant fertilizer such as 20-20-20 diluted to one fourth the strength suggested on the label. Propagate by dividing the fleshy roots in late winter or early spring. Stem cuttings will root easily in moist vermiculite.

MEXICAN SNOWBALL See *Echeveria*
MINIATURE CATTLEYA ORCHID See *Cattleya*
MINIATURE CYMBIDIUM ORCHID See *Cymbidium*
MINIATURE ROSE See *Rosa*
MINIATURE SINNINGIA See *Sinningia*
MISTLETOE FIG See *Ficus*
MOONSTONES See *Pachyphytum*
MOTH ORCHID See *Phalaenopsis*
MOTHER-OF-THOUSANDS See *Cymbalaria* and
    Saxifraga

N

NAEGELIA See *Smithiantha*
NEANTHE ELEGANS See *Chamaedorea*
NEANTHE PALM See *Chamaedorea*
NECKLACE VINE See *Crassula*
NEMATANTHUS See *Hypocyrta*

NEOREGELIA
N. ampullacea; N. carolinae 'Tricolor'; *N. marmorata; N. sarmentosa chlorosticta* (all called neoregelia)

With a reputation for durability, neoregelias have leathery leaves clustered tightly to form a cup in the center of the plant. The foliage of these bromeliads may be banded, marbled or spotted and the red markings on the leaf tips of some species resemble painted fingernails. *N. ampullacea's* glossy green, narrow leaves with purple flecks and crossbands form a tube 5 inches high; tiny white flowers with blue edges nestle inconspicuously in the cup. *N. carolinae* Tricolor's 1-foot leaves are banded with green, rose and white. The rose color becomes more pronounced under bright light and the cup turns dark red before the small lavender flowers appear in it. *N. marmorata* has red-tipped leaves 1½ feet long that are marbled purple and green on both sides; the small flowers are lavender. *N. sarmentosa chlorosticta,* a striking plant, has 1- to 1½-foot leaves that are red on top and splotched with silver below; the tiny flowers are pale lavender.

HOW TO GROW. Give neoregelias bright light, about 500 to 750 foot-candles, for 12 to 14 hours daily. Place plants 3 to 6 inches below a two-tube fixture. Night temperatures of 60° to 65° and day temperatures of 70° or higher are best. Keep

NEOREGELIA
Neoregelia sarmentosa chlorosticta

SCARLET BALL CACTUS
Notocactus haselbergii

SWEET BASIL
Ocimum basilicum

humidity as close to 50 per cent as possible by misting plants and setting pots on a moisture tray. Plant in a soilless mix of equal parts of sphagnum peat moss, vermiculite and perlite; do not add lime. Otherwise, use a packaged soilless mix. Allow the mix to dry slightly between waterings, and do not let it become soggy or the plant's base may rot. Keep the cup in the center of the leaf rosette filled with water.

Feed weekly with a water-soluble balanced fertilizer such as 20-20-20 at one fourth the strength recommended on the label. To encourage a mature plant to bloom, enclose it in a plastic bag with a sliced apple for five or six days. The ripening fruit gives off ethylene gas, which induces bromeliads to produce a flower spike in about two months. After blooming, the mother plant slowly dies over one to two years while producing offshoots. These can be left in the original pot as a multiple rosette or they can be removed and potted individually. Offshoots bloom when two years old. Neoregelia can be grown from seed to blooming plants in three years.

NOTOCACTUS
N. crassigibbus; N. haselbergii (scarlet ball cactus, white-web ball cactus) (both called ball cactus)

Young ball cacti are small, flattened globes but they become round with age and develop clusters of offsets around their bases to form clumps 18 inches across. The notched ribs bristle with clusters of spines. Funnel-shaped flowers grow on top of the cactus during the spring-through-fall growing season. Prickly fruits follow the blossoms. *N. crassigibbus* has a deep depression in the center of its 2- to 3-inch globe, which is green to black; the flowers are yellow. The scarlet ball cactus is so covered with short white spines that the green below is barely visible. Its red-to-orange flowers appear in the early spring.

HOW TO GROW. Provide ball cacti with 1,000 to 1,500 footcandles of light by placing them 6 inches or less below a four-tube fixture. Illuminate the plants for 14 to 16 hours daily while they are actively growing and for 10 to 12 hours daily during their winter resting period. Temperatures ranging from 65° at night to 85° during the day are best from spring through fall; maintain temperatures of 40° to 65° during the winter. Plants grow slowly and need repotting only every three to five years. Wear gloves to protect your hands from the spines and use rolled newspapers as tongs when you handle the cacti. Plant in a soilless mixture of 1 part sphagnum peat moss, 2 parts perlite and 2 parts vermiculite, adding 1 teaspoon of bone meal and either 1 teaspoon of ground limestone or ¼ cup of crushed eggshells per quart of mix; or use a packaged soilless mix for cacti, adding bone meal and a lime source in the same proportions.

From spring through fall, let the soil dry almost completely between waterings and feed the plants biweekly with a high-phosphorus fertilizer such as 15-30-15 diluted to one fourth the strength recommended on the label. During winter, water only enough to keep the cacti from shriveling and do not feed. Propagate by removing an offset from the base of a mature plant; let the juicy cut surface dry 24 hours before inserting it in moist vermiculite.

NUT ORCHID See *Achimenes*

OAK-LEAVED CREEPING FIG See *Ficus*

OCIMUM
O. basilicum (sweet basil); *O. minimum* (bush basil)

In Italy, basil is a symbol of love. And for generations,

Italian and French chefs have added this delicate herb to tomatoes and to a basic green sauce called *pesto* or *pistou,* which gives zest to soups, fish and pasta. Grown under light, basil produces bushier growth than if grown in a window-sill pot. An annual when grown outdoors, basil puts forth an abundance of shiny, dark green leaves year round in the light garden; when they are slightly brushed, the leaves exude a clovelike aroma.

Sweet basil grows 15 to 24 inches with 1- to 2-inch leaves and circles of ⅛- to ¼-inch white blossoms on spikes at the tips of its upright stems. Bush basil grows 6 to 12 inches with ¼- to ½-inch leaves.

HOW TO GROW. Give basil a medium amount of light, 400 to 600 foot-candles, by placing plants 6 to 12 inches from a two-tube fixture 14 to 16 hours daily. Night temperatures of 60° to 65°, daytime temperatures of 70° or more and 30 to 40 per cent humidity are ideal. Plant in a pot 1 inch larger in diameter than the herb's root ball in a soilless mixture of equal parts sphagnum peat moss, perlite and vermiculite, or use a packaged soilless mix, adding 1 teaspoon ground lime-stone or ¼ cup crushed eggshells per quart of either mix. Keep soil evenly moist but never soggy. Feed weekly after watering with a balanced fertilizer such as 20-20-20 diluted to one quarter the strength recommended on the label. Prop-agate from stem cuttings, which take about 10 days to root in moist vermiculite. Basil also grows easily from seed sown on sphagnum moss that is warmed from the bottom to 70°.

ONCIDIUM

O. cheirophorum (Colombia buttercup); *O. ornithorhynchum; O. pulchellum; O. pusillum; O. triquetrum* (all called dancing lady orchids, oncidium orchids)

Oncidium orchids are called dancing ladies because they have an airy look in their long, arching flower stalks covered with up to a hundred tiny flowers. Several varieties are small enough to be grown in the limited space of a light garden. The plants send up fleshy pseudobulbs from which leaves or flower stems grow. The dainty flowers are often used in tiny corsages or as hair ornaments; each one has an exaggerated lower petal, the lip, with a bump on it called a crest. In fall or winter, each of the Colombia buttercup's pseudobulbs sends up a single 6-inch leaf and an arching flower stalk covered with waxy ½-inch yellow flowers with a lemon scent.

O. ornithorhynchum has sprays of ¾-inch flowers that smell like the herb heliotrope. Twin 10-inch leaves grow from its pseudobulbs. The flowers that appear in autumn or winter are rose to purple with dark, fiddle-shaped lips that have yellow crests. Flower stalks of *O. pulchellum* grow from fans of overlapping folded leaves; its summer-blooming, 1-inch flowers are white tinged with pink and rose with lips spotted with yellow. *O. pusillum* usually blooms in summer but its arching sprays of 1-inch yellow flowers marked with purple sometimes appear at other seasons; like *O. pulchellum* it has a fan of leaves at its base. *O. triquetrum* sends up a tuft of 4- to 5-inch leaves and a spray of unusual 1-inch flowers in the fall; each has green petal-like outer sepals, rose inner petals bordered with white and spotted with red, and a yellow-throated lip.

HOW TO GROW. Oncidium orchids need 1,500 to 2,400 or more foot-candles. This can be achieved by growing them under a bank of eight to 10 4-foot cool- and warm-white fluorescent tubes, or six to eight 4-foot high-output tubes, or four to six 4-foot very-high-output tubes. *O. cheirophorum* and *O. ornithorhynchum* will bloom at less light than the other species. Place plants as close to the tubes as possible without touching them; use the lights 14 to 16 hours daily.

ONCIDIUM ORCHID
Oncidium triquetrum

Night temperatures of 55° to 60° and day temperatures of 65° to 70° suit these orchids, although *O. cheirophorum* and *O. ornithorhynchum* sometimes bloom better if temperatures are 5° to 10° cooler than this. A 10° temperature drop at night is necessary to make these orchids bloom. Provide 50 to 75 per cent humidity by misting plants twice daily, placing pots on a moisture tray and using a room humidifier. Since humid, stagnant air promotes fungus growth, maintain space for good air circulation around plants.

Grow plants in a mixture of 2 parts fir bark or shredded tree-fern fiber, 1 part perlite and 1 part coarse peat moss. Oncidiums can also be fastened with nylon thread to a suspended slab of tree fern. Allow the soil to dry slightly between waterings; water standing around roots can quickly rot orchids. Feed each week with a fertilizer formulated for orchids such as 30-10-10 or 18-18-18, diluted to one fourth the strength recommended on the label. Repot every two or four years when a plant and its creeping rhizome grow over the edge of the container. For additional plants, propagate when repotting by dividing the rhizome, with five or six pseudobulbs per division.

OPUNTIA

O. chlorotica (flapjack cactus); *O. microdasys* (bunny-ears cactus)

Opuntias are cacti notable for their unusual forms and spine configurations. The two species listed can grow 3 to 6 feet tall, but their unusual shapes, colorful bristle tufts (the glochids) and satiny flowers make young plants attractive to light gardeners. Both species grow in flat, jointed, paddle-shaped segments called pads that are dotted with glochids. Beware of these glochids; they can be extremely painful if they stick in your skin. The flapjack cactus has blue-green pads dotted with yellow-to-brown glochids bristling with a tangle of yellow spines. Growing more slowly than most opuntias, it bears yellow flowers 3 inches across. On the bunny-ears cactus, young pads branch from the top of older ones. These pads are dotted with yellow glochids, spines are inconspicuous, and yellow flowers are carried on short stalks growing in pad joints. The variety *alba* has white glochids and the variety *rufida* has red-to-brown glochids. Both produce yellow flowers.

HOW TO GROW. Give opuntias 1,000 to 1,500 foot-candles of light by placing the tops of the plants 6 inches or less below a four-tube fixture. Illuminate plants for 14 to 16 hours daily during their spring-to-fall season of active growth and for 10 to 12 hours during the winter when they are resting. Temperatures ranging from 65° at night to 85° by day during the growing season and from 40° to 65° during the winter are best. Humidity of 25 to 30 per cent is adequate. Repot when roots crowd the container; wear heavy gloves to protect your hands and use rolled newspapers as tongs to handle the cacti. Pot in a soilless mixture of 1 part sphagnum peat moss, 2 parts perlite and 2 parts vermiculite, adding 1 teaspoon of bone meal and either 1 teaspoon of ground limestone or ¼ cup of crushed eggshells per quart of mix; otherwise, use a packaged soilless mix for cacti, adding bone meal and a lime source in the same proportions.

During periods of growth, let the soil become nearly dry between waterings and feed the plants biweekly with a high-phosphorus fertilizer such as 15-30-15, diluted to one fourth the recommended strength. During dormancy, do not feed; water only enough to keep the cacti from shriveling. Brown or gray spots develop on the pads if they receive too much water; pads may drop if the cacti become too dry. Opuntias that grow too tall can be shortened by removing pads at the

RED BUNNY EARS
Opuntia microdasys rufida

top, but this may delay flowering. Propagate by cutting pads from the cacti, letting the juicy cuts dry for 24 hours, then inserting cut ends in moist vermiculite.

ORANGE COB CACTUS See *Lobivia*
ORCHID, BUTTERFLY See *Epidendrum*
ORCHID, CLAMSHELL See *Epidendrum*
ORCHID, COMPARETTIA See *Comparettia*
ORCHID, CORAL See *Rodriguezia*
ORCHID, DANCING LADY See *Oncidium*
ORCHID, JEWEL See *Haemaria*
ORCHID, LADY'S-SLIPPER See *Paphiopedilum*
ORCHID, LAELIA See *Laelia*
ORCHID, MINIATURE CATTLEYA See *Cattleya*
ORCHID, MOTH See *Phalaenopsis*
ORCHID, NUT See *Achimenes*
ORCHID, SPIDER See *Brassia*
ORNAMENTAL PEPPER See *Capsicum*

OXALIS

O. hedysaroides rubra (firefern); *O. regnellii; O. siliquosa* (all called oxalis)

Spindly and rangy when grown on a window sill, oxalis is a compact, profusely blooming plant in the light garden. Growing to a height of 8 to 16 inches, most oxalis have clover-like leaves with three heart-shaped blades. The clusters of five-petaled 1-inch flowers are pink, white, red or yellow. Some oxalis bloom all year round, but flowering generally peaks in summer and fall. The firefern, which resembles neither fire nor fern, is a fibrous-rooted oxalis with yellow flowers that grows to a height of 4 to 8 inches. Its deep red leaves move up and down in response to slight changes in light or air movements. *O. regnellii,* one of the best plants for beginning light gardeners, can be depended on to flower. Its leaf blades are triangular rather than heart-shaped and are green on top, purple below. The plants bear white flowers and reach a height of 4 to 8 inches. *O. regnellii*'s stems stand upright better than those of most oxalis; they grow from tuberous underground roots called pips. *O. siliquosa* is another fibrous-rooted oxalis; it produces lush red, green and purple foliage and bright yellow flowers under artificial light. If it receives too much or too little light, or if the soil dries out, the leaves fold until conditions improve. Its readily branching red stems must be regularly pruned to maintain a compact shape.

HOW TO GROW. Place oxalis so it will receive bright light, 500 to 750 foot-candles, for 12 to 14 hours daily. A two-tube fixture placed 4 to 6 inches above the plants provides the needed amount of light. Maintain night temperatures of 50° to 60° and day temperatures of 68° to 72°, with a moderate humidity of about 40 per cent. Pot fibrous-rooted oxalis in a mix of 2 parts sphagnum peat moss, 1 part vermiculite and 1 part perlite. Pot tuberous oxalis from pips in equal parts sphagnum moss, vermiculite and perlite. To either of these mixes, add ½ teaspoon of ground limestone or ½ cup of crushed eggshells per quart. Keep the soil evenly moist but not soggy. Feed weekly after watering with a balanced 20-20-20 water-soluble fertilizer at one fourth the strength recommended on the label. Remove dead leaves, stems and faded flowers. If plants become too tall, cut them down to 3-inch stubs and new growth will soon appear. Fibrous-rooted oxalis is propagated by rooting three or four 3-inch tip cuttings in a 4-inch pot of moist perlite or vermiculite. Propagate oxalis that grows from pips by dividing crowded plants and potting each pip separately in potting mix.

OX TONGUE See *Gasteria*

FIREFERN
Oxalis hedysaroides rubra

P

PACHYPHYTUM

P. bracteosum (silver bract); *P. brevifolium* (sticky moonstones); *P. compactum* (thick plant); *P. oviferum* (moonstones, sugared almonds) (all called pachyphytum)

The plump, fleshy leaves of pachyphytums, radiating from short stems in loose rosettes, develop more color variations under the dependable illumination of a light garden than they do when grown on a window sill. Under lights, these succulents are also more likely to bloom, sending up tall stalks with nodding flowers from the centers of their rosettes. Silver bract grows 6 inches tall with pointed, tongue-shaped gray leaves that curve upward; under lights, the leaves take on a rosy tint and red flowers may appear. Sticky moonstones has blunt-tipped, fleshy blue leaves that develop red edges under lights. The tacky surfaces of these thick leaves have a waxy sheen. Flowers are red. On the thick plant, 30 to 60 round, cylindrical leaves develop a blue-gray tinge under lights; plants grow 1 to 2 inches tall and bear pink-to-red flowers tipped with blue. The 2-inch-long, egg-shaped silver-to-gray leaves of moonstones are delicately shaded from pink to mauve; these plants grow only 2½ inches tall and bear red flowers.

HOW TO GROW. Grow pachyphytums 6 inches or less below a four-tube fixture, where they will receive 1,000 to 1,500 foot-candles of light. Illuminate plants for 14 to 16 hours daily during the period of active growth, spring through fall. Gradually reduce this level to 10 to 12 hours during the winter resting period. Maintain temperatures of 50° to 55° at night, 75° or higher during the day, with humidity of 25 to 30 per cent. Repot every three to five years when roots crowd their container. Use a soilless mixture of 1 part sphagnum peat moss, 2 parts perlite and 2 parts vermiculite, adding 1 teaspoon of bone meal and either 1 teaspoon of ground limestone or ¼ cup of crushed eggshells per quart of mix; otherwise, use a packaged soilless mix prepared for cacti, adding bone meal and a lime source in the same proportions. During active growth, let the soil dry almost completely between waterings and feed biweekly with a high-phosphorus fertilizer such as 15-30-15 diluted to one fourth the recommended strength. During the plant's resting period, withhold fertilizer and water only enough to keep the fleshy leaves from shriveling. Propagate from stem or leaf cuttings, letting the surface of the juicy cuts dry for 24 hours before inserting the cuttings in moist vermiculite.

PAINTED LADY See *Echeveria*
PAN-AMERICAN FRIENDSHIP PLANT See *Pilea*
PANAMIGA See *Pilea*
PANAMIGA, SILVER TREE See *Pilea*

PAPHIOPEDILUM

P. bellatulum; P. charlesworthii; P. godefroyae; P. insigne (all called lady's-slipper orchid)

Paphiopedilums defy the usual light laws that govern orchid culture and make it possible for gardeners with modest lighting arrangements to enjoy these exotic flowers. These lady's-slipper orchids, though not the American woodland wildflowers known as lady's-slippers (orchids of the *Cypripedium* genus), will bloom under only four to six flourescent tubes. Their low-growing tufts of leathery leaves and 15-inch or shorter flower stalks are well suited to light gardening spaces. These lady's-slippers will produce waxy 3- to 5-inch blooms with large petal-like sepals at the backs of the flowers. The spreading horizontal petals are frequently hairy and bumpy. The flower's lower petal is a pouch that resembles a

STICKY MOONSTONES
Pachyphytum brevifolium

slipper. Paphiopedilums are most frequently green or brown, but other colors including white and red are available; the blooms are usually veined or spotted in contrasting hues. Each flower stem rises from a cluster of evergreen leaves and bears either a single flower or small cluster of blooms. Flowers last as long as three months on the plant or a month as cut flowers. The leaf clusters multiply into clumps so mature plants produce several flowers annually.

P. bellatulum has leaves mottled in two shades of green and shell-shaped flowers with short pouches that are not as prominent as those of most lady's-slippers. A single bloom, creamy white to pale yellow and dotted with bumps and purple spots, grows on each flower stalk, sometimes lasting eight weeks. *P. charlesworthii* has a white back sepal veined with purple; its slightly hairy petals and its slipper-shaped pouch are yellow to green. Flower stalks rise from tufts of mottled leaves in summer. Similar in appearance to *P. bellatulum, P. godefroyae* bears small clusters of white flowers spotted with red or purple in summer; the green foliage is checkered with silver above and red below. *P. insigne* bears flowers that rise from tufts of 1-foot green leaves, sometimes lasting from fall to early spring. The broad back sepal is yellow-green with purple spots, the horizontal petals are streaked with brown and the slipper is yellow to brown.

HOW TO GROW. When temperature and humidity needs are met, paphiopedilum orchids can be grown with the 1,000 to 1,200 foot-candles of light available under four to six cool- and warm-white fluorescent tubes. They bloom more reliably, however, when grown in collections of orchids provided with 1,200 to 2,400 foot-candles of light, achieved by using eight to 10 4-foot cool- and warm-white fluorescent tubes, or six to eight 4-foot high-output tubes, or four to six 4-foot very-high-output tubes. Place the plants as close to the tubes as possible without touching them; illuminate plants for 14 to 16 hours daily. Temperatures of 55° to 60° at night and from 65° to 70° during the day are best for the mottled-leaf species like *P. bellatulum, P. charlesworthii* and *P. godefroyae;* green-leaved species such as *P. insigne* need cooler temperatures ranging from 50° to 55° at night and from 60° to 65° during the day. In either case, a 10° drop in temperature at night will help ensure bloom.

While paphiopedilums are less demanding about humidity than other orchids and will survive in humidity as low as 30 per cent, for best blooms provide 50 per cent or more by placing pots on a moisture tray and misting plants twice daily. Use a fine mist so water does not remain long on the foliage, where it could cause rot. Use a room humidifier to achieve consistently high humidity.

Since humid conditions promote the growth of fungus diseases, maintain good air circulation around plants. Grow lady's-slippers in a mixture of 2 parts fir bark or shredded tree-fern fiber, 1 part perlite and 1 part coarse peat moss. Keep the soil evenly moist but never soggy; water standing around the roots of orchids will rot them. Feed weekly with a fertilizer formulated for orchids such as 30-10-10 or 18-18-18, diluted to one fourth the strength recommended on the label. Repot the plants every two to four years when leaf clusters begin crowding over the sides of the containers. Propagate lady's-slipper orchids when repotting, breaking the leaf clusters apart with your fingers so there are three or four clusters per division.

LADY'S-SLIPPER ORCHID
Paphiopedilum bellatulum

PARLOR PALM See *Chamaedorea*
PARTRIDGE BREAST See *Aloe*
PATIENT LUCY See *Impatiens*
PEARLY HAWORTHIA See *Haworthia*

LEMON-SCENTED GERANIUM
Pelargonium crispum 'Prince Rupert Variegated'

MINIATURE COMMON GERANIUM
Pelargonium hortorum 'Minx'

PELARGONIUM

P. crispum (scented-leaf geranium); *P. hortorum* (common or zonal geranium)

The geranium is valued in the light garden because it is easy to grow, blooms frequently in such colors as red, white, pink and lavender, and has leaves that in some cases can fill a room with fragrance. *P. crispum* varieties are grown for their abundant, crinkly, lemon-scented foliage that is often dried and used in potpourris; Prince Rupert variegated geranium is a variety with lavender-colored blooms that is recommended for light gardening. The zonal geranium compensates for the faintly fishy odor of its leaves with abundant blooms on plants in three sizes: miniature varieties that grow to a height of only 4 inches and include the scarlet-flowered Minx; dwarf varieties that grow to 10 inches and include Pixie with salmon-pink flowers; and semidwarf varieties that reach 12 to 15 inches and include the scarlet Red Spider.

HOW TO GROW. Geraniums grow best when given very bright light, 1,000 foot-candles or more, for 14 to 16 hours daily. If they receive four hours or more of natural sunlight in addition to artificial light, enough light can be achieved by placing them 6 inches or less below a two-tube fixture; otherwise, a four-tube fixture is needed. Abundant bloom is encouraged by cool night temperatures of 50° to 55° and day temperatures of 68° to 72°. Good air circulation with 40 per cent humidity promotes sturdy growth. Grow geraniums in a soilless mix of 1 part sphagnum peat moss, 2 parts vermiculite and 2 parts perlite, adding 1 teaspoon of ground limestone or ¼ cup of crushed eggshells per quart of mix; alternatively, use a packaged soilless mix and add limestone or eggshells in the same proportions. To encourage vigorous roots, keep the potting mix evenly moist but never soggy. Varieties with fragrant foliage may be watered more often, but avoid saturating the soil lest you encourage rot. Geraniums bloom best when their roots fill the pots. Feed weekly after watering with a high-phosphorus, water-soluble fertilizer such as 10-30-20, at one fourth the strength recommended on the label. To encourage new blooms, pinch back straggly stems and remove faded flowers promptly. Although geraniums are perennial plants, most of the hybrid varieties grown in light gardens are treated as annuals. Take stem cuttings for propagation before discarding an aging plant. If misted frequently, such cuttings will root in moist vermiculite in about three weeks and flower in two to three months.

PELLAEA

P. rotundifolia (button fern, New Zealand cliff brake)

In light gardens, the button fern puts forth more luxuriant growth than it will when grown under ordinary houseplant conditions. With its low, spreading, 18-inch fronds and button-shaped, polished leaflets only ½ inch wide, this species bears slight resemblance to most ferns. New leaves are red-green when they emerge but change to a waxy, dark green as they grow.

HOW TO GROW. Button ferns grow well if given 14 hours of medium light, 200 to 500 foot-candles, each day. Place plants 6 to 12 inches below a two-tube fixture. Temperatures from 50° to 60° at night and from 70° to 80° during the day, with 40 to 50 per cent humidity, promote best growth. Pot in a soilless mixture of 2 parts sphagnum peat moss, 1 part perlite and 1 part vermiculite, adding 1 teaspoon of bone meal per quart of mix. Feed biweekly during periods of active growth with a high-nitrogen (5-2-2) fertilizer such as fish emulsion, diluting it to one fourth the strength suggested on the label. Keep the soil constantly moist; moisture fluctuations can kill this fern. Propagate by dividing mature plants.

PEPEROMIA

P. caperata (wrinkled-leaved peperomia); *P. incana; P. obtusifolia* (blunt-leaved peperomia, pepper-face peperomia); *P. rotundifolia* (yerba linda); *P. sandersii,* also called *P. arifolia argyreia* (watermelon peperomia, watermelon begonia)

Better able to tolerate a gardener's mistakes than most plants, peperomias are a good choice among foliage plants for a beginner. In addition to being tough, they offer color, texture and sizes that fit well into limited spaces. Although their thick, almost succulent leaves are their chief attraction, these members of the pepper family produce minute flowers on slender, tapering spikes that resemble miniature cattails. The wrinkled-leaved peperomia is probably best known. Its green, heart-shaped leaves are deeply corrugated; the ¾-inch to 1½-inch leaves grow on compact plants only 3 to 4 inches tall and 5 inches across. *P. caperata variegata* is a variety of the wrinkled-leaved peperomia that has edges broadly banded in white. *P. incana* has heart-shaped, 2-inch leaves covered with hairs that turn white when the plants are grown in strong light; this peperomia can become 15 inches tall. The blunt-leaved peperomia has waxy, oval 2- to 3-inch leaves, fleshier than those of most peperomias, on plants 8 to 10 inches tall. The variegated blunt-leaved peperomia, *P. obtusifolia variegata,* has leaves heavily banded with white. Yerba linda is a good choice for terrariums where its oval, waxy ½-inch green leaves creep along to form a ground cover. The watermelon peperomia takes its common name from the silver-to-white bands that run down its glossy dark green leaves; the 2- to 4-inch, heart-shaped leaves grow on 8- to 10-inch plants.

HOW TO GROW. Give peperomias a medium amount of light, 200 to 500 foot-candles, by placing the plants 12 inches or less below a two-tube fixture. Illuminate plants for 14 to 16 hours daily. Temperatures of 65° to 70° at night, 75° to 85° during the day, and humidity as close to 50 per cent as possible are best. To raise the humidity level, grow peperomias in a terrarium or place pots on a moisture tray. Repot only when roots become crowded. Use a soilless mixture of 2 parts sphagnum peat moss, 1 part perlite and 1 part vermiculite, adding either 1 teaspoon of ground limestone or ¼ cup of crushed eggshells per quart of mix; otherwise, use a packaged soilless mix prepared for African violets, adding a lime source in the same proportions. Allow the soil to dry only slightly between waterings but water less in winter when growth slows. Peperomias are susceptible to rot if their roots are kept too wet. Feed weekly with a balanced houseplant fertilizer such as 20-20-20 diluted to one quarter the recommended rate. Propagate by dividing clumps of mature plants or by rooting stem cuttings in moist vermiculite.

PERENNIAL GLOXINIA See *Gloxinia*

PHALAENOPSIS

P. hybrids (moth orchids)

The flat blooms of phalaenopsis orchids with their petals shaped like butterflies have long been prized in bouquets for their velvety elegance. Most orchids need extremely bright light to flower satisfactorily but moth orchids bloom under a modest arrangement of only four to six fluorescent tubes. Each of the plant's clusters of leaves sends out an arching flower stalk with as many as 30 blooms that last as long as five months on the plant. New buds open along the stalk as older ones fade, and if the stalk is cut off just above its last joint after the last flower has faded, the plant often sends up another flower stalk and thus stays in bloom nearly year round. The moth orchid hybrids produce 2- to 5-inch flowers

BUTTON FERN
Pellaea rotundifolia

VARIEGATED WRINKLED-LEAVED PEPEROMIA
Peperomia caperata variegata

MOTH ORCHID
Phalaenopsis Heistaway 'Jeanette'

PANAMIGA
Pilea involucrata

in shades of white, yellow, pink and rose, frequently shaded or striped with other colors. The plants are less than a foot tall, making them suitable for small light gardens.

HOW TO GROW. Moth orchids will bloom when given 1,000 to 1,200 foot-candles of light, the amount available under four 4-foot cool- and warm-white fluorescent tubes. Place plants as close to the tubes as possible without touching them, lowering the plants as flower stalks grow. Light the orchids for 14 to 16 hours daily. Provide temperatures of 60° to 65° at night, 70° to 75° by day; orchids require a 10° temperature drop at night to flower. Maintain humidity of 60 to 70 per cent by placing pots on a moisture tray, misting plants twice daily and using a room humidifier. Since humid, stagnant air can promote fungus growth, good air circulation around the plants is essential.

Pot the orchids in a mixture of 2 parts fir bark or shredded tree-fern fiber, 1 part perlite and 1 part coarse peat moss. Keep the soil evenly moist but never soggy; orchids quickly rot if water stands around their roots. Feed weekly with a fertilizer formulated for orchids such as 30-10-10 or 18-18-18, diluted to one fourth the strength recommended on the label. Repot every two to four years as the clusters of leaves multiply and both the plants and their roots begin creeping over the edges of the containers. Propagate when repotting, separating the clumps with fingers so there are three or four leaf clusters in each division.

PHEASANT WING See *Aloe*
PIGTAIL PLANT See *Anthurium*
PIGTAIL, VARIEGATED See *Anthurium*

PILEA

P. cadierei (aluminum plant, watermelon pilea); *P. involucrata* (panamiga, Pan-American friendship plant); *P.* 'Silver Tree' (Silver Tree panamiga) (all called pilea)

Fast-growing pileas seldom develop into plants more than a foot tall. Besides their compact size, they offer light gardeners puffy, quilted leaves that are pleasantly streaked and blotched with color. Each blue-green leaf of the 9- to 12-inch aluminum plant seems to be brushed with shiny gray paint on either side of the leaf's main rib; the end of each 2½- to 3½-inch elliptical leaf tapers abruptly to a point. *P. cadierei minima* is a dwarf aluminum plant that grows only 5 or 6 inches tall. The panamiga's 1½- to 3-inch oval leaves with scalloped edges grow on branching plants 6 to 8 inches tall; the slightly hairy leaves are usually deep green when the plant is grown on a window sill but become a copper color under more intense light. The branching Silver Tree variety has 1- to 3-inch red-to-green leaves on stalks covered with white down; each pointed leaf has a broad silver band down its center and silver spots near its edges.

HOW TO GROW. Pileas need medium light, 200 to 500 foot-candles, achieved by placing them 6 to 12 inches below a two-tube fixture. Light the plants for 14 to 16 hours daily. Provide temperatures of 65° to 70° at night, from 75° to 85° during the day, with humidity as close to 50 per cent as possible. Place plants on a moisture tray to raise humidity. When roots fill the plant's container, repot in a soilless mixture of 2 parts sphagnum peat moss, 1 part perlite and 1 part vermiculite, adding either 1 teaspoon of ground limestone or ¼ cup of crushed eggshells per quart of mix; otherwise, use a packaged soilless mix for African violets, adding lime in the same proportions. Keep the soil evenly moist but never wet or soggy. Feed plants weekly with a balanced house-plant fertilizer such as 20-20-20, diluted to one fourth the strength recommended on the label. For additional plants, propagate by dividing mature plants or by rooting stem cuttings in moist vermiculite.

PINEAPPLE See *Ananas*
PINEAPPLE SAGE See *Salvia*
PINK POLKA DOT PLANT See *Hypoestes*
PLAID CACTUS See *Gymnocalycium*

PLECTRANTHUS
P. australis (Swedish ivy); *P. coleoides marginatus* (white-edged Swedish ivy, candle plant)

These two Swedish ivies are vigorous trailing plants that are especially attractive in hanging baskets or cascading over the edge of a shelf. Both have succulent, waxy round leaves with scalloped edges along translucent stems. Under lights, leaves grow larger and closer together; spikes of tiny white flowers tinged with purple grow at the tips of the trailing stems. Swedish ivy's bright green leaves grow 1 to 1½ inches across. Its stems and the veins of new leaves are red when young, gradually turning green. Stems grow 1½ to 2 feet in length. White-edged Swedish ivy is a bushier species with more erect stems. Its 2- to 3-inch leaves are hairy and their scalloped edges are white.

HOW TO GROW. Grow Swedish ivy in low to medium light, 200 to 400 foot-candles, for 12 to 14 hours daily. Place plants 6 to 12 inches below a two-tube fixture. Provide temperatures of 50° to 65° at night and 65° to 75° during the day, with humidity kept as close to 50 per cent as possible. Place pots on a moisture tray to raise the humidity around plants. Repot when roots become crowded in their containers, using a soilless mixture of 2 parts sphagnum peat moss, 1 part perlite and 1 part vermiculite, adding either 1 teaspoon of ground limestone or ¼ cup of crushed eggshells per quart of mix. Alternatively, use a packaged soilless mix prepared for African violets, adding a lime source in the same proportions. Keep the growing medium evenly moist but never let it get soggy. Feed weekly with a balanced house-plant fertilizer such as 20-20-20 diluted to one fourth the recommended strength. Pinch off stem tips to encourage branching. Propagate by rooting cuttings in moist vermiculite.

PLUSH PLANT See *Echeveria*
POWDER PUFF CACTUS See *Mammillaria*
PRAYER PLANT See *Maranta*
PROPELLER PLANT See *Crassula*

PUNICA
P. granatum nana (dwarf pomegranate)

A doubly rewarding plant to include in a light garden, the dwarf pomegranate bears 2-inch fruits as well as 1- to 1½-inch red bell-shaped flowers from the time plants are only 3 inches tall. The narrow leaves are small and shiny in contrast to the large, graceful flowers and fruit. The branches are thin and spiny. An untrimmed plant grows to 15 inches.

HOW TO GROW. Dwarf pomegranates require medium light, 400 to 600 foot-candles, for at least 14 hours daily. Place plants 3 to 6 inches beneath a two-tube fixture. Maintain night temperatures of 55° to 60° and day temperatures of 70° to 80°. Keep humidity as close to 50 per cent as possible by misting and placing pots on a moisture tray. Plant in a soilless mix of 2 parts sphagnum peat moss, 1 part vermiculite and 1 part perlite, adding 1 teaspoon of ground limestone or ¼ cup of crushed eggshells per quart of mix; otherwise, use a packaged soilless mix, adding limestone or eggshells in the same proportions. Keep the soil evenly moist but never soggy while the plant is growing and flowering. Fertilize

SWEDISH IVY
Plectranthus australis

DWARF POMEGRANATE
Punica granatum nana

RED CROWN CACTUS
Rebutia minuscula

weekly after watering with a high-nitrogen water-soluble fertilizer such as 30-10-10 applied at one fourth the strength recommended on the label. To encourage branching, pinch back new growth. Blow a puff of air into mature flowers to pollinate them and produce pomegranates. Allow only one or two pomegranates to form, because the bearing of abundant fruit weakens the tree. Propagate from stem cuttings rooted in moist vermiculite.

PURPLE PASSION VINE See *Gynura*
PUSSY EARS See *Cyanotis*
PYGMY PAPYRUS See *Cyperus*

Q

QUEEN VICTORIA CENTURY PLANT See *Agave*
QUEEN'S-TEARS See *Billbergia*

R

RATTAIL CRASSULA See *Crassula*

REBUTIA

R. krainziana; R. minuscula (red crown cactus); *R. senilis* (fire crown cactus) (all called crown cactus)

As many as 15 flowers at one time may crowd atop a mature crown cactus during the spring-summer blooming period. A crown cactus forms compact clusters of 1- to 3-inch globes with flattened tops; bumps called tubercles spiral up its sides. The trumpet-shaped blossoms, on short stalks growing from the base of the plant, may be as large as the globes. *R. krainziana* has 2-inch globes; its white spines rise from conspicuous white tufts of woolly barbs and its 2½-inch flowers are red. The red crown cactus has small, almost harmless spines on its 1- to 2½-inch globes; the red flowers are 1½ inches in diameter. The fire crown cactus has white spines that form a dense network over the 3-inch globes; its 1½-inch flowers also are red.

HOW TO GROW. Give crown cacti 1,000 to 1,500 foot-candles of light by placing them 6 inches or less below a four-tube fixture. Keep the plants lighted for 14 to 16 hours daily during their spring-through-fall growing season, reducing the illumination to 10 to 12 hours during the winter resting period. While they are actively growing, provide temperatures ranging from 65° at night up to 85° by day. In winter, temperatures of 40° to 45° at night and up to 65° during the day are best to ensure bloom the following spring. Humidity of 25 to 30 per cent is adequate. Plants grow slowly and need repotting only after three to five years. Wear gloves to protect your hands from the spines and use rolled newspapers as tongs when you handle the plants. Repot in a soilless mixture of 1 part sphagnum peat moss, 2 parts perlite and 2 parts vermiculite, adding 1 teaspoon of bone meal and either 1 teaspoon of ground limestone or ¼ cup of crushed eggshells per quart of mix; otherwise, use a packaged soilless mix prepared for cacti, adding bone meal and a lime source in the same proportions.

During active growth, let the potting mix become almost dry between waterings and feed every two weeks with a high-phosphorus fertilizer such as 15-30-15, diluted to one fourth the recommended strength. During winter, do not feed and provide only enough water to keep the globes from shriveling. Propagate by severing small globes that develop alongside mature plants. Allow the cut surface to dry for 24 hours before inserting these globes in moist vermiculite.

RECHSTEINERIA

R. cardinalis, also called *Sinningia cardinalis* (cardinal flower); *R. leucotricha,* also called *Sinningia leucotricha* (Brazilian edelweiss)

Rechsteinerias are South American gesneriads that bear clusters of nodding, tubular flowers, each blossom 1¼ to 2 inches long, above layers of velvety foliage. Pairs or whorls of heart-shaped leaves grow on hairy stems 10 to 18 inches tall. The cardinal flower's 3- to 6-inch leaves and scarlet flowers are covered with fine white hairs; the plant can be kept in bloom for months at a time if old flower stalks are removed when flowers fade. The stems of Brazilian edelweiss are covered with downy hairs that turn from silvery white to gray as plants mature. The thick, 6-inch leaves and the rose-to-coral flowers are blanketed with silky white hair. The plant blooms intermittently for six months, then rests for six months, although the attractive foliage remains. Both rechsteinerias grow from fleshy tubers.

HOW TO GROW. Rechsteinerias need medium light, 400 to 600 foot-candles, for 12 to 14 hours daily and grow best when they are placed 6 inches below a two-tube fixture. Night temperatures of 65° to 70° and day temperatures of 75° to 85° are best, with humidity kept as close to 50 per cent as possible. Raise humidity around the plants by placing the pots on a moisture tray. Plant tubers slightly exposed in a 4-inch pot, using a soilless mixture of equal parts sphagnum peat moss, perlite and vermiculite, adding either 1 teaspoon of ground limestone or ¼ cup of crushed eggshells per quart of mix; otherwise, use a packaged soilless mix adding a lime source in the same amounts. Let the soil dry slightly between waterings and avoid wetting the leaves.

Feed weekly with a high-phosphorus fertilizer such as 10-15-10 diluted to one fourth the strength recommended on the label. When blooming ceases, water less often and withhold fertilizer; rest the plants in their pots at 50° to 55° for four to six months, then repot for a new blooming cycle. If the foliage begins to wither, gradually decrease water until leaves and stems have dried. Store these tubers in dry vermiculite at 50° to 55° for four to six months, then repot. Plants that are grown from tubers will flower in seven to nine months. Rechsteinerias can be propagated by rooting stem cuttings in moist vermiculite.

RED BUNNY EARS See *Opuntia*
RED CROWN CACTUS See *Rebutia*
RED-FLOWERING CRASSULA See *Crassula*
RED-NERVED FITTONIA See *Fittonia*
REX BEGONIA See *Begonia*
RIBBON PLANT See *Chlorophytum*
RIEGER BEGONIA See *Begonia*
ROCHEFORD'S HOLLY FERN See *Cyrtomium*

RODRIGUEZIA
R. secunda, also called *R. lanceolata* (coral orchid, rodriguezia orchid)

Small orchids that fit easily into limited light-gardening space, the rodriguezias grow from clumps of thick water-storing stems called pseudobulbs. Each of these produces a single strap-shaped 9-inch leaf and a 12- to 15-inch spray of boat-shaped flowers once a year between midwinter and fall. *R. secunda* has ½-inch flowers that are rose to pink.

HOW TO GROW. Give rodriguezia orchids 1,200 to 2,400 foot-candles of light by growing them under a bank of eight to 10 4-foot cool- and warm-white fluorescent tubes, or six to eight 4-foot high-output tubes, or four to six 4-foot very-high-output tubes. Place plants as close to the tubes as possible, lowering them as the flower stalks grow. Keep lights on 14 to 16 hours daily. A temperature range of 55° to 60° at night

BRAZILIAN EDELWEISS
Rechsteineria leucotricha

CORAL ORCHID
Rodriguezia secunda

MINIATURE ROSE
Rosa hybrid 'Eleanor'

and from 65° to 70° by day is best; orchids require a 10° drop in temperature at night to bloom. Maintain 50 to 75 per cent humidity by placing pots on a moisture tray, misting plants twice daily and using a room humidifier. Since humid, stagnant air promotes fungus growth, space enough for good air circulation around the plants is essential.

Grow rodriguezia orchids in a mixture of 2 parts fir bark or shredded tree-fern fiber, 1 part perlite and 1 part coarse peat moss. They can also be fastened to a suspended slab of tree fern, with nylon thread. Allow the soil to dry slightly between waterings; plant roots will quickly rot if water is allowed to stand around them. Feed each week with a fertilizer formulated for orchids such as 30-10-10 or 18-18-18, diluted to one fourth the strength recommended on the label. Repot every two to four years when plants and their aerial roots creep over the edges of their containers. Propagate by dividing when repotting, with five or six pseudobulbs per division.

ROSA
R. hybrids (miniature roses)

All year long, even in midwinter, a light gardener can enjoy the beauty and fragrance of tiny counterparts of large summer-blooming roses. Miniatures of all types of roses have been developed—tea roses, moss roses, cabbage roses, even climbing roses that cascade from hanging pots. The more than 200 varieties available offer a wide array of colors, forms and fragrances. The smallest roses are micro-minis that grow only 4 to 6 inches tall. Among popular varieties are Bo-peep, with double-petaled pink blooms; Baby Cheryl, a disease-resistant plant with pink flowers that is suited to dwarf-tree treatment; Littlest Angel, a vigorous rose that bears long-lasting, fragrant yellow blooms almost constantly; and Pearl Dawn, an ever-blooming rose in shades of pink. Medium-sized miniatures that grow 6 to 10 inches tall include Baby Darling, a profusely blooming apricot-to-pink rose that requires less light than most miniatures; and Little Linda, which produces quantities of fragrant yellow blooms.

Larger miniature roses grow 15 inches tall and produce showier flowers than the smaller ones. Good varieties are Starina with fragrant, orange-to-red flowers tinted with yellow at their bases; Tiny Warrior, with white-veined red flowers that last up to two weeks; and Eleanor, a pink double-flowered rose. Among the climbing miniatures suitable for hanging baskets are Baby Gold Star, a yellow rose with flowers that are splashed with red; and the free-flowering Green Ice, with apricot-colored buds that open to white flowers, then turn green as they mature.

HOW TO GROW. Give miniature roses very bright light, 1,000 foot-candles or more, for 14 to 16 hours daily. This intense light requires a four-tube fixture placed no more than 6 inches above the plants. To stimulate flowering, maintain day temperatures of 65° to 70° and night temperatures about 10° lower. Keep humidity as close to 50 per cent as possible by placing the pots on a humidity tray. Enclosing each pot in a plastic bag at night to increase humidity further stimulates lush foliage. Start plants in 3-inch pots, using a soilless mix of equal parts of sphagnum peat moss, vermiculite and perlite. Move to pots one size larger before roots become crowded. Keep the soil evenly moist, firm and springy to the touch, but never soggy. Never let the roots dry out.

Fertilize roses each week, alternating a special liquid fertilizer for potted roses with a low-nitrogen house-plant formula such as 5-8-7, applying each fertilizer at one fourth the strength recommended on the label. After they flower, the plants need to rest; move them further from the lights, withhold fertilizer and reduce water for three months. To renew blooming, prune off the previous year's growth, place the plants closer to the lights and resume regular watering and feeding. Miniature roses cannot be propagated from seed, but stem cuttings can be rooted in moist vermiculite.

ROUGH MAIDENHAIR FERN See *Adiantum*
ROVING SAILOR See *Saxifraga*

S

SAINTPAULIA

S. hybrids (African violets)

Because they flower abundantly and almost continuously under lights, African violets have been credited with popularizing light gardening. They hybridize so readily that the variety of plant sizes, leaf shapes and flower forms and colors can seem endless. Miniatures may be 3 inches across when fully grown, while standard-sized African violets can become 2 feet across. The thick, hairy leaves growing in compact rosettes like spokes of a wheel may be spoon-shaped, appear quilted, have curled edges or be variegated. The 1- to 2-inch single or double flowers may be smooth, ruffled or wavy. Lower petals are sometimes larger than upper ones, sometimes symmetrical and occasionally star-shaped. Colors include deep purple, blue, violet, lavender, pink and white. Some blossoms are edged, streaked or splotched with contrasting colors. Just as all hybrids are not equal in size, shape or color, neither are they equal in their response to fluorescent light, their flowering periods or their ability to form neat, compact plants. Reliable plants for beginners are the Rhapsodie, Ballet and Diana hybrids.

HOW TO GROW. While African violets tolerate light intensity as low as 150 foot-candles, they grow best when they receive a medium amount of light, 250 to 500 foot-candles, for 11 to 16 hours daily. Place them 6 to 12 inches beneath a standard two-tube fixture. African violets are not damaged if they are closer to the tubes, but they should not touch the fixture. Night temperatures of 65° to 70° and day temperatures of 75° are best. Keep the humidity high, as close to 50 per cent as possible, by using a moisture tray. African violets bloom best when their roots crowd the pots; use 3- to 4-inch pots for standard-sized violets and plant miniatures in 2-inch pots. Plant in a soilless mixture of 2 parts sphagnum peat moss, 1 part vermiculite and 1 part perlite, adding 1 teaspoon of ground limestone or ¼ cup crushed eggshells per quart of mix; otherwise, use a packaged soilless African violet mix adding limestone or eggshells in the same proportions. Feed weekly with a water-soluble high-phosphorus fertilizer such as 12-36-14 that has been compounded especially for African violets; dilute the fertilizer to one fourth the strength recommended on the label. Pinch off small plants that appear around the base of the violet to form a single-crowned, symmetrical plant. (Any plant with multiple crowns can be divided.) African violets can be propagated from leaf cuttings rooted in moist vermiculite or from seed.

SALVIA

S. rutilans, also called *S. elegans* (pineapple sage)

Although pineapple sage has little use as a flavoring, light gardeners grow this herb for its brilliant-red tubular flowers, 1½ inches long, and for its fruity aroma. The downy, spear-shaped leaves, 2 to 4 inches long, are sometimes used as a garnish for fruit salads. The plant grows as tall as 3 feet unless regularly pinched back.

HOW TO GROW. Give pineapple sage a medium amount of light, 400 to 600 foot-candles, by placing plants 6 to 12 inches below a two-tube fixture for 14 to 16 hours daily. To

VARIEGATED AFRICAN VIOLET
Saintpaulia ionantha 'Cordelia'

MINIATURE TRAILING AFRICAN VIOLET
Saintpaulia ionantha 'Pixie Blue'

PINEAPPLE SAGE
Salvia rutilans

WINTER SAVORY
Satureia montana

bloom well, pineapple sage also requires some natural sunlight each day. Night temperatures of 60° to 65°, day temperatures of 70° or higher and 30 to 40 per cent humidity are best. To maintain humidity, set pots on a moisture tray. Plant in a pot 1 inch larger in diameter than the herb's root ball, using a soilless mixture of equal parts sphagnum peat moss, perlite and vermiculite, or use a packaged soilless mix. Add 1 teaspoon ground limestone or ¼ cup crushed eggshells per quart of either mix. Allow the soil to dry slightly between waterings, and feed weekly after watering with a balanced fertilizer such as 20-20-20 at one quarter the strength recommended on the label. Propagate from tip cuttings rooted in moist vermiculite. Sage can also be grown from seed; germinate seeds on moist sphagnum moss in a container that is warmed from the bottom to 70°.

SANDER'S DRACAENA See *Dracaena*

SATUREIA

S. hortensis (summer savory); *S. montana* (winter savory)

Some cooks call savory the "bean herb" because of its compatability with dishes that have a base of beans or peas. This peppery-tasting herb also diminishes the cooking odors of turnips, cabbage and other strong-smelling vegetables. Plucked from a light garden for stew or stuffing, the fresh herb's flavor is more delicate than that of the dried variety.

Summer savory is larger than the winter variety, often reaching 18 inches. Its narrow, lance-shaped ½- to 1½-inch leaves are covered with downy hairs, and weak, woody stems give the herb a straggly appearance. Winter savory grows no higher than 12 inches, with smooth, shiny, 1-inch-long leaves. Both savories bloom with tiny white-to-lavender or pink flowers, but the flavor of the herb is best if the leaves are harvested before the plant blooms.

HOW TO GROW. Savory requires a medium amount of light, 200 to 500 foot-candles, for 14 to 16 hours daily. Place plants 6 to 12 inches from a two-tube fluorescent fixture. Night temperatures of 60° to 65°, day temperatures of 70° or higher, and 30 to 40 per cent humidity are best. Set pots on a moisture tray to maintain the proper humidity. Choose a pot 1 inch larger in diameter than the herb's root ball and plant in a soilless mixture of equal parts sphagnum peat moss, perlite and vermiculite, adding 1 teaspoon ground limestone or ¼ cup crushed eggshells per quart of mix; otherwise, use a packaged soilless mix, adding limestone or eggshells in the same proportions. Allow the soil to dry slightly between waterings. Feed weekly after watering with a balanced fertilizer such as 20-20-20 at one quarter the strength recommended on the label. Propagate new plants from stem cuttings rooted in moist vermiculite. Savory can also be grown from seed sown on moist sphagnum moss that is warmed from the bottom to 70°.

SAVORY See *Satureia*

SAXIFRAGA

S. stolonifera, also called *S. sarmentosa* (strawberry geranium, strawberry begonia, roving sailor, mother-of-thousands, Aaron's beard)

Eye catching as a foliage plant, the strawberry geranium reaches its fullest potential under controlled light conditions where it will bear clouds of wispy white flowers. The blossoms usually appear in summer, rising on slender 9- to 12-inch stalks from a rosette of white-veined green leaves with pink edges. These hairy, nearly round leaves with scalloped edges grow as broad as 3 inches under lights. Mature plants reach 20 inches in width and bear tiny new plants that trail from them on bright red runners.

HOW TO GROW. Give the strawberry geranium very bright light, 1,000 foot-candles or more. Place a four-tube, 48-inch fixture 3 to 6 inches above the top of the plant. But use the light for only 10 to 12 hours daily in the spring because the plant requires long nights to bloom. Night temperatures of 45° and a day temperature under 68° are best for encouraging bloom. Humidity as low as 20 to 30 per cent is adequate. Pot in a soilless mix of 2 parts sphagnum peat moss, 1 part vermiculite and 1 part perlite, adding ½ teaspoon of ground limestone or ¼ cup of crushed eggshells per quart of mix; otherwise, use a packaged soilless mix adding limestone or eggshells in the same proportions. Keep the mix evenly moist but never soggy.

After the plant blooms, water less frequently, keeping the mix barely moist, until flower buds form again in spring. Except during this winter resting period, feed weekly after watering with a balanced water-soluble fertilizer such as 20-20-20 at one fourth the strength recommended on the label. Remove flowers as they fade. Propagate by removing the plantlets that form at the ends of runners and placing them in water until they root. Or pin plantlets atop separate small pots of moist vermiculite while they are still attached to the mother plant, and sever them after roots are established.

SCARLET BALL CACTUS See *Notocactus*
SCARLET PAINT BRUSH See *Crassula*

SELAGINELLA

S. kraussiana, also called *S. denticolata* (spreading selaginella, spreading spikemoss)

Given dependable light, spreading selaginella will rapidly spill out of its pot or fill a terrarium with tiny, ⅛-inch leaflets. Actually a fern, this creeping plant's slender stems take root wherever they sprawl. *S. kraussiana aurea* has yellow-green leaflets, while *S. kraussiana brownii* is a slower-growing dwarf variety with bright green leaflets.

HOW TO GROW. Give spreading selaginella 14 hours of medium light, 200 to 500 foot-candles each day, by placing plants 6 to 12 inches from a two-tube fixture. Night temperatures from 50° to 60° and day temperatures of 70° to 80° are best. Since these ferns require between 60 and 80 per cent humidity, they grow best in a terrarium. Plant in a soilless mixture of 2 parts spaghnum peat moss, 1 part perlite and 1 part vermiculite, adding 1 teaspoon of bone meal per quart of mix; otherwise, use a packaged soilless mix prepared for African violets, adding bone meal in the same amount. Feed plants biweekly during periods of active growth with a high-nitrogen (5-2-2) fertilizer such as fish emulsion diluted to one fourth the strength recommended on the label. Keep the soil evenly moist, but never soggy. Propagate by pinning stem cuttings to moist potting medium; mist until new roots are well established.

SENECIO See *Kleinia*
SHORT-LEAVED ALOE See *Aloe*
SILVER BRACT See *Pachyphytum*
SILVER-NERVED FITTONIA See *Fittonia*
SILVER TREE PANAMIGA See *Pilea*

SINNINGIA

S. pusilla, *S. regina* (violet slipper gloxinia); *S. speciosa* (all called gloxinia)

With their large slipper-shaped or bell-shaped blossoms, gloxinias have long been favorites with light gardeners be-

STRAWBERRY GERANIUM
Saxifraga stolonifera

DWARF CLUB MOSS
Selaginella kraussiana aurea

VIOLET SLIPPER GLOXINIA
Sinningia regina

GLOXINIA
Sinningia speciosa hybrid

cause they grow and bloom so readily under dependable light conditions. Under fluorescent tubes they grow from seed in half the time they otherwise would take, although many gardeners prefer to start them from dormant tubers, the thick underground stems. *S. pusilla* is a miniature species, under 2 inches tall, that forms flat rosettes of ½-inch leaves. The ¾-inch violet flowers that rise from the center of each rosette on minute stems last about a week. Among the miniature hybrids of *S. pusilla* are White Sprite, with white flowers; Bright Eyes, with purple flowers that are white on the underside; and Doll Baby, with lilac flowers tinged with white. The clear purple hue of the violet slipper gloxinia blooms is almost unmatched among gloxinias; its 2-inch flowers have narrow tubes and the 4- to 6-inch bronze-to-green leaves have white veins.

S. speciosa is the plant most people have in mind when they ask a florist for a gloxinia. The many *S. speciosa* hybrids bear large flowers, 3 to 6 inches across, in single and in many-petaled double forms. Colors range from white to red, purple, pink or lavender, and the bell-shaped blooms are often bordered, spotted or streaked with a contrasting color. The flowers are carried above rosettes of soft, velvety oval leaves 5 to 8 inches long. Among the hybrids are Delight, a dwarf gloxinia whose white flowers have red throats; Emperor William, with dark purple flowers edged in white; Emperor Frederick, whose red blooms are bordered with white; and Queen of Hearts, a double-petaled gloxinia in shades of pink and salmon. Both the violet slipper gloxinia and *S. speciosa* go through periods of dormancy after they bloom.

HOW TO GROW. *S. pusilla,* the miniature gloxinia, grows best with a low level of light, about 150 foot-candles, for 12 to 16 hours daily. Place it 18 inches below a standard two-tube fixture. Give it temperatures of 60° to 70° at night, 70° to 75° or more by day. Because it requires humidity of 70 per cent or more, the miniature gloxinia grows best in a terrarium. Pot each tuber individually, dented side up, in a 2½-inch or smaller pot and barely cover it with soil. Use a mixture of equal parts sphagnum peat moss, vermiculite and perlite, adding 1 teaspoon ground limestone or ¼ cup of crushed eggshells per quart of mix; otherwise, use a packaged soilless African violet mix, adding limestone or eggshells in the same proportions. Water sparingly until growth appears, then keep barely moist, watering only when the top of the mix is dry to the touch. When the leaves have grown above the rim of the pot, feed weekly after watering with a water-soluble high-phosphorus fertilizer such as 10-30-20 diluted to one fourth the recommended strength. *S. pusilla* seeds itself; small plants appear around each parent.

The violet slipper gloxinia and *S. speciosa* require bright light, about 500 to 750 foot-candles, for 14 to 16 hours daily. Place them 6 to 12 inches beneath a standard fixture. They grow best when night temperatures are 60° to 70° and day temperatures are 70° to 75° or higher. Maintain humidity as close to 60 per cent as possible by misting plants and placing pots on a moisture tray. Plant each tuber individually with the dented side up in a 4- to 6-inch pot, barely covering it with soil. Use the same soilless mix recommended for *S. pusilla* and water and fertilize in the same manner. These tubers will bloom in about five months. After flowers fade and leaves turn yellow, cut the foliage off at the soil line and store the tubers in their pots at 60°, watering just enough to keep the mix from drying completely. When growth appears in four to six months, repot the tubers. Gloxinias can also be propagated from leaf cuttings, which, under lights, take about six months to develop into blooming plants. Plants grown from seed will bloom in six to eight months.

SLENDER UMBRELLA PLANT See *Cyperus*
SMALL-LEAVED CREEPING FIG See *Ficus*

SMITHIANTHA, formerly known as NAEGELIA
S. cinnabarina, S. hybrids (temple bells)

The light gardener who chooses temple bells is compensated for the space they occupy by spectacular slipper-shaped flowers that bloom readily under uniform illumination. These gesneriads have heart-shaped, velvety leaves. Nodding 1½-inch flowers are clustered along tall spires. *S. cinnabarina* with 6-inch red, hairy leaves bears red and cream flowers on spikes 1 to 2 feet tall. This species and the other four *Smithiantha* species have been so extensively hybridized that flowers come in combinations of white, pink, red, orange or yellow. Little Tudor, with flowers that combine orange, red and yellow, and Little Wonder, with red-and-yellow flowers, are two dwarf hybrids most suitable in size to light gardening; they grow 8 inches tall and have green leaves mottled with dark red.

HOW TO GROW. Give temple bells medium light levels, 250 to 500 foot-candles, for 14 to 16 hours daily. To prevent stems from becoming long and spindly, keep the tallest plant no more than 6 inches from a standard two-tube fixture. Flower spikes can touch the tubes without harm. Night temperatures of 65° to 70° and day temperatures of 75° or higher are best. Maintain high humidity, as close to 60 per cent as possible, by using a humidity tray. Plant each rhizome, a thickened stem, 1 inch deep in a 4- to 6-inch pot containing a soilless mixture of 2 parts sphagnum peat moss, 1 part vermiculite and 1 part perlite. Add 1 teaspoon of ground limestone or ¼ cup of crushed eggshells per quart of mix. Water sparingly until growth appears, then keep the soil barely moist, watering when the top of the mix feels dry. Use tepid water; cold water may spot leaves. Feed weekly after watering with a high-phosphorus water-soluble fertilizer such as 10-30-20 at one fourth the strength recommended on the label. Plants usually begin blooming three months after a rhizome is planted. After blooming, diminish watering gradually until the foliage turns yellow. Cut the foliage back to the soil line and store the rhizomes in their pots for three months, watering only enough to keep the mix from drying completely. Propagate by dividing the rhizomes from leaf cuttings or grow from seed. Leaf cuttings root best in moist vermiculite if cut without the stalk. Plants grow to blooming size from seeds or cuttings in six to nine months.

SPIDER ORCHID See *Brassia*
SPIDER PLANT See *Chlorophytum*
SPIDER PLANT, MANDA'S See *Chlorophytum*
SPIDER PLANT, VARIEGATED See *Chlorophytum*
SPOTTED CHINESE EVERGREEN See *Euonymus*
SPOTTED GASTERIA See *Gasteria*
STICKY MOONSTONES See *Pachyphytum*
STRAWBERRY BEGONIA See *Saxifraga*
STRAWBERRY GERANIUM See *Saxifraga*

STREPTOCARPUS
S. hybrids (Cape primrose)

Under lights, Cape primroses bear 2- to 3-inch trumpet-shaped flowers almost continuously. This gesneriad's flowers range from white to pink, blue, violet or red and often have throats in contrasting colors. Young plants form rosettes of stalkless, strap-shaped, wrinkled leaves that hug the edges of their pots. Mature plants produce multiple rosettes, become bushy, then bear two to six flowers on each of several tall, arching stalks that rise from the centers of the rosettes. The

TEMPLE BELLS
Smithiantha cinnabarina

Constant Nymph hybrids have wrinkled leaves that grow up to 1 foot long and 2 inches wide; each of their 6- to 8-inch flower stalks has as many as six 3-inch blue or violet blossoms that last for several days. *S. rexii* hybrids, which have quiltlike leaves, are larger and produce 2- to 5-inch flowers in a range of colors.

HOW TO GROW. Give Cape primroses medium to bright light, about 500 foot-candles, for 14 to 16 hours daily. Set plants 6 to 8 inches below a standard two-tube fixture. Maintain night temperatures of 50° to 60°, day temperatures of 65° to 75°, and keep humidity between 30 to 45 per cent, using a humidity tray if necessary. Pot in equal parts of sphagnum peat moss, vermiculite and perlite, adding 1 teaspoon of ground limestone or ¼ cup of crushed eggshells per quart of mix. Keep the mix evenly moist but not soggy. Feed weekly after watering with a water-soluble high-phosphorus fertilizer such as 10-30-20, applied at one fourth the strength recommended on the label. Start small plants in 3-inch pots and gradually move to 5-inch pots as the roots fill the containers. Take care when repotting; the leaves are brittle. Propagate by dividing rosettes, by rooting leaf cuttings in moist vermiculite or by planting seeds. Plants started from seeds or cuttings bloom in six to nine months.

STRING OF BUTTONS See *Crassula*
SUGARED ALMONDS See *Pachyphytum*
SUMMER SAVORY See *Satureia*
SWEDISH IVY See *Plectranthus*
SWEET BASIL See *Ocimum*

T

TEDDY-BEAR VINE See *Cyanotis*
TEMPLE BELLS See *Smithiantha*

THYMUS

T. vulgaris (common thyme, garden thyme, black thyme); *T. citriodorus* (lemon thyme)

There is hardly a soup, stew or ragout that cannot be improved with a pinch of pungent thyme plucked from a nearby light garden, where it can be easily cultivated. This aromatic herb has thin, woody stems that form bushy plants up to a foot in height. Its small (¼- to ½-inch-long), shiny leaves range in color from gray to green; its flowers vary from pale rose to lilac.

Common thyme has a more pungent flavor than lemon thyme, though both are popular with cooks. There are three varieties of common thyme: English thyme, which has variegated leaves; German thyme, which has broad leaves; and French summer thyme, which has narrow leaves. Lemon thyme can be distinguished from common thyme by its fragrance and its semitrailing stems. *T. citriodorus aureus* is a variety of lemon thyme with leaves edged in gold.

HOW TO GROW. Give thyme a medium amount of light (400 to 600 foot-candles) for 14 to 16 hours daily. Place plants 6 to 12 inches from a standard two-tube fixture. Temperatures of 60° to 65° at night and 70° or higher during the day and humidity ranging from 30 to 40 per cent are best. Plant thyme in a pot 1 inch larger in diameter than the herb's root ball. Use a soilless mixture of equal parts sphagnum peat moss, perlite and vermiculite, adding 1 teaspoon of ground limestone or ¼ cup crushed eggshells per quart of soil mix; you can also use a packaged soilless mix, adding limestone or eggshells in the same proportions. Allow soil to dry slightly between waterings. Feed weekly after watering with a balanced fertilizer, such as 20-20-20, diluted to one-quarter strength. Propagate new plants by rooting stem cut-

CAPE PRIMROSE
Streptocarpus hybrid 'Constant Nymph'

tings or root cuttings in moist vermiculite; thyme also can be grown from seed on moist sphagnum moss that is warmed to 70° from the bottom.

TIGER ALOE See *Aloe*
TIGER'S JAWS See *Faucaria*

TILLANDSIA
T. cyanea; T. ionanatha; T. lindenii (all called tillandsia)

The largest genus of bromeliads are the tillandsias, bizarre and variable plants. Those commonly grown indoors have stiff rosettes of arching or twisted leaves covered with silver-gray scales. In nature, most tillandsias grow on trees and shrubs where they take moisture and nutrients from the air through these scales. Their roots function only as anchors that hold them to their perch. Generally, the bright bracts (modified leaves) and the tubular flowers rise on spikes from the center of the plant. The 8- to 10-inch *T. cyanea* has 12- to 14-inch green leaves striped with brown; the flower spike has rose-colored bracts and large violet flowers. *T. ionanatha*, 1½ to 4 inches high, has overlapping 2-inch leaves that turn red at blossom time; red bracts surround the violet flowers. *T. lindenii* looks much like *T. cyanea;* it has a rosette of 40 to 60 thin 1- to 1½-foot leaves penciled with red-to-brown lines. In both species, the leaves turn red in bright light and the flat flower spike has red bracts below blue flowers.

HOW TO GROW. Tillandsias require medium to bright light, about 500 foot-candles, for 12 to 14 hours daily. Place them 6 inches from a two-tube fixture. Night temperatures of 60° to 65° and day temperatures of 70° or higher are best. These plants can be grown tied to a suspended slab of wood with nylon fishing line. If the plants are grown in containers, pot them in fir bark to allow swift drainage; otherwise the base of the plant will rot. Mist plants with tepid water daily. Fertilize plants by spraying the leaves weekly with a water-soluble balanced fertilizer such as 20-20-20 used at one fourth the strength recommended on the label. Propagate by removing the small plants that appear around the base and planting them individually in fir bark.

TRADESCANTIA
T. albiflora albo-vittata (giant white inch plant); *T. fluminensis variegata* (variegated wandering Jew); *T. sillamontana* (white velvet wandering Jew)

Fluorescent lights strengthen the leaf colors of inch plants and wandering Jews. Strong, dependable light also ensures bushy plants with leaves closely spaced on the creeping stems and can stimulate production of tiny white or violet flowers. These pot or hanging-basket plants are closely related to the zebrinas, also called wandering Jews, differing only slightly in botanical detail. The giant white inch plant has 2- to 3-inch pointed leaves banded with white. The smaller leaves of the variegated wandering Jew, 1 to 1½ inches long, are green or green striped with white or yellow. The white velvet wandering Jew has narrow 1½- to 2½-inch green leaves covered with woolly white fluff above and colored purple below. In strong light, the entire leaf turns red under the dense white fuzz.

HOW TO GROW. Give inch plants and wandering Jews medium light, 200 to 500 foot-candles, for 14 to 16 hours daily. Place plants 6 to 12 inches below a two-tube fixture. Temperatures of 50° to 55° at night, 68° to 72° during the day, and humidity of 30 to 40 per cent are best. When a plant's roots become crowded, repot in a soilless mixture of 2 parts sphagnum peat moss, 1 part perlite and 1 part vermiculite, adding either 1 teaspoon of ground limestone or ¼ cup of

GOLDEN LEMON THYME
Thymus citriodorus aureus

TILLANDSIA
Tillandsia ionantha

WHITE VELVET WANDERING JEW
Tradescantia sillamontana

VRIESIA
Vriesia scalaris

crushed eggshells per quart of mix; otherwise, use a packaged soilless mix prepared for African violets, adding a lime source in the same proportions. Allow the soil to dry slightly between waterings. Feed plants each week with a balanced house-plant fertilizer such as 20-20-20 diluted to one fourth the strength recommended on the label. Stem cuttings root easily in moist vermiculite; the variegated wandering Jew can be rooted in water.

TRAILING BEGONIA See *Cissus*
TRICHOSPORUM See *Aeschynanthus*
TROUT BEGONIA See *Begonia*
TRUE ALOE See *Aloe*

U
URN PLANT See *Aechmea*

V
VARIABLE DIEFFENBACHIA See *Dieffenbachia*
VARIEGATED CREEPING FIG See *Ficus*
VARIEGATED KENILWORTH IVY See *Cymbalaria*
VARIEGATED PIGTAIL PLANT See *Anthurium*
VARIEGATED PINEAPPLE See *Ananas*
VARIEGATED SPIDER PLANT See *Chlorophytum*
VARIEGATED WANDERING JEW See *Tradescantia*

VRIESIA
V. carinata (lobster claws); *V. heliconioides, V. scalaris, V. splendens* (flaming sword)

Under lights, these bromeliads grow and flower as well as they do in their native tropics. Vriesias have exotically marked, straplike leaves that form shapely rosettes. A brilliant flower that lasts for several months rises from the cup-shaped center of the rosette. The flat flower spike is covered with multicolored bracts, the scalelike 1- to 2-inch modified leaves. The vriesia known as lobster claws has 6- to 8-inch light green leaves; when it blooms, red, yellow and green bracts overlap along the foot-tall flower spike and a yellow flower, about an inch long, emerges from each bract. The 8-inch green leaves of *V. heliconioides* are flushed with red underneath; white flowers emerge from red, green and yellow boat-shaped bracts on 6-inch spikes. *V. scalaris* has pale green leaves 6 inches long and ¾ inch wide; its pendant, 1-foot flower spike has yellow flowers with green-tipped petals that emerge from red bracts. Flaming sword, among the most spectacular of all bromeliads, has blue-green leaves 1 to 1½ feet long that are marked with dark purple crossbands. Its sword-shaped flower spike grows up to 2 feet tall and bears 2- to 3-inch yellow flowers in red bracts.

HOW TO GROW. Give vriesias a medium amount of light, about 250 to 500 foot-candles, for 12 to 14 hours daily. Adjust a standard two-tube fixture so that it is about 6 to 12 inches above the plant. Maintain night temperatures of 55° to 65° and day temperatures of 65° or higher. Keep humidity as close to 50 per cent as possible by misting plants and standing pots on a moisture tray.

Plant vriesias in 5-inch or smaller pots using a soilless mix of equal parts sphagnum peat moss, vermiculite and perlite; otherwise, use a prepackaged soilless mix. Keep the cup in the center of the plant's leaf rosette filled with water; water the planting mix only when the top feels dry when pinched between the fingers. Too much water will rot the base of a bromeliad. Fertilize vriesias weekly with a water-soluble, balanced fertilizer such as 20-20-20 diluted to one fourth the strength recommended on the label.

To encourage flowering in a mature plant, place it in a

plastic bag with a sliced apple for five or six days. The ethylene gas given off by the ripening fruit will induce the bromeliad to produce a flower spike in about two months. After it has bloomed, the mother plant will slowly die during a period of one to two years but will produce offshoots. These can be left in the original pot as a multiple rosette or they can be removed and potted individually. The offshoots bloom when they are two years old. Vriesias can also be propagated from seed to bloom in three years.

W

WANDERING JEW See *Zebrina*
WART PLANT See *Haworthia*
WATERMELON PEPEROMIA See *Peperomia*
WATERMELON PILEA See *Pilea*
WAX BEGONIA See *Begonia*
WAXPLANT See *Hoya*
WHITE-EDGED SWEDISH IVY See *Plectranthus*
WHITE VELVET WANDERING JEW See *Tradescantia*
WINDOW PLANT See *Haworthia*
WRINKLED-LEAVED PEPEROMIA See *Peperomia*

Y

YELLOW QUEEN EUONYMUS See *Euonymus*
YOUTH-AND-OLD-AGE See *Aichryson*

Z

ZEBRA PLANT See *Aphelandra*

ZEBRINA
Z. pendula, also called *Cyanotis vittata, Tradescantia tricolor* or *T. zebrina* (wandering Jew)

Creeping plants with variegated foliage, these wandering Jews have richer color when they are grown in a light garden than they do as pot plants or hanging-basket plants at the window. Under fluorescent lights the leaves are spaced closely along trailing stems that can become 5 or 6 feet long if they are not pinched back regularly. Tiny violet flowers may appear, usually in the summer. *Z. pendula* has narrow 3-inch-long leaves with silver bands on either side of each leaf's main rib; the undersides are purple. *Z. pendula discolor,* the two-color wandering Jew, is a variety with narrower silver bands on leaves that are copper to green above and purple below. The four-color wandering Jew, *Z. pendula quadricolor,* has leaves that are irregularly striped above with green, purple, silver, pink or red; the leaf edges and undersides are purple. These plants are closely related to those of the *Tradescantia* genus, also called wandering Jews, but these require higher temperatures.

HOW TO GROW. Zebrinas have the best color when they are grown in medium light, 200 to 500 foot-candles, provided for 14 to 16 hours daily. Place plants 6 to 12 inches below a two-tube fixture. Night temperatures of 65° to 70°, day temperatures of 75° to 85° and humidity as close to 50 per cent as possible are best. To raise the humidity, place pots on a moisture tray. When roots become crowded in a container, repot the plant in a soilless mixture of 2 parts sphagnum peat moss, 1 part perlite and 1 part vermiculite, adding either 1 teaspoon of ground limestone or ¼ cup crushed eggshells per quart of mix; otherwise, use a packaged soilless mix prepared for African violets, adding a lime source in the same proportions. Keep the soil evenly moist at all times but never soggy, and feed weekly with a balanced house-plant fertilizer such as 20-20-20 diluted to one fourth the strength recommended on the label. Propagate zebrinas from stem cuttings rooted in moist vermiculite.

WANDERING JEW
Zebrina pendula

Characteristics of 192 light-garden plants

	LIGHT				NIGHT TEMP.			HUMIDITY			PLANT TYPE				FLOWER COLOR					LEAF COLOR		PLANT HEIGHT		
	75 to 200 foot-candles	200 to 500 foot-candles	500 to 1,000 foot-candles	Over 1,000 foot-candles	45° to 50°	50° to 60°	60° to 70°	30 to 45 per cent	45 to 60 per cent	Above 60 per cent	Flowering	Foliage	Succulent	Herb	White	Yellow to orange	Pink to red	Blue to purple	Multicolor	Green	Variegated	Under 1 foot	1 to 2 feet	Over 2 feet
ACHIMENES HYBRID (magic flower)		●	●			●		●			●						●			●		●		
ADIANTUM HISPIDULUM (rough maidenhair fern)		●		●					●			●								●		●		
ADIANTUM RADDIANUM (delta maidenhair fern)		●		●					●			●								●		●		
AECHMEA CHANTINII (aechmea)			●			●		●		●	●	●							●	●		●		
AECHMEA FASCIATA (urn plant)			●			●		●		●	●	●						●		●		●		
AESCHYNANTHUS HYBRID 'BLACK PAGODA' (lipstick plant)		●									●						●			●				●
AGAVE FILIFERA COMPACTA (dwarf thread-bearing century plant)			●	●		●			●				●						●		●	●		
AGAVE VICTORIAE-REGINAE (Queen Victoria century plant)			●	●		●			●				●						●		●	●		
AGLAONEMA COMMUTATUM (Chinese evergreen)	●					●		●				●								●				●
AICHRYSON BETHENCOURTIANUM (aichryson)			●		●		●			●		●			●					●		●		
ALOE HUMILIS (crocodile jaws)			●	●		●							●			●				●		●		
ALOE VARIEGATA (tiger aloe)			●	●		●							●			●				●		●		
ALOE VERA (true aloe)			●	●		●							●			●				●			●	
ANANAS COMOSUS VARIEGATUS (variegated pineapple)			●			●		●		●	●						●		●		●			
ANANAS NANUS (dwarf pineapple)			●			●		●		●	●						●		●			●		
ANTHURIUM CRYSTALLINUM (crystal anthurium)		●				●			●			●								●	●			
ANTHURIUM SCHERZERIANUM (flamingo flower)		●				●			●								●			●	●			
APHELANDRA SQUARROSA 'DANIA' (zebra plant)		●				●			●											●	●			
ASPARAGUS PLUMOSUS (asparagus fern)		●		●					●			●								●		●		
BEGONIA BELVA KUSLER HYBRIDS (Belva Kusler begonia)		●				●		●									●				●	●		
BEGONIA BOWERAE (eyelash begonia)		●				●		●			●						●			●	●	●		
BEGONIA CUBENSIS (holly-leaved begonia)		●				●		●	●			●						●		●		●		
BEGONIA ELATIOR HYBRIDS (Rieger begonia)		●				●		●									●				●	●		
BEGONIA HYBRID ARGENTEO-GUTTATA (angel wing begonia)		●				●		●	●		●								●				●
BEGONIA HYBRID 'DUSCHARFF' (hairy-leaved begonia)		●				●		●	●		●								●				●
BEGONIA REX 'SILVER QUEEN' (rex begonia)		●				●		●				●								●	●	●		
BEGONIA SEMPERFLORENS 'GENEVA SCARLET BEAUTY' (wax begonia)		●				●		●									●				●			
BILLBERGIA NUTANS (Queen's tears)		●				●		●			●							●		●				
BRASSIA CAUDATA (spider orchid)		●		●		●	●	●			●							●		●				
BRASSIA LANCEANA (spider orchid)		●		●		●	●	●			●							●		●				
CALADIUM HORTULANUM 'CANDIDUM' (fancy-leaved caladium)		●				●			●			●								●	●			
CAPSICUM ANNUUM 'FIESTA' (ornamental pepper)		●				●	●		●					●						●				
CATTLEYA LUTEOLA (miniature cattleya orchid)			●				●		●					●						●				
CHAMAEDOREA ELEGANS (parlor palm)	●					●		●				●						●		●				
CHIRITA SINENSIS (chirita)		●			●				●			●					●		●	●	●			
CHLOROPHYTUM COMOSUM MANDAIANUM (Manda's spider plant)		●				●			●			●			●					●	●			
CISSUS RHOMBIFOLIA (grape ivy)		●				●			●			●								●		●		
CISSUS QUADRANGULARIS (cissus)		●				●							●							●		●		
CODIAEUM VARIEGATUM PICTUM (croton)			●			●			●			●									●			●
COLEUS BLUMEI HYBRIDS (common coleus)			●			●	●		●			●					●			●	●			
COLUMNEA HYBRID 'CHANTICLEER' (columnea)	●					●			●							●				●				●
COLUMNEA HYBRID 'ROBIN' (columnea)	●					●			●								●			●				●
COMPARETTIA FALCATA (comparettia orchid)			●		●			●	●								●			●		●		
COMPARETTIA MACROPLECTRON (comparettia orchid)			●					●	●								●			●		●		
CRASSULA FALCATA (scarlet paint brush)			●			●			●				●				●			●	●	●		
CRASSULA SCHMIDTII (red flowering crassula)			●			●			●				●				●			●		●		
CROSSANDRA INFUNDIBULIFORMIS (firecracker flower)		●				●			●	●							●			●				●
CRYPTANTHUS BIVITTATUS (earth stars)			●			●		●	●	●				●						●	●			

Plant	75 to 200 foot-candles	200 to 500 foot-candles	500 to 1,000 foot-candles	Over 1,000 foot-candles	45° to 50°	50° to 60°	60° to 70°	30 to 45 per cent	45 to 60 per cent	Above 60 per cent	Flowering	Foliage	Succulent	Herb	White	Yellow to orange	Pink to red	Blue to purple	Multicolor	Green	Variegated	Under 1 foot	1 to 2 feet	Over 2 feet
	LIGHT				NIGHT TEMP.			HUMIDITY			PLANT TYPE				FLOWER COLOR					LEAF COLOR		PLANT HEIGHT		
CUPHEA HYSSOPIFOLIA (elfin herb)		●				●	●	●	●	●	●						●				●			
CYANOTIS KEWENSIS (teddy-bear vine)			●			●	●			●			●				●				●			
CYANOTIS SOMALIENSIS (pussy ears)			●			●	●			●			●				●				●			
CYMBALARIA MURALIS VARIEGATA (variegated Kenilworth ivy)		●				●		●		●	●	●					●				●			●
CYMBIDIUM HYBRID 'FLIRTATION' (miniature cymbidium orchid)			●		●			●			●						●				●			
CYPERUS DIFFUSUS (dwarf umbrella plant)			●			●		●				●								●	●			
CYRTOMIUM FALCATUM ROCHEFORDIANUM (Rocheford's holly fern)	●	●				●		●				●								●			●	●
DIEFFENBACHIA EXOTICA (exotic dieffenbachia)	●	●					●		●			●									●			●
DRACAENA SANDERIANA (Sander's dracaena)		●					●		●			●									●	●	●	
ECHEVERIA DERENBERGII (painted lady)				●		●		●				●	●			●					●			
ECHEVERIA ELEGANS (Mexican snowball)		●		●		●		●				●	●			●	●				●			
ECHEVERIA PULVINATA (plush plant)		●		●		●		●				●	●			●	●				●			
ECHINOCACTUS GRUSONII (golden barrel cactus)		●		●		●		●				●	●			●			●		●	●	●	●
EPIDENDRUM COCHLEATUM (clamshell orchid)			●	●		●		●	●	●	●							●				●	●	
EPIDENDRUM TAMPENSE (butterfly orchid)			●	●		●		●	●	●	●							●				●	●	
EPISCIA HYBRID 'MOSS AGATE' (flame violet)		●	●			●		●	●	●							●			●	●			
EPISCIA HYBRID 'PINK BROCADE' (flame violet)		●	●			●		●	●	●							●			●	●			
EUONYMUS JAPONICUS AUREO-VARIEGATUS (Yellow Queen euonymus)		●			●			●				●								●	●	●	●	
EUPHORBIA SPLENDENS 'BOJERI' (dwarf crown of thorns)			●			●		●			●		●				●				●			
EXACUM AFFINE (Arabian violet)	●	●				●		●			●							●			●			
EXACUM AFFINE 'BLITHE SPIRIT' (Arabian violet)	●	●				●		●			●				●						●			
FAUCARIA TIGRINA (tiger's jaws)			●			●		●			●		●			●					●			
FICUS DIVERSIFOLIA (mistletoe fig)		●				●		●				●							●					●
FICUS PUMILA VARIEGATA (variegated creeping fig)		●				●		●				●									●	●		
FITTONIA VERSCHAFFELTII (red-nerved fittonia)		●					●	●				●						●			●	●		
GARDENIA JASMINOIDES VEITCHII (gardenia)		●					●		●		●				●								●	●
GASTERIA LILIPUTANA (Lilliput gasteria)		●				●		●				●	●				●			●	●			
GASTERIA MACULATA (spotted gasteria)		●				●		●				●	●				●			●	●			
GESNERIA CUNEIFOLIA (gesneria)		●				●			●	●	●						●			●	●			
GESNERIA HYBRID 'LEMON DROP' (gesneria)		●				●		●		●	●					●				●	●			
GLOXINIA PERENNIS (Canterbury bells)		●				●		●			●							●			●			
GUZMANIA LINGULATA CARDINALIS (guzmania)		●				●			●	●	●				●						●			
GUZMANIA MONOSTACHYA (guzmania)		●				●			●	●								●			●			
GYMNOCALYCIUM MIHANOVICHII FRIEDRICHIAE 'RED CAP' (plaid cactus)		●			●			●				●					●				●			
GYNURA SARMENTOSA (purple passion vine)		●				●		●				●									●	●		
HAEMANTHUS KATHERINAE (blood lily)		●			●		●		●		●						●				●		●	
HAEMANTHUS PUNICEUS (blood lily)		●			●		●				●						●				●		●	
HAEMARIA DISCOLOR DAWSONIANUS (jewel orchid)			●			●		●	●	●	●	●			●						●			
HAWORTHIA MARGARITIFERA (pearly haworthia)		●	●			●		●				●	●		●					●	●			
HAWORTHIA TRUNCATA (window plant)		●	●			●		●				●	●		●					●	●			
HEDERA HELIX 'CHICAGO' (English ivy)		●				●		●				●								●		●		
HEDERA HELIX 'GLACIER' (English ivy)		●				●		●				●									●	●		
HEDERA HELIX 'MAMORATA' (English ivy)		●				●		●				●									●	●		
HELXINE SOLEIROLII AUREA (golden baby's tears)	●					●		●				●		●						●		●		
HOYA BELLA (wax plant)		●				●	●			●					●		●				●			
HYPOCYRTA HYBRID 'TROPICANA' (goldfish plant)	●	●				●		●		●					●		●			●	●			
HYPOCYRTA WETTSTEINII (goldfish plant)	●	●				●		●		●					●		●				●			
HYPOESTES SANGUINOLENTA 'SPLASH' (freckle-face plant)						●				●										●	●			

151

	LIGHT				NIGHT TEMP.			HUMIDITY			PLANT TYPE				FLOWER COLOR					LEAF COLOR		PLANT HEIGHT		
Plant	75 to 200 foot-candles	200 to 500 foot-candles	500 to 1,000 foot-candles	Over 1,000 foot-candles	45° to 50°	50° to 60°	60° to 70°	30 to 45 per cent	45 to 60 per cent	Above 60 per cent	Flowering	Foliage	Succulent	Herb	White	Yellow to orange	Pink to red	Blue to purple	Multicolor	Green	Variegated	Under 1 foot	1 to 2 feet	Over 2 feet
IMPATIENS WALLERANA 'ORANGE BABY' (patient Lucy)		●		●		●				●	●					●					●			
JASMINUM SAMBAC 'GRAND DUKE OF TUSCANY' (Arabian jasmine)	●	●				●	●			●				●									●	
JASMINUM SAMBAC 'MAID OF ORLEANS' (Arabian jasmine)	●	●				●	●			●				●									●	
KLEINIA REPENS (blue chalk sticks)			●		●	●				●			●		●						●			
KOELLIKERIA ERINOIDES (koellikeria)		●				●		●	●	●									●	●	●			
KOHLERIA BOGOTENSIS (kohleria)		●				●	●			●								●			●			
KOHLERIA HYBRID 'CARNIVAL' (kohleria)		●				●	●			●							●				●			
LAELIA LUNDII (laelia orchid)			●		●		●	●	●								●				●			
LAELIA PUMILA (laelia orchid)			●		●		●	●	●								●				●			
LAGERSTROEMIA INDICA 'CRAPE MYRTLETTE' (crape myrtlette)		●				●				●							●				?	●	●	
LAVANDULA DENTATA (fringed lavender)	●				●	●				●			●					●			●			
LOBIVIA FAMATIMENSIS (orange cob cactus)			●		●	●							●		●						●			
MALPIGHIA COCCIGERA (holly malpighia)		●			●	●				●	●						●		●		●			
MAMMILLARIA BOCASANA (powder puff cactus)			●	●		●				●			●		●						●			
MAMMILLARIA ELONGATA (golden star cactus)			●	●		●				●			●		●						●			
MARANTA LEUCONEURA KERCHOVEANA (rabbit's tracks)	●					●		●				●								●	●			
NEOREGELIA CAROLINAE 'TRICOLOR' (neoregelia)		●			●		●			●		●						●		●	●			
NEOREGELIA SARMENTOSA CHLOROSTICTA (neoregelia)		●			●		●			●	●							●		●	●			
NOTOCACTUS CRASSIGIBBUS (ball cactus)			●			●	●			●			●		●						●			
NOTOCACTUS HASELBERGII (scarlet ball cactus)			●			●	●			●			●		●	●					●			
OCIMUM BASILICUM (sweet basil)	●	●				●	●			●			●	●					●		●			
OCIMUM MINIMUM (bush basil)	●	●				●	●			●			●	●					●		●			
ONCIDIUM CHEIROPHORUM (Colombia buttercup)			●		●		●	●	●							●					●			
ONCIDIUM PULCHELLUM (dancing lady orchid)			●		●		●	●					●								●			
ONCIDIUM TRIQUETRUM (dancing lady orchid)			●		●		●	●	●										●		●			
OPUNTIA CHLOROTICA (flapjack cactus)			●			●	●			●			●		●						●		●	●
OPUNTIA MICRODASYS (bunny ears)			●			●	●			●			●		●						●		●	●
OPUNTIA MICRODASYS RUFIDA (red bunny ears)			●			●	●			●			●		●						●		●	●
OXALIS HEDYSAROIDES RUBRA (firefern)		●			●		●			●			●		●						●			
OXALIS REGNELLII (oxalis)		●			●		●						●		●						●			
OXALIS SILIQUOSA (oxalis)		●			●		●			●			●		●						●			
PACHYPHYTUM BRACTEOSUM (silver bract)			●		●		●			●		●					●				●			
PACHYPHYTUM BREVIFOLIUM (sticky moonstones)			●		●		●			●			●			●					●			
PACHYPHYTUM OVIFERUM (moonstones)			●		●		●			●			●			●					●			
PAPHIOPEDILUM BELLATULUM (lady's-slipper orchid)			●		●		●	●	●		●	●						●		●	●			
PAPHIOPEDILUM CHARLESWORTHII (lady's-slipper orchid)			●		●		●	●	●		●	●					●			●	●			
PAPHIOPEDILUM GODEFROYAE (lady's-slipper orchid)			●		●		●	●	●		●	●					●			●	●			
PAPHIOPEDILUM INSIGNE (lady's-slipper orchid)			●		●		●	●	●								●				●			
PELARGONIUM CRISPUM 'PRINCE RUPERT VARIEGATED' (lemon-scented geranium)		●			●		●			●							●				●			
PELARGONIUM HORTORUM 'MINX' (miniature common geranium)		●			●		●			●									●		●			
PELLAEA ROTUNDIFOLIA (button fern)	●				●		●	●				●								●		●		
PEPEROMIA CAPERATA VARIEGATA (variegated wrinkled-leaved peperomia)	●					●		●				●								●	●			
PEPEROMIA INCANA (peperomia)	●					●		●				●								●		●		
PEPEROMIA OBTUSIFOLIA (blunt-leaved peperomia)	●					●		●				●								●	●			
PEPEROMIA ROTUNDIFOLIA (yerba linda)	●					●		●				●								●	●			
PEPEROMIA SANDERSII (watermelon peperomia)	●					●		●				●								●	●			
PHALAENOPSIS HEISTAWAY 'JEANETTE' (moth orchid)			●		●		●	●	●								●				●			
PILEA CADIEREI (aluminum plant)	●					●		●				●								●	●			

	LIGHT				NIGHT TEMP.			HUMIDITY			PLANT TYPE				FLOWER COLOR					LEAF COLOR		PLANT HEIGHT		
	75 to 200 foot-candles	200 to 500 foot-candles	500 to 1,000 foot-candles	Over 1,000 foot-candles	45° to 50°	50° to 60°	60° to 70°	30 to 45 per cent	45 to 60 per cent	Above 60 per cent	Flowering	Foliage	Succulent	Herb	White	Yellow to orange	Pink to red	Blue to purple	Multicolor	Green	Variegated	Under 1 foot	1 to 2 feet	Over 2 feet
PILEA INVOLUCRATA (panamiga)		•					•		•			•								•	•	•		
PLECTRANTHUS AUSTRALIS (Swedish ivy)	•	•				•			•			•						•			•	•		
PLECTRANTHUS COLEOIDES MARGINATUS (white-edged Swedish ivy)	•	•				•			•			•									•	•		
PUNICA GRANATUM NANA (dwarf pomegranate)		•	•			•			•		•						•				•			
REBUTIA KRAINZIANA (crown cactus)			•			•	•		•		•		•				•				•			
REBUTIA MINUSCULA (red crown cactus)			•			•	•		•		•		•				•				•			
REBUTIA SENILIS (fire crown cactus)			•			•	•		•		•						•				•			
RECHSTEINERIA CARDINALIS (cardinal flower)		•	•			•			•		•						•				•		•	
RECHSTEINERIA LEUCOTRICHA (Brazilian edelweiss)		•	•			•			•		•						•				•	•		
RODRIGUEZIA SECUNDA (coral orchid)			•		•			•	•	•	•						•				•			
ROSA HYBRID 'BABY CHERYL' (miniature rose)		•				•			•		•						•				•			
ROSA HYBRID 'BABY DARLING' (miniature rose)		•				•			•		•					•	•				•			
ROSA HYBRID 'BO-PEEP' (miniature rose)		•				•			•		•						•				•			
ROSA HYBRID 'ELEANOR' (miniature rose)		•				•			•		•						•					•		
ROSA HYBRID 'GREEN ICE' (miniature rose)		•				•			•		•				•							•		
ROSA HYBRID 'LITTLEST ANGEL' (miniature rose)		•				•			•		•				•							•		
ROSA HYBRID 'PEARL DAWN' (miniature rose)		•				•			•		•						•					•		
ROSA HYBRID 'STARINA' (miniature rose)		•				•			•		•					•	•					•		
ROSA HYBRID 'TINY WARRIOR' (miniature rose)		•				•			•		•						•					•		
SAINTPAULIA IONANTHA 'CORDELIA' (variegated African violet)	•					•			•		•							•		•	•	•		
SAINTPAULIA IONANTHA 'PIXIE BLUE' (miniature trailing African violet)	•					•			•		•							•			•	•		
SALVIA OFFICINALIS (garden sage)	•	•				•	•		•					•			•					•		
SALVIA RUTILANS (pineapple sage)	•	•				•	•		•					•			•					•		
SATUREIA HORTENSIS (summer savory)	•					•	•		•					•			•					•		
SATUREIA MONTANA (winter savory)	•					•	•		•					•			•				•	•		
SAXIFRAGA STOLONIFERA (strawberry geranium)		•		•			•		•					•						•	•	•		
SELAGINELLA KRAUSSIANA AUREA (dwarf club moss)		•				•			•	•									•		•	•		
SINNINGIA HYBRID 'BRIGHT EYES' (miniature sinningia)	•					•		•	•		•						•				•			
SINNINGIA HYBRID 'DOLL BABY' (miniature sinningia)	•					•		•	•		•						•				•			
SINNINGIA PUSILLA (miniature sinningia)	•					•		•	•		•						•				•			
SINNINGIA REGINA (violet-slipper gloxinia)		•				•		•	•		•						•				•			
SINNINGIA SPECIOSA (gloxinia)		•				•		•	•		•							•			•			
SMITHIANTHA CINNABARINA (temple bells)	•					•		•	•		•							•			•		•	
SMITHIANTHA HYBRID 'LITTLE TUDOR' (temple bells)	•					•		•	•		•							•			•			
SMITHIANTHA HYBRID 'LITTLE WONDER' (temple bells)	•					•		•	•		•							•			•			
STREPTOCARPUS HYBRID 'CONSTANT NYMPH' (Cape primrose)	•					•		•			•						•				•			
THYMUS CITRIODORUS AUREUS (golden lemon thyme)	•					•	•		•					•						•	•			
TILLANDSIA CYANEA (tillandsia)	•	•				•		•			•						•					•		
TILLANDSIA IONANTHA (tillandsia)	•	•				•		•			•						•				•			
TRADESCANTIA ALBIFLORA ALBO-VITTATA (giant white inch plant)		•		•			•			•		•			•						•	•		
TRADESCANTIA FLUMINESIS VARIEGATA (variegated wandering Jew)		•		•			•			•		•			•						•	•		
TRADESCANTIA SILLAMONTANA (white velvet wandering Jew)		•		•			•			•		•					•		•	•	•	•		
VRIESIA CARINATA (lobster claws)		•				•			•		•						•				•			
VRIESIA SCALARIS (vriesea)		•				•			•	•	•						•				•			
VRIESIA SPLENDENS (flaming sword)		•				•			•	•	•						•				•			
ZEBRINA PENDULA (wandering Jew)		•				•			•			•									•	•		
ZEBRINA PENDULA DISCOLOR (two-color wandering Jew)		•				•			•			•									•	•		
ZEBRINA PENDULA QUADRICOLOR (four-color wandering Jew)		•				•			•			•									•	•		

153

Picture credits

The sources for the illustrations that appear in this book are listed below. Credits for pictures from left to right are separated by semicolons, from top to bottom by dashes. Cover—Richard Jeffery. 4—Jack Murphy. 6—Lynn Pelham/Kay Reese & Associates, Inc. 9—Charlie Brown; drawing by Great, Inc. 11—Drawing by John Drummond. 12,13—Peter B. Kaplan. 15—Drawing by Kathy Rebeiz. 18—John Arapoff. 23—Drawing by John Drummond. 33—Marina Schinz. 34 through 37—Peter B. Kaplan. 38,39—Marina Schinz. 40, 41—Peter B. Kaplan. 42—Richard Jeffery. 46 through 54—Drawings by Kathy Rebeiz. 57 through 64—Charles Phillips. 69—Drawing by Kathy Rebeiz. 71—Peter B. Kaplan. 72,73—Peter B. Kaplan; drawings by Great, Inc. 75,76—Drawing by Kathy Rebeiz. 78—Illustration by Eduardo Salgado. 80 through 149—Illustrations by artists listed in alphabetical order: Anne Anderson, Adolph E. Brotman, Patricia Caley, Richard Crist, Deborah King, Charlotte Knox, Annabel Large, John Murphy, Donald Myall, Trudy Nicholson, Nina Roberts, Eduardo Salgado, Joan Thompson.

Acknowledgments

The index was prepared by Anita R. Beckerman. For their help in the preparation of this book, the editors wish to thank the following: Rita Arapoff, Marshfield, Mass.; Els Benjamin, Horticulturist, Brookside Gardens, Wheaton, Md.; James Alfred Buck, Lamp Marketing Department, General Electric Company, Cleveland, Ohio; Buell's Greenhouses, Inc., Eastford, Conn.; Lowell E. Campbell, Agricultural Equipment Laboratory, Agricultural Research Service, U.S. Department of Agriculture, Beltsville, Md.; Dr. Henry M. Cathey, Chief, Florist and Nursery Crop Laboratory, Agricultural Research Service, U.S. Department of Agriculture, Beltsville, Md.; Dr. Charles A. Conover, University of Florida Agricultural Research Center, Apopka; R. J. Downs, Director, Phytotron, North Carolina State University, Raleigh; Dr. P. Allen Hammer, Associate Professor of Horticulture, Department of Horticulture, Purdue University, Lafayette, Indiana; Howard Haynes, Illuminating Engineering Society of America, New York City; Mr. and Mrs. Ernest Heise, Highland, Md.; Barbara Joe Hoshizaki, Professor of Botany, Los Angeles City College, Los Angeles, Calif.; Ruth Ihara, Washington, D.C.; Barbara Jackson, Washington, D.C.; Mr. and Mrs. George Kackley, Washington, D.C.; Michael J. Kartuz, Kartuz Greenhouses, Wilmington, Mass.; Dr. Anton M. Kofranek, University of California, Davis; Mr. and Mrs. Herman Lambert, New York City; Harry R. Lobdell, Vice President, Research and Engineering, Columbia Company, Spokane, Wash.; Jane Maurice, New York City; Martha Meehan, Wheaton, Md.; Mr. and Mrs. Richard E. Meissner, Silver Spring, Md.; Cecile Middleton, Washington, D.C.; Hildreth Morton, Bittersweet Hill Nurseries, Davidsonville, Md.; Richard Peterson, American Orchid Society, Botanical Museum, Harvard University, Cambridge, Mass.; Dr. Richard T. Poole, University of Florida Agricultural Research Center, Apopka; Daryl Puterbaugh, New York City; Robert Ricketts, Frederick, Md.; Gladys Scheer, Falls Church, Va.; Bill Seaborn, Seaborn Del Dios Nursery, Escondido, Calif.; Robert R. Wylie, GTE Sylvania Inc., Danvers, Mass.

Bibliography

Asimov, Isaac, *Photosynthesis*. Basic Books, 1969.

Ballard, Ernesta D., *The Art of Training Plants*. Harper & Row, 1974.

Banucci, Phyllis Wolff, *Light Garden Construction: A Do-It-Yourself Manual* (Cultural Guide No. 7). Indoor Light Gardening Society of America, Inc., 1976.

Bickford, Elwood D., and Dunn, Stuart, *Lighting for Plant Growth*. The Kent State University Press, 1972.

Brooklyn Botanic Garden, *Gardening Under Artificial Light*. BBG, 1976.

Brooklyn Botanic Garden, *Handbook on Gesneriads (African-Violets, Gloxinias and Their Relatives)*, revised. BBG, 1976.

Brooklyn Botanic Garden, *Handbook on Propagation*. BBG, 1957.

Buck, James, *High Intensity Discharge Lamps for Plant Growth Application* (reprinted from *Transactions* of the ASAE Vol. 16, No. 1). American Society of Agricultural Engineers, 1973.

Campbell, L. E., and Cathey, H. M., *Horticultural Lighting* (Conference Paper No. C-74-912-21A). IEEE 1974 Rural Electric Power Conference, 1974.

Campbell, Lowell E., Thimijan, Richard W., and Cathey, Henry M., *Spectral Radiant Power of Lamps Used in Horticulture* (reprinted from *Transactions* of the ASAE Vol. 18, No. 5). American Society of Agricultural Engineers, 1975.

Cathey, H. M., and Campbell, L. E., "Lamps and lighting—a horticultural view." *Lighting Design & Application,* November, 1974.

Cathey, Henry M., Klueter, Herschel H., and Bailey, William A., *Indoor Gardens with Controlled Lighting* (USDA Home and Garden Bulletin No. 187). U.S. Department of Agriculture, 1971.

Chittenden, Fred J., ed., *The Royal Horticultural Society Dictionary of Gardening,* 2nd ed. Clarendon Press, 1974.

Cronin, Evelyn D., and Ritzau, Fred, *Seed Propagation* (Cultural Guide No. 2). Indoor Light Gardening Society of America, Inc., 1975.

Elbert, George A., *The Indoor Light Gardening Book*. Crown Publishers, Inc., 1973.

Elbert, George A., *Multiplying Your Plants*. Indoor Light Gardening Society of America, Inc. (undated).

Elbert, George and Virginie, *Plants That Really Bloom Indoors*. Simon and Schuster, Inc., 1974.

Elbert, Virginie and George A., *Fun with Terrarium Gardening*. Crown Publishers, Inc., 1973.

Elbert, Virginie F. and George A., *Fun with Growing Herbs Indoors*. Crown Publishers, Inc., 1974.

Elbert, Virginie F. and George A., *The Miracle Houseplants: The Gesneriad Family*. Crown Publishers, Inc., 1976.

Evans, L. T., *Daylength & The Flowering of Plants*. W. A. Benjamin, Inc., 1975.

Finkbeiner, Frances, *Ferns Under Fluorescents* (Cultural Guide No. 1). Indoor Light Gardening Society of America, Inc., 1975.

Fitch, Charles Marden, *The Complete Book of Houseplants Under Lights*. Hawthorn Books, Inc., 1975.

Golding, Jack, *Light Garden Primer* (Cultural Guide No. 5). Indoor Light Gardening Society of America, Inc. (undated).

Golding, Jack, and Thompson, Edward J. and Mildred L., *Begonias for Light Gardens, Begonia Propagation* (Cultural Guide No. 5). Indoor Light Gardening Society of America, Inc., 1976.

Graf, Alfred Byrd, *Exotic Plant Manual,* 4th ed. Roehrs Co., Inc., 1974.

Graf, Alfred Byrd, *Exotica,* Series 3, 8th ed. Roehrs Co., Inc., 1976.

Haage, Walther, *Cacti and Succulents*. E. P. Dutton and Company, Inc., 1963.

Hessayon, D. G., *Be Your Own House Plant Expert,* 2nd ed. Pan Britannica Industries Ltd., 1974.

Hillman, William S., *The Physiology of Flowering*. Yale University Press, 1964.

Hoshizaki, Barbara Joe, *Fern Growers Manual*. Alfred A. Knopf, 1975.

Jacobsen, Hermann, *Lexicon of Succulent Plants*. Blandford Press Ltd., 1974.

Kartuz, Michael J., and Cronin, Evelyn D., *Flowering Plants for Light Gardens* (Cultural Guide No. 4). Indoor Light Gardening Society of America, Inc., 1976.

Kaufman, John E., ed., *IES Lighting Handbook,* 5th ed. Illuminating Engineering Society, 1972.

Kranz, Frederick H., and Kranz, Jacqueline L., *Gardening Indoors under Lights*. The Viking Press, 1971.

Lamb, Edgar, *The Illustrated Reference on Cacti & Other Succulents,* Vol. 1. Blandford Press, 1955.

Lamb, Edgar and Brian, *The Illustrated Reference on Cacti & Other Succulents,* Vol. 2. Blandford Press, 1968.

Lamb, Edgar and Brian M., *The Illustrated Reference on Cacti & Other Succulents,* Vol. 3. Blandford Press, 1971.

Lamb, Edgar and Brian M., *The Illustrated Reference on Cacti & Other Succulents,* Vol. 4. Blandford Press, 1975.

McDonald, Elvin, *The Complete Book of Gardening Under Lights*. Popular Library. 1965.

Morrison, R. D. (Pat), *Learn to Grow Under Fluorescent Lights*. Indoor Light Gardening Society of America, Inc. (undated).

Noggle, G. R., and Fritz, George J., *Introductory Plant Physiology*. Prentice-Hall, Inc., 1976.

Northen, Rebecca Tyson, *Home Orchid Growing,* 3rd ed. Van Nostrand Reinhold Co., 1970.

Northen, Rebecca Tyson, *Orchids as House Plants,* 2nd rev. ed. Dover Publications, Inc., 1976.

Peterson, Richard, *Orchid Culture Under Lights* (Cultural Guide No. 3). Indoor Light Gardening Society of America, Inc., 1975.

Staff of the L. H. Bailey Hortorium, Cornell University, *Hortus Third: A Dictionary of Plants Cultivated in the United States and Canada*. Macmillan Publishing Co., Inc., 1976.

Steeves, Taylor A., and Sussex, Ian M., *Patterns in Plant Development*. Prentice-Hall, Inc., 1972.

Wilson, Helen Van Pelt, *The African Violet: Saintpaulia*. M. Barrows and Company, Inc., 1948.

Index